FEETS...
(Around the World)

~~~

A True Story of Love and Adventure

Love you Kim!

Mark

By Mark Brown
With Karen Spencer

Copyright © 2017 by Mark Brown
feetsaroundtheworld@gmail.com

ISBN: 978-1-54391-628-7

"In love, you and I, we can conquer the world."
Stevie Wonder

PROLOGUE

My heart jumped when the phone rang. For a brief moment, I was afraid it might be her, but then I told myself no, it couldn't be. I had only gotten here about 10 minutes ago, hardly enough time for anything to have happened. I was just being jumpy from not having gotten any sleep last night, I thought, and tried to relax.

I'd come to Steve's apartment that morning to sell him my darkroom equipment, in preparation for my big trip, and we were right in the middle of negotiations. The phone rang again as he was reaching to answer it. He said hello, paused a moment, then shot me a quick glance. At that moment, I knew that my fears had just been realized; something had indeed gone wrong and now she was in trouble. It was, after all, the reason I had given her his phone number in the first place. "Call me if you need any help," I'd said to her as I dropped her off at her house that morning, but I didn't think it would ever actually come to that. At least I'd hoped not. Now, though, I was afraid it had.

With a puzzled look on his face, Steve looked up and held the phone out to me. "It's for you," he said, as though I hadn't already guessed. I felt awkward as I took it from his hand and I turned my back toward him as if to keep him from hearing the conversation. "Is everything alright?" I half-whispered, fearing her reply. I was self-conscious talking to her in front of Steve like that, for he worked with Karen, too, and I knew how odd he must be thinking it that she should be calling me, particularly here at his place since neither of us knew Steve very well nor had ever been to his apartment before.

"Yes," was all she answered. Her simple reply took me by surprise. Why the hell, then, was she calling me? Surely she wasn't so impetuous as to take a risk like this just to tell me everything was okay. It would be much too difficult now to deny all the rumors at work and she had to know that, too. There had to be something else, I thought as I stood there, and I soon found out that indeed there was. It was what she said next that was the reason for her call: a short little sentence that tumbled out of her mouth so matter-of-factly but one that was to change both our lives so quickly and so drastically on that sunny August morning.

I listened for a moment, not really believing what I was hearing. "I'll be right there," was all I could manage to say. My heart started to race at the thought of what was unfolding and I quickly hung up the phone. Flushed with a sudden sense of urgency, I turned to Steve, who was eyeing me even more curiously now. I knew he wanted to ask but I didn't give him the opportunity.

"Something's come up, Steve; I gotta go. You can have the whole thing for a hundred bucks," I said, referring to the equipment laid out before us. It was a bargain, I knew, but I couldn't afford to have him refuse it at this point. I scribbled down my mother's address in Los Angeles and handed it to him as I made for the door. "Mail the money to me as soon as you can," I said to him. I knew that I'd soon need every penny I could muster up. "Is there something wrong?" he managed to squeeze in before I made it out the door. "No," I replied, pausing for a moment as a smile slowly crept across my heart, "everything's fine. I can't explain it to you just now but you'll find out soon." With that I dashed out of the apartment, hopped into Otto (my 1974 Toyota Corolla) and sped away to Karen's house as fast as I dared, still not fully believing the way things were turning out so suddenly.

As I neared her house, I saw her standing there, outside by the side of street, just like she said she would be. That was a good sign; it meant I'd made it in time. She looked like a forlorn little orphan standing out there all alone, albeit a very nervous little orphan. At her feet was a large cardboard box which contained all the things she thought she would need or want for the next three years. All the things she would need or want to go around the world with her. Indeed, all the things she could pack in the five minutes it took me to get there.

When she saw me coming down the street, she quickly grabbed her "luggage" and, as I pulled up, threw it in the back seat and then jumped in. She looked over at me and smiled. It was a nervous, uncertain smile, yet a happy one, for it was finally over now. She had done it. She had just committed herself to something that would change her life forever, something the likes of which she never thought she'd do.

I, of course, understood all this, but I could only sit there and smile back at her, as I'm afraid I was just as nervous and unsure as she was, for at that precise moment Karen had just left not only her husband of two years, but also her mother (with whom they both lived), her brothers, sister, cats and dogs. She left the house in which she had been born and raised, the friends she had known all her life. She left virtually the only life she had ever known and was trading it in for one with me. One that was soon to be full of strange people and strange places, one whose direction was unknown and outcome uncertain. A life that could no longer be predicted. The slamming of the door behind her as she got into my car was to be the starting gunshot of a race that would take us far into an unknown world. And together, armed with little more than our love for each other, we put our noses to the wind and we ran.

PREFACE

It's been ten years, almost to the day, that I sit here in my little house telling this story and as I think back on it I'm sometimes not sure that it all really happened. Karen and I split up long ago and there is little left of our trip to remind me that it actually did happen except for a few photographs and a million or so memories that become ever more vague as time skips by. So now, before it totally slips from me, I will put this story down for the sake of posterity and for my own peace of mind, knowing that I can finally let the memories fade without the fear of losing perhaps the most important chronicle of my life. Certainly the happiest.

If it sounds, by this telling, overly sweet and simple it's because that's exactly what it was and if it seems that we were both somehow blessed, well, that too is exactly what we believed as well.

HUMBOLDT COUNTY

Way up on the Northern California coast, sitting alongside the muddy banks of Humboldt Bay, lies the humble little city of Eureka. Since its nearest neighbor of any size is San Francisco, about 270 miles to the south, it serves, in effect, as the capitol and regional center for the entire north coast area, much as it has for the past 150 years.

In those days, the area that is now called "Olde Town" was pretty much the only town. It was a bustling seaport then and in its prime, as in most seaport towns, Eureka's Victorian waterfront section had been alive with saloons, brothels, shipyards and merchant shops of all sorts servicing mostly the needs of not only the transient sailors but also the thousands of redwood loggers and gold miners that lived and worked throughout this remote corner of the state.

But that was over a century ago and, despite a recent attempt to turn Olde Town into a charming tourist center, the quiet, dead-end streets that ran through this part of town and the dilapidated remains of many of the original warehouses and shops that still loomed darkly around its fringes were now home mostly only to the odd assortment of fishing boats and the scores of hobos and transients that had found their way in here over time but had somehow never managed to find their way back out again.

Here, too, along the old, rotting docks of the waterfront, was Lazio's Seafood Restaurant. Despite the fact that it was set up in a corner of the crumbling, decrepit, and otherwise deserted fish packing plant that it once had been, it was nonetheless a very well-known and extremely busy restaurant. It was here, in the winter of 1978, that I first met Karen and where this story begins.

She was working nights there as a salad maker when I returned to Lazio's from a brief absence to resume my work as a dishwasher that January and I was quick to notice the new girl they'd hired while I'd been gone. She was no raving beauty, in the classic sense anyway, and would probably sound fairly average if I were to try to describe her looks here, she was in actuality a very attractive woman, by almost all accounts.

Though she was indeed pretty, it wasn't on her looks alone that the strength of her appeal rested. Rather, she simply had a way about her that seemed to attract not only one's attention but one's affection as well. It was more of an essence of childlikeness really and carried through with such an honest sincerity that you couldn't help but become endeared to her, indeed much as you would be to a child. She also had a certain sparkle in her eyes (particularly when she smiled, which was always) that seemed to emanate from the very depths of her heart and it didn't take much more than a single look into them to become ensnared. Apparently, I wasn't the only one to feel this way for I soon found out that just about every guy in the place had a similar crush on her.

As is so often the case with such women, though, she had been scooped up at an early age by the first guy to realize what a prize she was and it was to him that she was in fact married.

I was disappointed, to be sure, to learn of this since I had always considered marriage a fairly sacred institution and I didn't feel that this was a good time to violate my otherwise dubious ethics by making a play for her. I was just coming out of a very long dry spell, so to speak, in regard to relationships, and a married woman was not what I needed to help bring me out of it. I needed a "real" girlfriend, someone I could call my own - certainly not another man's wife.

The funny thing about emotions, though, is that they don't seem to follow anybody else's rules but their own and these rules always seem to be contrary to the ones we're supposed to live by. In spite of my good and honorable intentions I couldn't help but be drawn to her more and more as time went by. Her positive, happy-go-lucky approach to life somehow seemed to just ooze all on its own into the hearts of those around her, making it almost impossible to keep a distance, and I'm afraid my heart was not immune.

A few weeks after my return to work, my position changed to that of night clean-up man, which meant coming in to work at about 11:00 every night. As the rest of the staff rarely got finished and out of my way before midnight, I usually just strolled around the kitchen during this hour of overlap and chatted with everyone while I had the chance to. Soon, they would all be going home, leaving me alone with only the wharf rats out back for company.

It was during these nightly intervals that my friendship with Karen eventually took root and I soon found myself holding up the wall over in her corner of the kitchen more times than not, talking on and on with her about anything and everything that happened to cross our minds.

From these talks, we soon discovered how much we really had in common with each other. Not in terms of background or lifestyle, for those were very different, but in our general view of the world. We had the same values, the same sense of spirit, the same taste in music and, perhaps most importantly, the same sense of humor. Indeed, we seemed to approach life from an identical point of view.

Neither of us took the daily machinations of life very seriously and our nightly talks were usually nothing more than highly animated, nonsensical banterings about absolutely meaningless things. There were no points to make or any arguments to propound; they were strictly recreational talks and would often go on for great lengths of time. A sort of verbal abstract art, if you will. Some would call it flirting.

Many times, other people would see us having such an obviously good time together that they'd come over and attempt to join into our conversation. After only a few minutes of our inane gibberish, however, they'd usually just walk away shaking their heads in bewilderment, never to try again. As a result, it wasn't long before we became known around the restaurant as a couple of loonies.

This, of course, only served to draw us together all the more, as like-minded people so often tend to collect together in the face of such mass incomprehension. Birds of a feather, I suppose.

This was compounded even more by the fact that we were the only two vegetarians in the entire place and this at a time when not eating meat was still associated with shaving your head and chanting on street corners. Almost anti-social, in other words, and not very well understood.

And so it was that Karen and I became best of buds, while at work anyway, and we continued to stand off in our corner of the kitchen every night with our backs to the world, discussing such fundamentally relevant topics as the probable sex life of French fries and other such profundities. Soon however our friendship began to quietly slip the confines of the restaurant.

As it was, we both also happened to be taking classes at the local College of the Redwoods (CR) during the day and in our nighttime chats we often spoke of the virtues of our respective classes. It shouldn't have come as much of a surprise, really, when on the first day of the very next semester we both just happened to show up in the exact same two classes together, but it was nevertheless.

Our two classes conveniently met back to back on the same days so now, not only were we working together every night of the week but we were also going to school together three days a week. And of course, the more we were together, the closer we got.

Our first class was recreational soccer and was immediately followed by recreational swimming. The soccer class, being unsupervised, gave us the opportunity to run around and play together like the kids we felt we really were, though I was in fact twenty-two at the time and she nineteen. The swimming class, also unsupervised, gave us the opportunity to flirt with each other at closer range, without the fear of being seen by anyone we knew. Of course, we also played in the pool a lot, too, chasing each other around, getting in water fights and the like. It was something we did well together, playing, and it was always the inevitable result whenever we were together.

And yet, as testimony to the mind's ability for selective thinking, we still somehow managed to bypass any conscious acknowledgment of affection or attraction to each other. It was, however, becoming increasingly harder to do so as time went by, to convince ourselves that we were really only platonic friends. Deep down I'm sure we both knew that the time would soon come when we would have to face up to the fact that, in spite of our otherwise childlike and innocent approach to this relationship, we were indeed adults with very adult feelings, regardless of how much we tried to ignore or even suppress them, subconsciously or otherwise.

But if we were suppressing the truth to ourselves about our feelings, it was only because to admit to them would be agreeing to hurt people that neither of us wanted to hurt. Specifically, her husband, Tom. Though I barely knew him, I didn't at all like the thought of being off with his wife like this. And if I felt that way about it, I can only imagine Karen's dilemma for she was the one who was married to the man. Though their marriage wasn't perfect, by any means, they did love each other very much and the thought of deceiving him certainly couldn't be something she enjoyed. And so we simply continued to deny it all.

As springtime blossomed, however, taking hold of the countryside and young hearts, I reached the point where I couldn't fool myself any longer. I finally allowed myself to consciously acknowledge that our relationship had indeed progressed far beyond the point where something needed to be done.

The thought of confronting Karen with this troubled me and I struggled with it for several days as I considered what to do. I had been painfully lonely prior to meeting Karen and now I was faced with becoming painfully frustrated in loving someone that I might never be able to have.

An even worse thought for me, though, was what I would feel like if I said or did nothing at all, if I just let it fade away without ever knowing what would have come of it. I had never felt with anyone else the way I now did with Karen. We seemed somehow made for each other, in my mind anyway, and I felt it would be a personal crime against myself and my happiness if she was indeed the person I had long hoped for and I let her go without at least making a try.

I knew that she would never bring up the subject of having an affair herself and that if we were to get past this turning point it would have to be at my suggestion, which I was very loathe to do. Though I knew in my heart that I wanted nothing more than to have her with me, I did not at all like the thought of suggesting to her that she betray her husband. All I knew was that whenever Karen and I were together, nothing felt so right with the world as did we.

***

It was an absolutely gorgeous spring day. The sun was up, the flowers were out and the grass was tall and glowing a vibrant green. Turkey vultures were high up in the deep blue sky with the cotton ball clouds, doing their slow, lazy circles above the redwood trees and sheep pastures that surrounded the beat-up old house I was presently living in. I had the day off from both work and school and my two roommates, Kathleen and Susan, had both gone on to their classes, leaving me home alone. I was supposed to be getting ready to do

16

some gardening work that morning at our landlord's house but I decided instead to just sit out in the sunshine on our front porch and dream up a good excuse why I wasn't.

We were living outside a very small town on a very small, dead-end lane just off an insignificant little highway that wasn't on the way to anywhere else in particular. We didn't get much traffic there, in other words, and so I was surprised, as I sat there basking in the sunbeams on our tiny little porch, when a big, old Pontiac Le Mans pulled around the corner not far away and came up the road toward the house. What was even more surprising was that it was this car in particular, for though I knew it and its driver well, it was the last car I expected to see driving up my street that day.

Some days ago, while sitting in my car after driving her home from swim class, I had finally drummed up my courage and broached the long-taboo subject. She was just getting her things up to leave and I knew that I had no more time to stall. "So," I blurted out anxiously, "when are we going to have an affair?" I had finally done it. For better or worse, there it was, out in the open, and with my heart on the line, I eagerly waited for her response. To my utter despair, however, she'd simply made a joke about it, got out and walked away laughing, leaving me sitting there alone and feeling like an idiot.

Not to be so easily daunted, I mentioned it again the following day but this time she'd deftly evaded answering me altogether and went on as though I hadn't even asked, leaving me to stew in my frustration. I had taken all this as a definite "not in this lifetime" and had resigned myself to the notion that it was a dead deal. I no longer expected her reply, nor would I ever mention it again.

As I sat there and watched, though, the big yellow battleship of a car pulled up and dropped anchor right across the lane from the house. The huge door creaked open and sure enough, pee-wee little Karen came falling out of it, wearing a smile as big as the car itself and as bright as the day.

17

She said she wasn't really sure why she'd come. She had just pulled into the parking lot at the college for class that morning when something in her head suddenly told her to come out and visit me instead. So that's just what she did. She started her car back up, turned around and drove the twenty some miles farther to come see me. She didn't really need to explain anything, though. I knew why she had come.

Although the house we lived in was a ramshackle little two-bedroom dump, it made up for any shortcomings by being situated on top of a high bluff overlooking a beautiful, big, green valley and surrounded by meadows, sheep pastures, forests and wild rivers.

Out back of the house, past the redwood trees and the garden, was a large open field of grass. It belonged with our property but wasn't being used for anything right then and so had just been left to grow wild. Off in the far corner of this field stood a lone, old cherry tree whose only company was the even older redwood stump that jutted up from the grass near the field's center.

Behind these, running along the back edge of the property, was a small brook that was lined on both sides by a narrow margin of woods. A ribbon of green grass, speckled with countless small, white English Daisies, carpeted the near side of the shaded banks and down its center ran a small foot trail. It followed along upriver for a short way before eventually veering away up a hill and continuing off into the trees.

Following the trail farther into these woods, it soon opened up into a small, grassy glade filled with the huge, black and gray remains of an ancient redwood forest that had been cut down ages ago. The dark stumps were twisted and weathered and in the misty fog or the darkness of evening they gave the place the feeling of a cemetery, grave markers of the giants that had lived there through the centuries before.

Sometimes, when I felt the pains of life too sharply, I would follow this trail and sit by the creek or farther up into the glade, amongst the giants, and bemoan my fate. It became a special place for me and it was out here that, only the night before, I had come and beseeched the gods to help me with this sordid thing called love. I'd pleaded that warm, cloudless night with the rising full moon to intervene in my sorrowful life.

It seemed only natural, then, that it was here I brought Karen that sunny morning and here alongside the creek, amongst the daisies, that she and I lay together for the first time. On a small grassy knoll, in the warm sunshine, with only the woods as our witness, we finally consummated our long-avoided affair.

As corny as I know this sounds, it was like being in a fairy tale. She truly was my long-lost princess and I felt like I was the misbegotten fool in the enchanted forest who had just discovered he was a prince unawares. We lay there for a while afterwards, soaking it all in, before finally getting dressed and meandering our way back to the house.

Karen must have felt the same way, for she came out several more times after that day. When she did, we usually headed straight out back, where we'd lie together in the tall, dry grass of the sunny field or in the cool, green grass of the shaded woods. Every time seemed like yet another fairy tale.

Almost every time, anyway. Once, while we were lost in our passion, the cows that lived out in these woods had quietly gathered around, unbeknownst to us. A short time later, we looked up and were momentarily startled to find ourselves almost completely ringed by a herd of Holsteins and Jerseys staring down at us from only a few feet away, thoroughly fascinated with what we were doing. We were a bit unnerved at first but it quickly became apparent that their curiosity had completely transfixed them where they stood and so we didn't let them deter us. We didn't really mind the company.

On one of Karen's visits we decided, instead of going out back again, to go down the highway a few miles to one of the nearby redwood parks that lined the banks of the Van Duzen river. There was a place I knew there that had a good-sized swimming hole at a bend in the river, with a nice patch of warm sand on one side and a high rock wall on the other to help keep the wind out. No one else was there that day so we promptly took off our clothes and jumped in the river. We spent the afternoon swimming and playing together in the clear, cool water, taking breaks occasionally to climb out and spread ourselves out on the sandy beach to warm up while we dried.

Across the river from this beach and a few feet up from the base of the rock wall, a little shelf had been cut into the cliff from previous floods. Inside this shelf was a small pocket of gray, slimy clay just big enough for two people to sit in. After we had lain out for a while in the sun, we swam over and climbed up in it. We couldn't resist the temptation in our illicit freedom and began smearing handfuls of the wet clay all over each other's naked body, head and face. We had a wonderful time heaving these gobs of muck on one another and then finger painting them onto any spot not yet covered, until only our white eyes remained visible through the viscous ooze. Any sensual arousal we may have felt from rubbing the slippery clay over each other's touchy parts was immediately offset by the total hilarity of our appearance when we were through. We looked like a couple of misplaced aborigines out of the jungles of New Guinea. The only things missing were bones in our noses.

We sat up there on the sunny ledge afterwards and played until all the mud on our bodies had become dry and flaky. We looked even funnier now and had a good laugh before finally diving off the ledge into the clear water below to wash off. Karen went first and left a long, gray plume behind her as she slid through the water looking, I thought, much like a torpedo shooting across the pool.

Later that day I climbed up on a large rock at the river's edge and watched Karen taking her last swim of the day. It was very much like watching an otter or a seal swim, I thought, as she

20

slipped in and out of the water looking for pretty stones on the river's bed. The reflection of the late afternoon sun on the ripples in the water turned the swimming hole into a brilliant, glittering golden pool and against its blinding sparkles I watched her dark silhouette silently disappear under the water and then, almost as silently, reappear on the other side of the pool from where she had just been, with only the slightest sound of her breath giving her away. I made a game of watching her slide under the water and then, scanning the limits of the pool, trying to guess where she would next appear but I never seemed to get it right. I think that's probably why I enjoyed it so much.

Truth is, I don't think there has ever been a day in my life, before or since, that I have enjoyed as much as I did this day, nor a time when I loved this woman more. Lying there on the beach after our romps in the river, watching the hawks high up in the sky doing their figure-eights above the steep, forested hills that surrounded us and Karen lying beside me, it seemed like yet another make-believe story come true. It was something I had previously thought only existed in dime store romance novels and I had a hard time believing that this was all real, let alone happening to me.

As our affair continued to grow, it became ever more difficult for us to wait until we could both be available to meet at my house. Fortunately, the college, being at the foot of a forested and otherwise deserted hillside, gave us a lot more opportunity and we didn't miss a chance to take advantage of its convenience. Several times, after our classes were finished, we'd sneak away to a grassy spot high up on the hill and commit our sordid crimes.

One day, while running downfield in our soccer class, our sense of romance (or maybe just our hormones) got the better of us and we decided to just keep going. When everyone else turned and headed back toward the other goal, we just kept on running - past the goal, out the gate and straight on up the hill - with our fellow teammates none the wiser. We sat up there overlooking the campus below and gloated in our cleverness as we watched the soccer game continue without us. Toward the end of class, we simply ran back down the mountainside, through the gate again, and rejoined them as though we'd never left.

Sometimes, for a change of pace, we'd drive to an old, abandoned pioneer farmhouse that we knew of about a half a mile down the two-lane road from the campus. It sat high up on a hillside overlooking the southern lobe of Humboldt Bay. To get up to it we had to jump a fence down by the roadway and walk another quarter mile along a winding, tree-lined dirt lane that served as its driveway.

Just before reaching the top we always stopped to raid the long-neglected apple and plum orchard before continuing on. Though the plums were hardly worth the effort, the apples were wonderful and worth the trip up for their own sake. Afterwards, we'd continue on up and lay out on the grassy hillside in front of the deserted, one-room pioneer shack that once had been the farmhouse and talk, make love or just sit and watch the afternoon sun as it slowly crept its way down to the sea before us. We fondly referred to this place as our "Summer Cottage" and came here several times. It was a truly magical time for us.

***

As spring grew into summer and our relationship continued to grow ever stronger, it became harder and harder to hide our secret from our coworkers. We were seeing each other for several hours every day now and people were beginning to notice that unspoken familiarity between us, no matter how hard we tried to seem otherwise. Rumors were beginning to circulate. I had since become night manager of sorts there at the restaurant and Karen was now working as a bus person, also at night, which put us in close working contact virtually every night and there were times I caught myself on the verge of forgetting where I was and doing something stupid.

Sneaking away when we could, we'd sometimes creep out back into the dark and abandoned, rat-infested depths of the old fish plant, past the gaping hole in the floor where a slab of concrete had fallen into the sloshing bay below and into one of the old fish filleting rooms. The moment we were inside we immediately launched into a hot and heavy make-out session, staying back there for as long as we thought we could get away with before sneaking back into the restaurant.

One night, early that summer, Karen came to tell me that the kitchen was out of iced tea so I went back with her into the old, onetime hallway that now served as the restaurant's storage pantry to try and find some.

As soon as we got inside, of course, the pantry's semi-seclusion overwhelmed us and within seconds we were hopelessly lip-locked. It was a very dangerous thing for us to do here since there was no way to know if anyone was coming until they rounded the corner at the entrance to the room and by that time it would be too late.

As exciting as this made the moment, I still felt uncomfortable at the thought of getting caught in such a compromising situation. At the same time, I was not at all ready to end our impassioned tryst quite so soon. Seeing the closed door at the far end of this pantry suddenly gave me a wonderful idea.

Though this door was kept locked all the time, it just so happened that, as the "Night Man", I had the only set of keys for the whole building, including the one to the wine room, which lay right on the other side of this now very opportune door. I quickly let us in and locked the door behind us. With the thrill of discovery having just added itself to the heat of our stolen moment and the knowledge that we were now only a few scant feet from the busiest part of the entire restaurant, we steamed up those wine bottles in there pretty good before we regrettably had cool down and return to work.

I let Karen out through the back door we'd come in and then waited several minutes before then letting myself out through the front door, which opened directly into the dining room up front. It couldn't have been a more perfect place.

If necessity is the mother of invention, then illicit passion must be the mother of great hiding places.

From then on, every time Karen had a few minutes to spare, she would come up to the fish counter where I normally based myself and coolly inform me, usually with a twinkle in her eye, that we were out of iced tea again. It was our code word now and whenever either one of us used it we would automatically put our system into operation. I would go directly to the wine room via the front door, lock it up again and then go wait by its rear door. After waiting several minutes, Karen would then go out back through the kitchen, around the corner and through the pantry. If the coast was clear, she would then tap gently on the door, her signal to me, and I'd quickly let her in. Five or ten minutes of heavy breathing later, we'd reverse the procedure and go back out into the restaurant, trying hard to act innocent but undoubtedly wearing the flush of passion all over our faces.

It was a terribly fun game and it seemed we looked for an awful lot of iced tea throughout the rest of that summer. For some reason, though, we never seemed to find any.

All this went on through the late spring and summer; the river, the grassy hills, the woods and cows, the iced tea, the Summer Cottage. But summer was drawing to a close by now and things would prove to be very different before it was over.

***

For some years now the notion of traveling around the world had been growing steadily in me. It seemed, though, that every time I considered it there was something missing that would serve to prevent me from actually doing it.

Closely related to this idea of travel was a blossoming concept I had that our society had somehow gotten the scheme of life backwards. The notion that a guy had to work 50 weeks out of the year at a job he didn't really like, just in order to save up enough money so that he could afford to spend it all in a mad rush trying to cram a year's worth of enjoyment and fulfillment into the remaining two weeks and then, when his allotted time was over, to go marching right back to work to start all over again saving up for the next year, all seemed so absurd and pitiful to me.

I was convinced that a person could do just about anything he wanted to in life if he just put his mind to it. Rather than making a job your living instead make living your job. I felt it a much better plan simply to go wherever it was you wanted to vacation, get a job there and stay as long as you wanted. This way you would make money instead of spending it; you'd have a better time, learn more and have all the time in the world to enjoy it. A free, non-stop vacation. All one need to do is put themselves to the task. It seemed so simple and obvious to me.

One day, as I sat musing on life, I thought about all of this again. Only this time when I ran the vital ingredients of my life through this picture, I included Karen and suddenly, the whole thing came together perfectly. I knew immediately that Karen would be the ideal travel mate for just such a trip as I envisioned, and the thought of her going with me proved to be the inspiration I had long been waiting for. It was too perfect. She was intelligent, endearing, fun, tough and resilient. More than anything, though, she had a wonderfully positive attitude towards people and life. All of the things that I felt were necessary (or at least helpful) for this type of travel.

The very next day, while on one of our hilltop outings out behind the college, I mentioned my idea to Karen and it was only then that she confessed to me for the first time her own long-held secret dreams of traveling the world. I should have been surprised, not only that she had such dreams but that they were, in fact, so similar to those of my own, but in truth I almost expected it. I had long ago gotten used to the revelations of these similarities in our character.

We had a great time in the weeks that followed, talking dreamily about traveling together, the places we wanted to go to, the things to see. We discussed what route would cover all of our destinations around the world and by what means we'd travel. We wanted to sail the Caribbean and the South Pacific, hitchhike South America and across Europe and to climb the Himalayas.

Karen particularly wanted to go to Africa. She'd always had a very profound compassion and admiration for all the various animals of the world and it was a lifelong goal of hers to go to Africa because it was where so many of them lived. Her dream, ever since a small girl, was to stow away on a freighter with her dog Toolie and sail off to the land of Tarzan.

It was all very romantic and much fun to talk about, serious or not. I say this because as much fun as it was to talk about all this, to actually do it was another thing altogether. There were many things that Karen would have to deal with if she were to do something like this, not the least of which was Tom.

It was easy for me to plan such an escapade. I was independent, unattached to anything in particular and had a very mobile past history; Karen, on the other hand, was anything but mobile and unattached and now that her dream had finally been awakened, it caused her a lot of turmoil as time went on. She wanted very much to go, to shed the grown-up responsibilities that she had somehow found herself in, and yet to leave would mean hurting the people she so dearly loved.

To make it even harder for her, with the exception of her older brother David she'd never before admitted to anyone that she harbored such ideas of traveling and a sudden revelation like this would be a big shock to all who knew her. Sadly, David had died about a year earlier as a result of a tragic car accident and, unfortunately now for Karen, had taken her secret with him.

All of this aside, however, it was still fun to think and talk about going and we enjoyed the excitement of imagining us cavorting around the world without a care. It was a fantasy, to be sure, but then one never really knows how life may swing next.

In time our talks began to sound more like plans and less like dreams. Despite the ever-increasing love I felt for Karen and the intense desire to run away with her, I knew that any decision on something of this nature had to be hers alone and I made it a point to try and be as neutral as possible on this subject. To leave one's family, friends, and hometown were not decisions to be taken lightly and a trip of this nature was sure to change a person's life in a big way. It was essential to me that Karen's decision be one she was comfortable with and one she could live with for the rest of her life, for she would most certainly have to.

This made it very difficult for me as well since my excitement and enthusiasm about all these wonderful changes in my life had to be constantly held in check and monitored so as not to provide any undue influence to her decision (if that were even possible).

It was a tangled, exciting time for both of us but it was really wearing on Karen. Every time I saw her she had changed her mind again. One day she was going, the next she could never leave, and the one after that she was back to going again.

There was little I could do to help her. I tried to be as objective about the whole thing as much as I could, explaining the pros and cons of both choices, but I have to admit it's not easy trying to help a married woman decide whether or not she wants to run off with you when you know that there is nothing else in the world that you want more to do than run off with her. Deep down, though, I knew it wouldn't end up being a decision based on rational logic and that when the final word came in it would be at the last possible moment. Little did I know.

***

As July came to a close, the whole idea of traveling was beginning to take on a life of its own. Too many things now were pointing me in that direction and since I couldn't know what Karen would end up doing, I had to take charge of my own life. I finally made the decision to quit my job and go, regardless of her decision. On August 1st, I gave my two weeks' notice and finally revealed to everyone my plans for global conquest.

Though I continued to see Karen at our usual rendezvous spots, I tried to give her some room and time on her own to work things out. I spent a lot of time driving in the hills and mountains outside of town, enjoying the scenery and doing a good share of sorting things out myself. There were many things to prepare for and to find out: passports, shots, job availability in different countries, etc. I didn't even know where I was going to go yet. I thought a lot about Karen, too. Would she decide to leave or stay? What would I do if she didn't go? What would we do if she did? This went on for nine days and the moment of reckoning was fast drawing near.

All these questions soon turned out to be academic, though. I had since moved out of the ramshackle house in the country and was now living by myself in a tiny two-room cottage just outside of Eureka. Late in the evening of the 10th day, I came home from one of my mountain drives and, as I let myself into the darkened house, I noticed an unusual shadow over in the corner of the room that hadn't been there before. When I looked closer, I was startled to find out that this shadow was a person, sitting there on my bed. Before I could react, though, I heard a plaintive, little "hi" squeak out from the dark blob that I now knew was Karen.

That was just my first surprise, though. The next one came a moment later when I asked her the obvious question of why she'd broken into my house and was sitting there alone in the dark. It was to warn me, she said, that my life was in danger, that an irate husband (hers, of course) and two of his friends (big ones, of course) were out at this very moment looking for me. It wasn't really the kind of news I was accustomed to coming home to hear and now that I had I wasn't real sure how to react. I climbed up on the bed beside her and we sat there in the dark while she explained the whole story to me.

Earlier that afternoon, she told me, she finally had resolved that she did indeed want to go traveling but that in fairness to Tom she should, at the very least, give him the first option and ask him if he would go travel the world with her. If he said yes, she reasoned, then the case was closed right then and there. She would go with him to live out her dream. When he in fact replied "No" to her question, however, that he had no desire to travel at all, she paused for a moment and then told him flatly, "Well, in that case I'm going to go with Mark Brown." She hadn't quite planned that response, she said, it just came out that way.

Well, had Tom not just finished drinking a bottle of tequila this news may have been a little bit easier to take. As it was, however, he had and it wasn't. He felt, and rightly so, that a little chat with me was in order here and tried to get Karen to give him my phone number. When she refused, he decided then to just get it for himself out of her purse. She resisted his attempt and they scuffled briefly as he tried to snatch her purse away from her. Fortunately, she prevailed (I said she was tough) and with frustration now added to his hurt and anger, he left the house to go get some friends together and to come looking for me.

She took that opportunity to head them off and immediately left for my house to tell me that Tom and his buddies were out to make quick work of convincing me that I shouldn't be doing what I was apparently about to do. And now here she was. Fortunately for me, she found me before they did.

Karen knew that it was no good going back home until the tequila had worn off some so we sat there together through the night, talking about all these new things and listening to the phone ring. It had started shortly after I'd returned home and since I hadn't given the number out to anyone yet, except to Karen, we knew that it had to be Tom. He would surely have gotten my number by now from someone at the restaurant. For my part, I didn't really think it wise just now to talk to him, however, so we did our best to ignore the phone's incessant call.

He didn't give up trying the entire night, calling three or four times an hour, each time renewing my growing apprehensions and concern. Since no one besides Karen knew where my little house was, though, we were at least safe as long as we didn't leave it. This all made our very first night together certainly a memorable one, if not the most ideal.

For Karen, though, each time the phone rang it was, perhaps, the sharp knife of guilt resting ever more heavily on her heart for in the late hour of the night, after seeing Tom's relentless attempts to deal with her absence, she changed her mind yet again; there was no way she could go now. It made her realize more fully just how much it would hurt him and all the others she loved if she were ever to leave.

To be honest, my heart went out to Tom as well and outwardly I accepted and supported her decision. Inside, however, I somehow knew that it wasn't over yet. After all, we still had another week to go before I was to leave. "Don't worry about it now," I told her, "a lot can happen in a week."

30

Little did I know then the truth to those words or just how soon I would be finding it out.

It was midmorning when we'd finally talked it all through. A few moments later Karen quietly asked me to drive her home. We were both pretty well beat from staying up all night but she wanted now to go straighten things out with Tom; she needed to go, to tell him that she was sorry, that she did love him and that she was staying.

I had an appointment that morning with Steve, one of the cooks from the restaurant to show him the darkroom equipment I was selling off, so I dropped her off in front of her house on my way over. Before I did, though, I jotted down his phone number and handed it to her. I knew that these kinds of situations can sometimes get ugly and I was concerned for her. I told her that if Tom started giving her any trouble to call me there immediately and I would come help, though, in truth, I had no idea what I'd actually be able to do. I just knew that I couldn't leave her stranded there if she needed help.

Sure enough, midway through my sales pitch with Steve, she called and said to me words that to this day still ring through me. "Mark, if we're going to go it has to be right now or never." There was a calm certainty in her voice as she quickly explained to me that Tom had just left the house for a few minutes to go to the market and that, despite promising to him that she'd be there when he returned, the same little voice that had sent her out to my house those many weeks before popped in her head again as soon as he'd left and she knew that this was her one, and only, moment to act.

It was the voice of her heart that spoke to her now for that is the voice that speaks in actions. Thoughts and words are the language solely of the mind and they spoke to her of only guilt and responsibility. Her heart, though, spoke of happiness and truth and, in this case, the truth, it seemed, was that she'd rather be traveling with me. She told me she'd be waiting for me outside her house. I had only five minutes, she said; if Tom

31

got home before I could get there then the deal was off, she wouldn't leave.

Suddenly, the full impact of all that we had talked about finally hit me. It wasn't talk anymore. This was a soap opera and a fantasy all in one. I was packing up and running away with a married woman, to go travel around the world, with no money, no real idea even of where we were going to go, and all in five minutes' time while her husband was shopping! The sense of drama was intense.

I quickly, and awkwardly, excused myself from Steve, leaving all my equipment with him as I bolted for my car. I sped all the way to her house, keeping an eye on the clock throughout, hoping beyond hope that I got there in time and wondering what I would do if I didn't.

Fortunately, I never found out for as I came racing up to her house I could see her lonely figure still out on the sidewalk with a cardboard box at her feet, waiting. We quickly threw her things in the car and then sped off back to my house, hoping now that we didn't pass Tom on way.

In less than two hours since her fateful phone call, we were all packed up and ready to go. We both agreed that we needed to return to the restaurant one last time before leaving to not only pick up our last paychecks but also because we wanted to explain to our boss what was going on and that we wouldn't be coming to work anymore. We knew that it was a very dangerous thing for us to do, as Tom surely must have figured things out by now and the restaurant would be the logical place for him to come looking for us. Our need for the money, however, and, ironically, our principles outweighed the danger so we took the chance. It added an extra dose of anxiety to our departure but this only served to make it all the more exciting. My heart hadn't stopped racing since I'd first gotten her call and it didn't slow down until we were far into the night and many miles down the road.

By early afternoon we were gone. In our wake, we left behind not only our friends, but everything else Karen knew, owned and loved. She felt very badly about leaving in this way, with nary a warning to anyone, nor even a good-by, but I think we both knew that this was the only way it could ever have possibly worked. I felt badly, too, and touched, when Karen told me that the restaurant had planned a surprise going away party for me on the following Sunday, which was to have been my last day.

We had too much future to think about just then, though, to spend much time mulling on the past. There was, after all, a whole world in front of us now that desperately needed conquering.

FEETS...Around the World

ON THE ROAD

Our first chosen destination was Los Angeles. My mother lived there and we thought it would be a good place to regroup and get ourselves organized a little bit before hitting the big road. It also offered me the luxury, the one so harshly denied Karen, of visiting with my mother first and telling of our plans. Sitting low in our seats and with a watchful eye in the rearview for any sign of Tom, we got on the southbound side of Hwy. 101 and made our escape.

On our way out of town, we stopped off at the "summer cottage," supposedly to pick a bagful of apples for the road but in reality, I think it was to stop and reflect on all that happened and to take one last look before heading off into the great, unknown world.

There was a touch of melancholy running through me as we meandered up the dirt road this last time. Never before in my life had I known such excitement and happiness as I did at this very moment and yet, at the same time, I knew that our magical springtime was fast coming to close now, even as we sat there on that sunny hillside. This old farm was our threshold now. Beyond it lay a whole new world for us, a whole new life, and the moment we stepped from it today would be the very moment the door to it would forever be closed behind us. It was as if I knew that it would be that irrevocable last step from our very own innocence.

The sun was beginning to lower itself from the sky, later, as we picked our apples, and the quietness that belongs to summer afternoons was gently soaking into the countryside around us, adding to the overall bittersweet feeling of the moment. In the contest of emotions that was revolving through me, however, it was excitement and happiness that held reign and despite the quiet and reflective nature of the setting, there was still a loud buzz of electricity spinning around my heart as we wound our way down the little dirt road and back to the car.

The hill on which we had lain so many times before and on which we had talked so often about our imagined escapades now bid us farewell as we neared the end of the winding drive. We jumped down from the board gate at its end into a brand-new world and drove away with the thrill of knowing that it was now ours.

The night was warm and dry as we made our way south, and the sky seemed filled to overflowing with stars. We pulled over to the side of the road a couple of times just to get out and gaze up at them, to let our spirits soar among them for a while.

Like the rest of the day had been, our drive down that night was a giant revolving bin of emotions for both of us, alternating between elation, sorrow, wonder and worry. We were doing what we knew was right with ourselves but what seemed wrong with everyone else. We broke the vows of possibly the world's foremost of institutions and were defying the accepted course of society. But, like school kids cutting class, we were regaling in our newfound sense of freedom. Freedom from Tom, freedom from Eureka and freedom from having to hide our relationship.

There were, of course, many concerns and doubts, yet the excitement of our departure held firm and somehow we both knew deep in our hearts that this was something we had to do. Not in the sense of an ultimatum; in fact, quite the opposite. Being true to oneself means knowing that we make our own options in life and that the best one to take is that one which feels the most right, and never in my life had I felt anything to be so right as that night, indeed as my whole relationship with this woman.

Somewhere along the highway that night, as we listened to Stevie Wonder on the tape player, the song "You are the

Sunshine of my Life" came on and I looked over to Karen and dedicated it to her from me.

When the next song came on, "You & I" ("In love, you and I, we can conquer the world"), I thought, *how appropriate*, and felt it surely must be a good omen. I was even more convinced when I then recalled that the two songs prior to "Sunshine" were "It Ain't No Use" (about someone declaring the end of their relationship to their lover) followed by "Please Don't Go" (an impassioned plea for his love not to leave him). I imagined them to be the words from Karen to Tom and his response back to her, respectively. This song list just happened to follow suit to our own lives that day and it allowed me to more fully appreciate the intensity and variety of emotions that were being lived just now. It seemed to put it all into a much broader perspective.

My heart went out to Tom, for whatever emotions Karen and I might be struggling with, they weren't anywhere nearly as bad as the ones he was having to deal with. We had each other; we had the future. Tom only had the past now, only loss.

We drove straight through to L.A. that starry, anxious night, drunk in our feelings of liberation the entire way. We stayed there for a couple of weeks getting the car fixed up a bit and ourselves outfitted as best we could for our upcoming adventures. Mostly, though, we just loafed around, going to the movies, the beach or visiting with my family.

Early on our second morning there, my mother walked into the front room where Karen and I were still asleep on the floor and woke me up to tell me that some guy proclaiming to be Karen's husband was on the phone wanting to talk to her. She had that tone of voice that said I had some fast explaining to do. It seems I forgot to mention that particular detail when I was telling my mother about our trip.

My mother, to her credit, had quickly sized up the situation and had discreetly avoided telling Tom that Karen was here. She was now standing there waiting for instructions. I woke Karen and asked what she wanted to do. There was no real decision, though; Karen knew she'd have to talk to him at some point. With an uneasy groan, she got up and took the phone.

Tom, it turned out, had called my father out of the Eureka phonebook and my dad told him that Karen and I had come here to L.A. and then gave him my mother's phone number. It was unfortunate because Karen had wanted just a little bit more time before confronting Tom but it turned out okay, anyway. At least as much as could be expected, under the circumstances. Karen told him how truly sorry she was but that it was something she had to do. She tried to allay his hurt but there was really nothing much she could do over the phone like that. All she could do was promise to talk to him about it again later. Maybe then it would be easier for both of them once their emotions settled down a little bit. [Though they did talk about it many times over the next several months, it was some time before it ever got any easier. In fact, initially, it got worse.]

Aside from all of this, it was a fairly uneventful visit and we were eager to get rolling so we soon hit the road again, aiming this time for Portland, Oregon, which was to be our next base. Our very limited money supply was already running out and we decided it would be good place to stop and work, plus I had some family and friends up there that I wanted her to meet and knew of some wonderful places that I wanted to show her. I'd had a whole lot of my life saved up to share with someone and now that I had a poor soul willing to be so endowed, I wanted to take full advantage.

To make the trip more exciting, or perhaps just to make it more nerve-wracking, the god of wayward-lovers-on-the-lam threw us a curve ball there in L.A. when we learned that we needed to return to Eureka for Karen's birth certificate. Without it she couldn't get a passport and without a passport, of course, no world.

It was with more than a little trepidation that we made our way back to the land that held the entirety of Karen's life. I think we both knew that this was going to be a major challenge of her resolve to continue on with me. Her decision to leave in the first place had obviously been a very difficult one and the thought that she would have to do it all again after only a few weeks was a tremendous weight on her. To make it worse, she had recently been having dreams about going back to Eureka and being confronted by her family and friends, which was making her very apprehensive about going anywhere near there.

This all made for a fairly nervous leg of our trip and there were many quiet spells as we both contemplated how well we were going to meet this first, and probably most difficult, test.

Two days later, however, as we approached Eureka, it was with our determination well in place. In order to keep this uncomfortable and dangerous situation from being a negative one we turned it into a game, playing like we were some kind of secret agents for the government on a mission to swipe some valuable documents.

Slunk low in our seats, our ever-watchful, shifty eyes darting to and fro, we slipped into town about midday and drove straight to the courthouse, which was conveniently right on the highway in the middle of town. We waited for a lull in traffic in order to keep the number of potential witnesses to a minimum, then Karen deftly slipped out of the car and disappeared through the front doors and into the big, ugly courthouse.

I was the getaway driver in this sensitive operation so I stayed out in the car and waited for her return, with only my eyes and the top of my head visible above the bottom edge of the window. She came scurrying out several minutes later and jumped in the car, certificate in hand. Mission complete! She sighed with relief when she drooped back down into the relative obscurity of the car, obviously relieved to finally have this over and our freedom once again restored. We sped straight out of town from there and didn't look back.

Aside from Karen's passport, our little ordeal seemed to have also given us a much finer hone on our resolve to make this trip work. After all, if Karen could come back to town so soon after her dramatic departure and remain true to her decision then it must have truly been the right one to make. It would have been so easy for her to say right then, "Never mind, Mark, take me home." It all could have ended that easily and quickly. Fortunately for us, though, she was as resolute as ever.

And it was a good thing, too, because soon, as if to make absolutely, positively sure of her decision to go, fate would tug once again at the rug 'neath our feet just to see, I think, how much we wobbled.

About fifteen miles out of town we pulled off the highway and took the little scenic road that went to the tiny town of Trinidad. Relieved now that Eureka was finally behind us for good (we thought, anyway), we decided to pay one last farewell to Humboldt County. The coastline all along through here was rugged, rocky, cliff-lined beach and I knew a spot along it that was particularly nice. I wanted to share it with Karen.

We followed the twisting roadway along the cliffs to an unmarked turnout and then got out and followed an ambling foot trail through the trees and bushes until it ended at the top of a gigantic boulder overlooking the whole of Trinidad Bay below us. It was so beautiful and pleasant out there that we didn't want to leave and decided right then to spend the night here.

As the day began to grow late, we went back to the car and got our new sleeping bags out and brought them out to the rocky bluff. It was a gorgeous place to stay, if not exactly the most comfortable, or safest. After all, it was a rocky cliff and not a very flat one at that. In fact, when we awoke the next morning after a long and lumpy night, we were startled to find that we'd slid partway down the rock during the night and were now only a few scant feet from the rock's precipitous edge and the frothing sea fifty feet below. It was such a beautiful fog-swirled morning though, that any feelings of near death quickly dissolved into it.

We stayed up there on the rock for a while, watching the nighttime fog begrudgingly cede its sovereignty to the bright sun of day before we decided that we'd better get going else we both end up changing our minds. We made our way back to the car and left, that old bittersweet feeling gripping our hearts once again. Not as much as before, to be sure, but it was a good squeeze, nonetheless.

It was only a short time later that Humboldt County would make its one last effort to hang onto Karen. Within only a few miles of its border, Otto seized up with a terrible noise and dashboard lights alit. We pulled off the road there in the middle of a large, ancient redwood grove.

The nearest (and only) town in the vicinity was about five miles behind us and not knowing what else to do, we locked up the car and started hitching back to it. We'd walked halfway there before someone finally pulled over for us. As soon as I'd explained our situation to the two men and the woman inside, they turned around and took us back so they could take a look at ole Otto themselves. The driver said that the symptoms I described sounded like a bad water pump. He was right, as it turned out, and he told us, luckily, that we could still drive it if we just took the fan belt off first. We did and were soon back on the road again in search of a new water pump. The only

41

place, of course, to get another one was, you guessed it, back in Eureka.

By the time we got back into town it was late in the evening and all the auto parts stores had already closed. Since this just happened to be the first day of Labor Day weekend, we were forced to wait until the following Tuesday before any of the stores would be open again. This was bad news since it meant we had to stay in town for three days without being seen and with nothing to do but wallow in our temptation to just give up on the whole affair, but we had no real choice.

We knew we couldn't stay out on the bluff for the whole three days so we imposed ourselves on a friend of mine, Doug, who didn't know Karen and was therefore neutral to our situation. It was the only place we could have stayed safely and he helped a lot by putting us up for the whole weekend, especially since it poured rain the entire two days of it.

There was nothing else we could do but wait so we just sat and whiled away the hours playing Monopoly with Doug's old, worn-out game. Perhaps "Monotony" would have been a better name for it that weekend, as we were becoming more and more anxious with each passing minute to finally break free of this determined town.

Tuesday finally did come, though. With the morning, I borrowed Doug's car and went into town to track down a new water pump. By midday we were up and rolling once more which was pretty good, I thought, considering that I had never worked on a car before other than replacing the starter back in L.A. I was quite proud of myself. Before leaving town, though, we both agreed that we should get some kind of gift for Doug to repay his much appreciated kindness. That, of course, meant one final trip into Eureka.

We must have been feeling overbold that day because both of us ended up going into town, which was not a very prudent thing to do. The chances of someone spotting Karen were much greater than for me alone since she knew so many more people here. But in we went, regardless, and sure as shootin', while cruising through Payless looking for a new Monopoly game, we spotted a former coworker of ours from Lazio's, Julie, at the end of our aisle doing some shopping of her own.

Luckily, she hadn't seen us before we'd seen her and we quickly ducked back out of sight behind the aisle end. We peeked furtively around the corners of the aisles now as we darted up and down through the store looking for the game aisle while deftly avoiding Julie's notice as she strolled through the store.

We made our way to the game aisle and grabbed a Monopoly box off the shelf as we whizzed by it without stopping. Karen ran forward lookout as I came up behind her with the game and headed straight to the checkout counter. We tossed down our money, grabbed the game and bolted out the door for the car.

It actually wasn't as serious a threat as we made it out to be. I guess we were still just a little bit jumpy. We went straight back to Doug's house and dropped off the game, our thanks and our goodbyes before trying once more to rid ourselves of this town's tenacious grip.

This time, though, we actually made it and with all the tests and trials of Eureka behind us now we were once again filled with the promise of the road ahead. There was no doubt about our resolve any longer. We were fully committed now and we hit the highway with confidence that this thing was going to happen.

We didn't stop until we got to Crescent City, just south of the Oregon border, and this just to get some new tires for Otto. His old ones were almost completely bald and we didn't want to break down again. This took a big swipe out of our mostly depleted money supply, giving our trip that uncertain dynamic quality that only true adventures have. It was time, we knew, to get serious about our finances and finally put our travel credo into full operation.

Way back at the very beginning of our trip, we decided that if we were to succeed in circling the globe without any real money we would have to follow pretty strict guidelines and we developed a set of rules from which we agreed we could not deviate. At least not without a good excuse.

The first rule was that we would not fly anywhere unless it was absolutely the only means available to us. This was included because not only was flying very expensive but it was also aesthetically inferior. It was cheating. We wanted to meet real people, not travel people, and we wanted to learn about the world, not about airports. We wanted adventure, not window seats.

The second rule of the road, and the one now up for implementation, was the "forage rule." This stipulated that, whenever possible, we would take advantage of any free food that might be available to us along the way. This could mean taking only restaurant jobs that came with meal allowances or simply nibbling on roadside edibles. This rule was for obvious reasons - simply to save money.

Rule three was a combination of the first two, actually. It was the one that prohibited us from taking busses when we could walk and trains when we could hitchhike. It also prevented us from paying any kind of superfluous fees or charges such as museum admissions or ferryboat crossings and the like.

While all of this might sound pretty drastic and untravel-like, we felt it was necessary, as we could never know how long we might have to travel on the money we had in hand since finding jobs would always be an uncertainty. More importantly, it promoted the creative side of travel, the adventure side. It would make us stop and think of ways to get by or alternatives that we felt would prove infinitely more interesting and memorable than the easy ways.

They were strict rules but certainly ones we could live with. After all, they were self-imposed and for very good reasons. Now that our original $600 had dwindled down to mere pocket change, it was time to put these rules to the test.

The first rule to come into play now was the "forage" rule. Fortunately, it was late summer and there were plenty of farms and orchards throughout Oregon that were in the midst of their bearing seasons. We stopped and picked wild blackberries whenever we came across a big enough patch on the roadside and sometimes apples or plums from the occasional orphaned trees that liked to grow in the ditches here. Sometimes, if the roadside didn't quite provide, we'd stage an orchard raid on some unsuspecting farm, dashing madly into the orchard and stuffing our shirts with as much ill-gotten booty as we could quickly drop into them before making a quick getaway in Otto. It was great fun and we enjoyed the spoils of our piracies much more than if we'd bought the things. It was just as well, too, for by the time we arrived in Portland we were indeed flat broke.

We had some time to kill before it was late enough to go surprise my friend Doug (another one) with the news of our arrival so we went to a big park I knew of in town where we could hang out for a while.

While we were sitting there enjoying the warm sunshine, we noticed a big three-tiered water fountain nearby that looked inviting to play in. As soon as we got up to its edge, we both stopped in our tracks and looked at each other with a wicked smile, for strewn all across the bottom of the fountain, were coins of all denominations (though mostly pennies) just ripe for the plucking. Still imbued with the plunder-lust of our recent forays into the orchards, we wasted no time now figuring a way to rob this unsuspecting fountain of its riches.

[This was great - foraging for money! We hadn't thought of that but we quickly incorporated it into our credo as a subparagraph of Rule #2 and from this point on collected any coin we happened to come across, even if it were only a penny.]

We rolled up our pants legs and hopped in the fountain. Karen then climbed up and stood on my shoulders and, while I waded around the bottom pool picking coins up with my toes, she held onto the edge of the second, smaller tier with her one hand and bent her other arm over its curved lip and fished out any coins she could get her little fingers on. When we had plucked all we could get hold of, we retreated back to the nearest park bench and counted out our loot. We had a whopping $1.27.

We left the park shortly afterwards and went through town and across the river to the Lloyd Center shopping mall where we blew the whole wad on a couple of ice cream cones from Baskin-Robbins. We stood and watched the ice-skaters there at the rink going round and round as we happily wolfed down the fruits of our stolen treasure, savoring every lick.

Early that evening we made our way over to Doug's house and spent our first night in town there. He was my very best friend from high school back in L.A. but was now living up here in Portland. We knew that we were going to be here for a while and we didn't want to impose on him to put us up for that length of time so the next morning we went out and found ourselves a nice park to camp out in for our second night. It was on a high bluff right on the Willamette River and, conveniently, only a few blocks from Doug's house.

Sellwood Park turned out to be so convenient, in fact, that we stayed there for the better part of the three weeks that we were here in Portland, sleeping in the car at night and playing in the park during the day.

Not only was Doug's house nearby, availing us occasional showers together, but so was Lewis and Clark College, just across the river from us, which gave us a place to take our everyday showers when we needed. As a bonus, it also gave us a place where we could hang out during our off hours with people our own age and watch TV, play pool or even crash the occasional dorm party.

With our accommodations all settled now it was time for us to find ourselves some work. We set out the following morning and both found jobs at the first restaurant we applied at. They didn't normally hire couples, the manager told us, but he liked us so he took us both on. Unfortunately, we didn't much like his place and quit it after only one day.

It turned out that restaurant work here in Portland was plentiful and we were offered jobs every single time we applied. This afforded us the luxury of being perhaps just a little too choosy. If for any reason we didn't like a place, we'd quit at the end of that particular day and simply pick up another job the next morning. Between the two of us we had, or were offered, about 10 jobs in the three weeks that we were there. After about a week or so of this, though, we finally settled down with two jobs each that satisfied us.

I was working days at a deli/restaurant, called Deja Vu, as a waiter/kitchen aid/busboy/dishwasher until 3 p.m., when I then had to race like a madman the few miles over to Mazzi's, an Italian restaurant, where I was supposed to start at 3 p.m. and work washing dishes until closing time, somewhere around midnight. Karen was working lunches at the Rafter's, right next to our park, bussing tables and working in the salad bar. Afterwards, she'd go downtown and wait tables at the Swashbuckler for the rest of the night.

Being faithful to our Rule #2, one of the main reasons I stuck with Mazzi's was because they had a very generous meal policy (always one of the first questions I asked when applying). In fact, when I asked the manager about it he rubbed his well-endowed belly with both hands and said, "Heck, that's the best part of working in a restaurant." In other words, I could have whatever I wanted.

47

Normally I'd order a large pizza before my break and when it was ready I'd sneak it out the back door and meet Karen in the parking lot, where she was patiently waiting for me in the car. Her jobs both made her pay for food which meant, excepting for the little bits of lettuce and bread she could occasionally filch, she didn't get any so this pizza was often our main meal of the day. Fortunately, when they said large pizza they meant it. This thing was huge. We sat there in the car and wolfed down as much as we could and then saved the leftovers for our breakfast the next morning in the park.

Mornings were about the only time we both ever had off together and we spent the majority of them just hanging out at the park, playing. Doug had given us an old leather football shortly after our arrival, and we liked to play one-on-one tackle football with it. We enjoyed wrestling (rassling) a lot too, and had great fun rolling around on the grass there, in the warm sunshine, like a couple of puppies fighting over a rubber ball. Of course, the only difference between "rassling" and one-on-one tackle football is that somewhere in between all the tangles of arms and legs is a football. Even so, it seemed we still preferred rassling for some reason.

If we weren't out on the turf beating each other up, though, it only meant that we were over at the children's playground, on the other side of the park, playing on the swings or the merry-go-round. Once, we dared each other to climb the big water tower that stood off in a corner of the park there. We hopped over the fence (the one with all the "Do Not Enter" signs all over it) and scaled up one of the stout legs of this giant metal spider, crossing over on its cable web and then farther on up until we reached the narrow catwalk that encircled the pill-shaped tank. We crawled around its perimeter like ants on a Coke can, admiring the fine views of the river below us, the city before us and the jagged, snow-capped peak of Mt. Hood off in the far distant east.

We very much enjoyed our life in the park these weeks. It was strangely idyllic, in a vagrant kind of way, which somehow, paradoxically, made it seem like home to us. Our first home away from home, in fact. Only twice did the park's friendliness let us down while we were there.

Although the police made nightly rounds through the park, turning a blind eye to our staying there for some reason, it still had its share of strange folk moving through its dark shadows and one night during our second week here one of these shadows came to pay us a visit.

FROM KAREN'S JOURNAL:

[03Oct78] - This one night as we were sleeping in the car at Sellwood Park, I awoke to find some guy with his arm reached inside the car. Don't ask how or why, but I just calmly whispered to him and asked him what he was doing. He pulled his arm out and said "nothing," then just stood there staring at me. I just didn't know what to do about this guy; finally I quietly asked him to go away, so he left. I just lay there stunned. About 5 min. later he came sneaking back to the car, then I was mad. I yelled at him and told him to get the hell out of there! I was now shaking and my heart was racing. It was all very upsetting. Mark, this whole time lay there peacefully asleep next to me. My prince and my protector. The more I think about it, it probably would have been a good idea to bring Toolie; at least I know she would have woken up. Well, not five mins. later here he came again. I sat up and really started yelling at him this time. He put his hand up to get me quiet. He asked me how long we were staying; like an idiot, I said all night. Then he said: (I should make a play out of this); he didn't say that, he said: Oh, so you're from out of town, huh? And then he walked away. Well, Mark, my hero, in the meantime had woken up. The guy was such a weirdo (the stranger, not Mark, though Mark's a

little weird himself) and he made me so upset and ruined my whole sleep. Me and Mark decided to leave, we went to another park to sleep the rest of that night. We did not get a good night's sleep that night, needless to say.

Some days later, we woke up in the morning to find Karen's purse missing from the dashboard where she'd left it the night before. This upset her greatly. Apparently, someone (maybe our old friend again) had reached in through the barely opened window and had somehow managed to pull the purse out without waking us. She had no money in it (we had none), only the million little things that were important to her, which is why it bothered her so much.

She had to work that morning so after dropping her off at the restaurant, I went back to the park and started looking through the bushes, thinking that whoever took it might have flung it in there after finding nothing of any value inside. I did find a piece of paper with her name on it and was encouraged but found nothing more.

About a hundred yards away, a group of park workers were clearing brush from the hillside. On the slight chance that maybe they had run across something, I went over and asked them if they had seen anything. Sure enough, they had found her purse earlier that morning, almost entirely intact.

After giving them a brief description of its contents and of Karen (they had her driver's license), they readily turned it over to me. The only thing missing turned out to be her birth control pills. Needless to say, Karen was overjoyed after work that day, when I surprised her with it. I was indeed her hero after all.

About a week later, however, my hero status was suddenly, and surprisingly, challenged, if only for a short time. As we neared the end of our third, and final, week in Portland, I noticed a very unusual mood in Karen when she picked me up from Deja Vu. She was uncharacteristically quiet and withdrawn and refused to answer me when I asked about it.

In default of any answer from her I was now free to make my own guesses and, being in a relatively good mood myself, I cavalierly offered that she was fooling around with another man and was feeling guilty. No one could have been more surprised than me when she coyly looked up and told me I was right.

Now that the story had been forced out, she readily explained to me its circumstances. It seemed that for some time now, one of the waiters at Swashbuckler had been making advances at Karen and, perhaps feeling emboldened by the fact that we were only days away from leaving town, she decided that she would finally accept his offer.

She explained further that what prompted her was nothing more than curiosity. Having only been with two men in her life before now, they being Tom and myself, of course, and both cases in the context of a relationship, she had been growing curious about what strictly casual sex must be like. Now that she was unhindered from her marriage vows for the first time in her adult life and there was a willing volunteer at the ready, she had her first opportunity to find out firsthand. Thankfully, for both of us, she wasn't much impressed.

She was visibly better afterwards for having confessed this all to me and seemed herself again once she had. I could certainly understand the rationale behind her actions and I could not blame her for that. I knew that prior to me, Karen had only been with one man. Tom had been her first, and only, boyfriend, meeting him when she was fourteen years old. She married him four years later, at age eighteen, because she figured that was what people do. It was two years later I showed up and messed up the plan. In a society inundated with images and notions of casual sex, it was very understandable for her to want to know what it was like and I could not fault her for that.

51

Putting rationale aside now for the moment, I must confess that when she first confirmed to me that she'd been with another man I was introduced to some very new feelings. My first reaction was, naturally, a strong upwelling of jealousy and hurt but, after a moment's thought, I realized how foolishly absurd that was. How could I be possessive and jealous of a woman that was, in truth, another man's wife? For a moment, this confused me and I wasn't sure how to respond to it in my own heart. It forced me to confront the whole notion of jealousy from a entirely new direction.

As a kid, you get jealous when your girlfriend or boyfriend flirts with someone one else and that's it; you have a right to. But this was grownup stuff, marriage, and I wasn't used to it. What does one do when his girlfriend, who happens to be someone else's wife, liaises with another man not himself? I simply had to accept the fact that she could do whatever she wanted and if I didn't like it, well, tough. I could never take possession of her in this regard and would only be with her until she saw fit to lose me. Of course, the reciprocal was just as true and from that moment on my whole concept of relationships, in general, became one based more on mutual respect than on ownership and I found, to my surprise, that I liked it much better that way.

It's a good thing, too, for this was a critical time in the formation of our relationship. That we could come through a situation as potentially lethal to it as this, and be better off for it, couldn't have been more important to our future just then.

Traveling with friends is always a little dicey anyway, but in our case, it was a make-or-break situation from the very beginning and the habits and attitudes we developed now were the ones we would end up carrying with us for the duration of our trip. We were planning on being together, side by side, for the next two to three years and it was vital that we enjoy each other's company (a lot). Indeed, the trip's very success depended on it.

Prior to leaving Eureka, however, we had only been together for short periods of time, and this while the lusts of our relationship were still steaming. We'd never even slept together before starting this trip, I mean actually sleeping, and we couldn't know before running off together if we'd even get along with each other once we did. We'd made a big gamble.

Fortunately, Portland couldn't have been a more ideal spot for us to put it to the test. The weather was warm and clear, work was plentiful and easy to find, we ate well, and took regular showers. We wanted for nothing. More than anything though, we found out that we really did enjoy being with each other. We lived literally side-by-side in my tiny little Toyota, sleeping in a park in a strange city, with no money, and we still liked each other. In fact, there was no question in our minds that we loved each other very much.

It was the perfect complement to our springtime, for if it had served to unite us, then this summertime was to lay the string work with which to bind us. And we couldn't have been happier.

***

If Sellwood Park could be called our home, then the Columbia Gorge was certainly our church. About 30 miles east of Portland, it's the cleavage that formed between the twin volcanoes of Mt. Hood and Mount St. Helens, midway along the Cascades mountain range, when the Columbia River found its only available pathway to the Pacific Ocean, a hundred miles farther away to the west.

Towering cliffs of solid rock line both sides of the river here, giving birth to the dozens of long, silvery waterfalls that plunge the several hundreds of feet to the river below. Foot trails run up along most of the creeks, going back into the thickly forested foothills of Mt. Hood for several miles.

53

I have yet to see a prettier place on Earth than this and we came up here as often as we could to hike along the cliff sides and swim in the clear, deep pools that formed at the bottom of the waterfalls.

Though it was all grandly beautiful, Oneonta Gorge was, I think, our favorite place to go. It is a very narrow rift in the rock, about a quarter mile long, that runs perpendicular to the main gorge, with steep, straight walls. At the far end of it, just out of view, the mist-filled gorge ends in a wonderful waterfall spilling through a smooth-worn cleft in the moss-covered stone bed.

The only way to get in to see the waterfall was by hiking up the creek bed itself and clambering along the rock sides of the gorge until finally rounding the corner and discovering the mighty cataract directly before you. Sometimes when the water level is too high to traverse the rock sides the only way to get in is to undress and swim through the deeper cuts while holding your clothes up over your head. Only the truly committed would go to this trouble but the final reward was always worth the effort.

It all seemed a cathedral to Karen and me. The floating spray was as a drifting cloud of incense and the long shafts of sunlight that beamed through it were like affirmations from God himself shining onto the steeply jutting walls of the gorge as though through stained glass panes onto mighty stone buttresses. The sense of majesty and reverence that it inspired in us was our holy rapture. We were humbled by it all.

Just before leaving Oregon, we came out here for one last visit. We couldn't know when, if ever, we'd be able to come back for another and we wanted to soak up as much of it as possible to carry with us. We went to Eagle Creek this time and spent the day hiking up the trail that ran alongside the creek and then up across a narrow path cut into the cliff face, through a little stone tunnel and eventually to the serenely beautiful Punchbowl Falls.

Because the source of these creeks is mostly snowmelt runoff from Mt. Hood, they were really too cold to comfortably swim in for most of the year and Eagle Creek was no exception. We were the only ones up here this particular day, though, and it just looked too inviting to pass up so we got naked and jumped into one of the crystal clear pools. Afterwards, still naked and still alone, we ran around in the sunshine exploring the nearby woods while we air-dried. Karen "discovered" a small waterfall hidden behind the boulders and trees. We officially dubbed it "Karen Falls" and played in it for a while before returning to our clothing and the trail.

We had a wonderful time out here and it made us sad to think that we were leaving it. Our time here in Oregon was through, though, and we both knew it. We had earned enough money by now to see us across the country (we hoped, anyway) and the season was growing late. Our next stop was to be New England and we wanted to catch it before fall ended. Since October was only a few days away now, it meant we'd need to hurry if we wanted to get there in time.

The thought of leaving Oregon was difficult for me for another reason as well. Up to this point we had been well within my world. A lot of this was new to Karen but not to me. She had already stepped into her unknown world some weeks earlier when we first left Eureka. Now it was to be my turn and I must confess that I felt just a little apprehensive about stepping across this final threshold, the boundary that separated the land I grew up in from the land that I had only ever heard about.

We left Portland the very next day. After picking up our last paychecks from work and saying our good-byes to Doug, we packed up and headed west for the coast. We were making a big detour down along the Oregon coastline to the south and then back over the coastal mountains and on up to the north again before heading east. It was obviously way out of the way but Karen really wanted to see the town of "Wonder" in southern Oregon before we left the west coast for good. This was the little town in which her brother, David, had lived and helped to build just before he died.

It really wasn't much of a town, as it turned out. Not much more than a small grocery store, in fact, and a handful of undistinguished wooden buildings, whose function wasn't immediately apparent, but she felt much better for having finally seen it after all that had happened.

It had been on a trip from his home here in Wonder down to Eureka one night that he was in the accident. He was asleep in a friend's car as they made their way south on the twisty highway when a deer bolted out in front of them. Swerving to miss it, the car went out of control and drove off an 80-foot embankment. David was so injured that he'd gone into a coma. Two years later, without ever waking up and with his family all standing beside him, he finally let go.

It was big blow to the whole family but I think it must have been even more so for Karen. Though she was the youngest of six kids, and he the second eldest, she was closer to him than to anyone else. He was her best friend, her confidant, and his loss was acutely felt by her. Whenever things went particularly well with us on our trip we liked to think it was David keeping a lookout for his little kid sis. [In light of all the many times of unbelievably good luck we actually had in our trip, I've come to feel there can be no doubt and it's to him alone that I give credit for much of what was to come.] We did a slow drive-by through Wonder. We didn't stop; Karen paid her respects to the meager outpost as we drove past and away.

Late afternoon of the next day found us approaching the Idaho border and the end of that which was familiar to me. We crossed just before sunset and pulled into a nearby freeway rest area to spend the night. As if to bid us farewell, the sun set gloriously behind the distant hills of Oregon, the very ones we'd just crossed.

This was as far as I'd ever been now and for all the mental melodrama that I'd made about this moment the next day was actually very ordinary and unimpressive. It wasn't until later, when we had gotten to Utah, that I actually felt my first pang of insecurity at being far from home and this, I think, only because it seemed so desolate and lonely there. These feelings soon passed though, and I enjoyed the drive across the rest of the country.

We were in a hurry to get to Connecticut before fall fell so we didn't stop much from that point on and did a lot of driving at night. Although I enjoyed going through Kansas, for some reason, I really had no interest in much of the other states we passed through and I didn't mind a bit passing through them in the dark. Actually, Karen did almost all of the driving at this point of our trans-national trek as she didn't like just sitting there doing nothing. I, on the other hand, quite liked just sitting there doing nothing so I was only too happy to let her take the reins. It gave me a chance to catch up on my reading.

When it did come time to change drivers, however, we would usually do it on the fly as we sped down the freeway. In a tightly coordinated maneuver, whoever was driving would set the seat back all the way flat and the in-coming driver would get behind and straddle the out-going driver who would then scoot their left foot over to the gas pedal and then slip the rest of themself over to the passenger side. At this, the incoming driver would then take the wheel and slide into position. Once fully in place, the out-going driver would remove their gas pedal foot as the in-coming driver quickly replaced with their own. There really was no need for such a potentially dangerous maneuver as we weren't in that much of a hurry, but it was an exciting way to break the monotony of the long drive and we pretty much did it each time we needed to switch.

Somewhere around Illinois I noticed that Otto started having an increasingly harder time getting up the meager hills of that part of the country and I begin to worry that the old boy might not survive this whirlwind cross-country dash intact. He continued to worsen as we made our way east but we managed to make it all the way to Connecticut, two days later, without incident.

We had come here not only to witness our first New England autumn but also to visit with my dear friend Susan, the same one that I had recently shared the old ramshackle house with back in California and who had since moved back home here. It was late in the afternoon when we arrived, unannounced, at her parents' house there. There was no one home when we got there and we had no way to know when anyone was due back so we decided to go off and do some exploring and come back in the morning. After driving around and marveling at all the colored trees, we found a dirt road that led to an isolated little lake out in the middle of a small wooded area. The woods were ablaze with the fires of autumn color, particularly with the late setting sun casting its yellow spotlight on them and contrasting them against the clear blue sky behind. We spent the rest of the afternoon hiking around the lake and through the woods in the dying light of the day and so enjoyed ourselves that we decided to stay here for the night.

As the full moon made its way up into the darkening night, we made ourselves comfy there in the car for what we knew would be a chilly sleep-out. We had been sleeping at freeway rest areas for the past three nights so it was a real treat to be able to park in a such a quiet, secluded and pretty place. We were in high spirits that night for some reason and we laughed and played well into the night before finally throwing the seats back and knocking off. We slept very well that night.

Despite the fact that I had told Susan some time ago that I was going to come out for a visit, she was literally dumbstruck the following morning when she came home to find us sitting in her driveway waiting for her. Apparently she hadn't believed me. California had been a whole 'nother life to her and very separate from her Connecticut one and now all of a sudden they were merging on her and causing a short-circuit somewhere.

At any rate, once she came to and got over the shock she was glad to have us and immediately set about introducing us to her various family and friends. When Susan had first moved to California a few years back, I had taken it upon myself to be her tour guide of the West Coast and had shown her much of it. Now it was her turn to return the favor and show us through her neck of the woods. She and her friend Harry drove us all around Connecticut and into parts of Vermont the next day.

Coming from the west, the land of the evergreens, I wasn't accustomed to seeing trees come in all the colors that they did here and after a while it started to seem too unreal to me. Everything up, down and in between was either red, orange, yellow or brown and I found myself desperately searching for anything green to reorient myself with and to bring me back to a sense of normalcy. Though it was all quite nice, I don't know that I could take a whole season of this autumn stuff. It did feel good to have finally seen it though. It's always been one of those things you have to see at least once and having now gazed upon it, I felt satisfied.

We stayed there at Susan's for three days before getting antsy for the road again and heading back out to it. We had so much ground still to cover and poor old Otto wasn't getting any better. My grandmother's house in Florida was our next destination and was pretty much going to be the end of the road for our (mostly) trusty steed. It was our plan to sell him there as soon as we figured out how we were going to get ourselves out of the country for our next leg. If he made it that far, that is.

Leaving Connecticut behind, we headed for the Big Apple next. Having scratched New England Autumn off our list of things to do, it was now time to give equal honor to New York City. Not that either of us was all that interested in New York City but it was something that had to be done. I had to see the Statue of Liberty just once.

The only map we had for that area was actually a map of the entire eastern coast and with only small insets of all the major cities, but we figured a city like New York would be pretty hard to miss so we didn't bother looking at it. We drove on. And on. And on. It was some time actually before I finally admitted that something was wrong. Not only should we have reached New York City by now but we should have been through it and well out the other side of it by now, too, and we hadn't even seen a sign for it yet.

I pulled off the freeway in search of a gas station to get us a real map, only to learn that they don't sell maps in gas stations here (at least at all the ones we went to). We also learned that somewhere along the way we had indeed made a wrong turn and were now at the very end of Long Island, only about 60 miles in the wrong direction! I guess now we could scratch off Long Island from our list, too. Anyway, I turned around and aimed us back in the right direction. We managed to find it this time.

While passing through midtown Manhattan, Otto stammered for a moment, threatening to stall, and I had a real fear that he might breakdown in the middle of the city. This was one thing definitely not on my list of "Do's" in New York City and with that thought in mind we quickly made our way to I-95 and went Florida-ho once again.

In fact, the only real goal I had for going to New York City was to see the Statue of Liberty. On the map it was shown right alongside the freeway and we thought we could just drive by and take a quick look. Unfortunately, little map insets don't match reality very closely and after several attempts to find

60

the blessed thing, crisscrossing freeways and rivers a couple times over, we finally gave up. I told myself that I'd catch up to old Madam Liberty some other time (and indeed I did, only from a very unexpected vantage point, but that story comes later) and we decided to just leave.

We got as far as Baltimore by that afternoon when Otto showed his first definite sign of expiration. The freeway we were on was still fairly new and the section that bypassed Baltimore hadn't been completed yet so all the traffic was being diverted right into the middle of the city. As we pulled up to the first stoplight, Otto sputtered and stalled dead. Now, downtown Baltimore wasn't any better in my mind than New York City when it came to breaking down and as I looked around the nearby environs I was even more convinced of that fact. Fortunately, Otto was only having a dizzy spell, though, and after a short rest he started back up and we were once again on our way, beginning now to think that we'd better hurry up and get to Florida soon.

It was late in the day by this time and as we approached the town of Laurel, Maryland, just a few miles further down the freeway, we came to a rest area and decided to pull in for the night. We all needed rest at this point.

The following morning our worst fears became real when we tried to start Otto up and the best we could get out of him was only a sickly cough. I knew that his valves had burnt to the point where there wasn't enough compression to start him up.

Knowing that, unfortunately, made very little difference, for we were stuck in some little nameless rest area with barely enough money for gas, let alone for towing and a valve job. We were woebegone and unsure what to do. There was a small hill nearby, there in the rest area, and in desperation we decided that we would push him up it and try to do a compression start by rolling him back down again and popping the clutch.

Fortunately, Corollas are very small, light cars and easy to push. Unfortunately, after about five trips up and down that stinkin' hill, all to no avail, this became meaningless, for we were totally spent by now and at a loss as to what to do next. We sat down on the hood of the car to rest and catch our breath, thoroughly beaten in our failure.

After a few moments, a Chevy pickup came toward us on his way out of the rest area and as he came past I impulsively stuck my thumb out. To my great surprise it pulled up and stopped and the fellow inside poked his head out and asked where we were headed. After a moment's hesitation to collect myself, I told him that what we actually needed was a push rather than a ride. He happily agreed to help and swung his truck around behind us.

We hopped in and gave him the thumbs up as he slowly nudged up to us and started pushing. As soon as we had built up some speed, I let the clutch out. Otto coughed and sputtered and spit but just short of the point where we'd have to cut loose and abort the mission, in a billowing cloud of black smoke, the old boy came to life with a jolt and shot out onto the freeway like a charging bull. Albeit an old, sick bull. At any rate, we were on our way again. We waved our vigorous thanks through the smoke to the kindly man and vowed now that we would not stop again until we were safely in my grandmother's driveway. It was a vow that Otto wouldn't let us keep for very long, though.

We agreed now that we couldn't take the chance of turning the car off again, for any reason. When we pulled in for gas, whoever was driving would sit there and rev the engine way up while the other got out, pumped the gas and paid. It was all simple enough to do, though somewhat embarrassing (not to mention illegal), as all the other drivers tended to stare as we sat there in the car doing about ninety miles an hour while we refilled.

Not quite so simple, however, were those infernal tollbooths, which seemed to pop up every third breath. To keep the car running I had to rev up the engine, of course, but because you never really come to a complete stop at them, I also had to do this stop and go routine while in line before I could even pay the toll. So, with my right foot pumping the gas pedal, my left foot holding the clutch in, my right hand working the emergency brake to slow us down and my left hand on the steering wheel, I would somehow maneuver us into position. I tried to time it so that there was no one immediately in front us by the time we actually got up to the booth. Meanwhile, Karen sat there next to me holding up the appropriate coins in her hand and, as we cruised through the tollbooth at about 10 miles per hour, I'd grab them from her just at the right moment and fling them into the coin hopper before popping the clutch and speeding away.

I felt like Kareem Abdul every time I slam-dunked those coins in the hopper and I was very proud of myself for not missing a single one, especially considering that I had to use my braking hand to throw the things, which was the only real control I had over the car.

This system worked pretty well. Up until we got to a certain tollbooth in Virginia anyway when, in the complicated maneuverings of my four limbs, I lost my co-ordination just long enough to forget to rev the engine as I was plunking the money in, and Otto stalled right in the station with a whole freeway of cars backing up behind us waiting to get through. We quickly jumped out and, thanking old man Toyota for making his cars so light, pushed Otto to the median on the fast lane side of the turnpike.

Once safely on the roadside, I walked back and asked the toll man if he might be able to give us a push, since I knew Otto would run if we could only get him started, but the man told me quite flatly that, no, he couldn't and that the only thing we could do was to just sit and wait for the next state patrol car to come by and call us a tow truck.

Since our money was getting very low by now, a tow truck and a cop were the last things we needed and so, once again, we took to pushing Otto up and down the freeway. I pushed from behind while Karen pushed from the open doorway on the driver's side. As soon as we got any speed up she'd jump in and engage the clutch. No luck. After several tries, we switched places and tried a couple more times, up and back, but it was futile. There was no hill there this time and we just couldn't get up enough speed.

Finally, in a last-ditch effort, I stuck my thumb out again, not thinking it would really work but not knowing what else to do. My thinking proved wrong, however, when only a few minutes later a guy pulled up and stopped for us. My heart was pumping fast as I came up to his window and I think my blood was about 75% adrenaline at this point, not only from pushing the car but also from trying to beat the cop that was supposedly not far behind. After quickly explaining the situation to guy, he somewhat reluctantly agreed to give us a push. He maneuvered behind us and slowly started us down the turnpike's median.

Sure enough, in our now familiar black cloud of smoke, we were off once again. We were only about five minutes down the road when the state patrolman passed us by, none the wiser. Again, we vowed not to stop. Again, we stopped.

This time it was in North Carolina. At about one o'clock the following morning I noticed that the alternator light had a slight glow to it but, not knowing what an alternator even did, I gave it little thought. As the night went on, however, the panel lights started getting very dim as did my headlights. In fact, people were beginning to flash their headlights at me, telling me to turn mine on. I realized then that my goal of at least making it to daylight, only a few hours away, before they conked out entirely was now about as dim as my headlights were and that we were going to have to stop somewhere very soon.

We figured we could just pull over on a side street somewhere and prop the accelerator on with a stone or something to keep the engine running, if not any of the electrics. We turned off the freeway in the town of Fayetteville and found a suitably dark little road immediately adjacent to it to spend the rest of the night. I wedged a stick and rock onto the gas pedal, being very careful not to kill the engine, and then climbed over to share the passenger seat with Karen and try to get some sleep. It was very cramped, to say the least, but I didn't want to accidentally knock my contraption out and leave us stranded.

At about 3 a.m. we awoke from a very uncomfortable sleep to an even more uncomfortable spotlight shining in our faces. After explaining to the nice officer what we were doing here, he kindly told us that we had to do it elsewhere.

Begrudgingly, I went back around to the driver's side and very carefully removed the stick and stone from the gas pedal that I had so meticulously placed only two hours earlier, while gently replacing them with my right foot. Once safely back in control, I cautiously turned Otto around and started back down the road toward the freeway. We made it a good 20 - 30 feet at best before Otto just up and quit, right there in the middle of the road. Worse, when I tried to restart him, the engine wouldn't even turn over. I discovered that now, along with the alternator, battery and valves, the starter was out, too!

There was nothing else we could do at this point but hop out of the car and push him into the parking lot of the small motel that was conveniently just across the street from us. It was now early (very early) Sunday morning and I knew that there was no way I'd find anybody open later that day so we reluctantly checked in into the motel and resigned ourselves to waiting out the remainder of the weekend here. It wasn't really what we wanted to do and it did go against our budget, but we didn't have much choice.

Although it was nice to sleep in a bed again and to lie around watching T.V. and playing cards, I was unsettled about what I was going to do with Otto. Our money was perilously low. Given the idleness of our day and the relative luxury of the motel room, it wasn't long before we degraded into a bout of rassling that soon grew into a major pillow fight, with both of us bouncing up and down on the beds like errant children, pulverizing each other as we did. It made me feel a lot better afterwards and allowed me to defer any further brainstorming until the next morning. I wouldn't be able to do anything till then anyway.

It proved to be a good strategy because after a good night's sleep the decision of what we were to do next was fairly easy to come to. There was obviously nothing I could do about the burnt valves so I promptly scratched that off the list and since the car wouldn't start without a push anyway there was certainly no reason to get the starter fixed. That only left the alternator to contend with and so I set about in earnest to see if I could track a new one down.

I called around town to see if I could get a rebuilt one somewhere and was disappointed when I failed to after several tries. I did manage to find a parts shop that had one very similar to mine, though, and we decided that it was worth a try. The best news was that this shop was just around the corner from the motel, sparing me a long walk.

To get to where the alternator lives in the car requires taking out a lot of other bits and pieces of machinery first and it took me a while to get the new one into place. With this in mind, it should be easy to understand my frustration when the blasted thing didn't work and I had to take it back out.

Not knowing the first thing about any of this didn't help and I wore a path in the roadway to the parts store asking the owner there all my multitudes of questions. He also charged my battery up for me and even loaned me some tools. He was a nice man. Anyway, I spent that whole day fooling around with it and I never did get it going. We spent that night in the motel again.

The next morning, I decided to see if the local Toyota dealership could help any and gave them a call. It proved too difficult to handle over the phone so I hesitatingly decided to go there in person. It was clear across town and since there were no buses going that direction, I had no choice but to walk the 10 miles or so there and back. I left late that morning and didn't get back until much later that afternoon.

Even with that, though, the mechanic I had talked to wasn't much help. Although he did give me some advice on a few things to check, without being able to look at the car in person there really wasn't much he could do and not knowing what I was talking about didn't make it any easier either. I came home exhausted and empty-handed.

Southerners, I found out, are a curious sort and as I went back to work on Otto a little while later I soon found myself the central figure in a small crowd that was growing around us. The man from the auto parts store finally closed his shop and came over himself to see if he could give a hand and as we worked on it, the garbage man, after emptying the motel's dumpster, pulled up in his truck and came over for a look, too. Soon after that, the motel owner and his nephew drifted over to see how things were coming along and, about this time, a passing taxicab happened by and he too stopped to see what was going on.

All these people gathered around the car and, as I lay underneath it, they would all take turns telling me to try something else. "Push that button," "Attach that wire to here," "Try this...", "Try that....", etc. It was somewhat confusing as none of us really knew what we were doing but after a while I finally got the old alternator and the radiator re-installed to everyone's satisfaction and it was generally agreed that I should hop in and see if I could get the old boy going.

Because the starter was still out of commission, the auto parts man offered to give me a push with his truck. After a quick run down the road, Otto once again jerked and wheezed and spit out a cloud of soot before he slowly lumbered back to life.

Everyone was so excited by the moment that they all began to shout at us to get going while we could (I think they just wanted to get rid of us). Getting caught up in the flurry myself, we scooped up all the loose nuts, bolts and miscellaneous parts that were still lying about, tossed them in the back seat and, yelling our thank-yous and waving wildly to everyone, we sped off down the highway, happy to be Florida-bound once more. Our glee lasted only about 10 minutes, however. That's when I noticed that the car was overheating rapidly and realized, that in the excitement of our hasty departure, I'd forgotten to refill the radiator with water.

I pulled over near a truck weigh station just outside of town and managed to talk Karen into going in and sweet talking some water and a push from the guys that worked there. I figured she would have a much better chance of succeeding than I would.

She did succeed, too, and we were soon off again. Breakdown number 6 now history. How many more to go we dared not venture to guess but our resolve to make it to Florida was by now nearly all-consuming.

Despite all these trials we kept our spirits up and looked at all of it as part of the adventure, rather than as setbacks, and we were encouraged by all the friendly and helpful people we had come across.

South Carolina distinguished itself by being the only state along the south-eastern coast that we didn't break down in.

How this happened I don't know but we were mighty glad for it. It was later that evening, however, just as it started to get dark that I noticed the now familiar alternator light faintly glowing once again as the power continued to drain away. Around eight o'clock the headlights had sufficiently conked out again that we had no choice but to pull over and wait out the night one more time. We were in Georgia by now so at least we were making some progress.

The following morning, we got our usual push from a passing stranger and resumed our trek. This time I decided to just stop periodically and get the battery recharged rather than fool with the alternator again. I'd had it with that thing. So, as the power drained away we kept a lookout for likely recharge spots along the freeway. When it looked like we weren't going to get much farther, we pulled into a small roadside gas station sitting all alone on a small service road.

After a couple of hours of waiting, the battery was finally recharged and we were ready to head out. The owner of the station didn't seem to have much interest in us and when we asked if he might give a push he pretty much said no and good luck trying to find someone who would. Fortunately, his station worker took pity on us and volunteered to push us with his old beat-up car. I got the impression that the owner wasn't real happy that he did, either, but we were certainly glad for his kindness.

Because the battery now needed to be conserved, we couldn't listen to the radio or the tape player anymore, which made for a very quiet ride. At least at first, for soon after leaving the station, as if having half of the car out of operation wasn't enough, the tailpipe broke loose and rattled violently on the undercarriage of the car if we drove any slower than 35 mph. Of course, with so little compression in the engine we couldn't go over 40 mph so we just crept along slowly but surely down the Georgia freeway, humming to ourselves in lieu of the radio and trying to keep our senses of humor about it all. We were beginning to wonder, though, if we would ever make it to Grandma's house.

At about two o'clock that afternoon, with whoops and cheers, we finally crossed the Florida state line. Even though we still had several hundred miles to go, we were elated at the thought of being so close and rolled down the windows so that we could yell our happiness out into the swamps that surrounded us.

Once across, though, our moods soon went quiet again. Florida wasn't a very stimulating or scenic place for us and we were tired. Of course, so was Otto. He just wasn't as amenable to sudden cross-country trips as we were and he was certainly letting us know it. When it started getting dark, we turned into a rest area and spent the night as we still couldn't drive in the dark. The next morning, another push and off again we were.

The poor old guy was getting feebler by the mile but we were optimistic that as long as we stayed on the freeway we just might make it all the way. As it happened, though, just about 30 miles shy of my grandma, the freeway was diverted onto the surface roads of Ft. Pierce while they finished constructing that portion of it.

Well, Otto could hold his own on the freeway when there were no stops and starts or even speed changes but, unfortunately, side streets were another story and it was within the first mile of leaving I-95 that, in a final spasm of coughs, sputters, chokes and backfires, he died. It was a sad death and we knew that this time it was for good. He'd brought us so far and had endured such an unfair amount of abuse. He had gotten us almost the entire way and only slipped into his coma a few short miles from the end of the road.

We sat there on the side of the road for a while and considered our options, finally deciding to hitchhike the rest of the way to Jensen Beach where my grandma lived and then come back for the car later. We packed up a few things and, after giving Otto a mournful last glance (for a while anyway), we pointed our thumbs southward.

It took us three different rides to get there. One of them made a very suspicious detour off the highway and onto a small dirt road that led into the nearby brush where we suddenly stopped. There was another car already parked out there, otherwise it was completely deserted. The two guys driving us seemed to know the driver of the other car and got out to talk with him as though he was waiting for them, I thought. For a moment, I began to have worries for our safety because it all seemed so very odd but a few minutes later they came back to the car and we returned to the highway and continued on as normal. It seemed even stranger when I reflected about it all later and I wondered just how close we'd actually come to some kind of harm. At any rate, we made it to my grandmother's house in short order, safe and unscathed.

My grandmother had no idea we were coming and was quite surprised to see us walking up her driveway that afternoon, particularly with no car in sight and virtually no possessions. In fact, she didn't even recognize me at first but I have to admit that I didn't really recognize her either. It had been a few years and she had gotten shorter and grayer since I had last seen her. But she was my "Mamaw" and I was glad to see her, nonetheless.

Later that day, we drove back up to Ft. Pierce with her husband Irving, tied a rope around Otto's bumper and dragged him back down to Jensen Beach with us. Once there, we unsaddled our dead horse, so to speak, and made ourselves at home as best as we could until we could figure out what we were going to do next.

FLORIDA

It had been our plan to sell Otto at the end of our stay here in Florida, but in the condition he was in now I was afraid we weren't going to get very much for him. That next day I called around to the local garages to see what they would charge to fix him back up again. The cheapest of the quotes that I ended up with came in at $800, which was about 80 times more than we could afford and more than the little guy was worth, so I had no real choice at this point but to try and do as much of it myself as I could. I had taken apart a lawnmower engine once in a class back at college and figured I could at least do that much and then have someone else put him back together. I started tearing him down that weekend.

It was going to take some time either way to get him back up again, so we did our best to settle into this new place for a while. We spent the better part of those next few days doing little more than swatting mosquitoes, eating papayas from my grandmother's tree and cutting down an unwanted bamboo grove out behind her house. In between we'd borrow my grandmother's car and go to the nearby beach or drive around and explore.

These days were fun for us. Everything here seemed so "tropical," especially the nightly thunderstorms; standing out in the 80-degree night in only my shorts watching the rain coming down in buckets and the thunder cracking like a train crash as the lightning forked itself across the blackened sky. I felt emboldened for some reason as I watched it all charge by on its way to somewhere else.

Our idyll laze was short-lived, however, as the reality of our new environs began to show its darker side. Our introduction to it had actually come on our very first morning there when Karen and I were suddenly awakened at 7 a.m. by my grandmother's husband, Irving, pounding violently on our bedroom door, accusing us of laziness and hollering at us to get up. It wasn't a very auspicious beginning to our visit here and unfortunately it proved to set the underlying tone for the remainder of our stay with them.

My grandmother had married this guy about four years earlier, against her better judgment. At his suggestion, she had sold her house in L.A. and moved to Florida with him, where they had bought a reasonably nice house on a dead-end street right off the Intracoastal Waterway. Irving was already well known by our family to be a dishonest, conniving opportunist, and a general all-around disreputable character. In fact, my grandmother had married him once before, several years earlier, but he'd run out and left her after only a month. She had the marriage annulled. Then, some twenty years later, with nary a word spoken between, he came back from out of the blue and sweet-talked his way back into her lonely life with bold tales of why he had ditched her all those years before. Of course nobody believed him, including my grandmother, but since she had nothing much else in her life to do or to look forward to, she overlooked his obvious character flaws and took him back.

In addition to these other qualities he also happened to be a pathological liar. He was at various times, by his own telling anyway, a college professor, a doctor, a sailor, an automotive engineer or anything else that might win a conversation. The only work any of us ever knew him to have actually done, however, was as a photographer of some sort. He also owned an island in the Caribbean, according to him, and was heir to a large family fortune, among other things at other times.

In actuality, of course, he owned nothing at all and was heir only to an active imagination. Once he got back into my grandmother's life and was protected by her fairly substantial savings he pretty much retired himself from any serious hustling and took to sitting around the house all day reading magazines and watching television. These provided him with the fodder for his constantly scheming mind and armed with these bits of information, he was always about the house ranting on about this or that. Since we were the new kids in town (literally), these fits were often aimed at Karen and me, which bred the discomfort that we were beginning to feel here. I felt sorry for Karen. The poor girl hardly had any solace at all what with being in a stranger's house in the first place and then having to put up with this guy's cantankerous fits to boot. At least I had my Mamaw, part of the time anyway.

Getting married and moving across the country had done nothing to lessen her fondness of drink and in fact had probably increased it. Every afternoon around 4 p.m. she would uncork the Gilbey's and do a slow fade into another person. Unfortunately, it was a person that I couldn't relate to very much and I spent most of the evenings trying to avoid having to deal with her as much as possible. During the day, however, she was still my Mamaw and I was glad to have her as long as she was.

A few days later, under pressure from my grandmother, Karen and I set out for the nearby town of Stuart to look for work. Unfortunately, we both found jobs. Unfortunate because neither of us really wanted to spend the time or trouble working when we could be spending that same time lounging about, which we were fond of, or getting the car fixed and moving again. She was pretty strong on the idea though and since we were here at her mercy we obliged her. In truth, once the parts for Otto had been sent away for machining there wasn't anything else we could do to him in the meantime, plus it did give us a good opportunity to get out of the house for a while and away from Irving's harangues.

I landed myself a job bussing tables at a trendy dinner restaurant but Karen only managed to scrounge up a day shift at the local Burger King. After all the stylish restaurants she'd worked in before she was pretty embarrassed now getting all dressed up in her cute little uniform and working with a bunch of perky teenagers as a burger jockey. She made me promise under threat of death never to tell anyone. It was money though, which we sorely needed, and it made my grandmother happy. I still admire Karen for her fortitude in going through with it all just for my grandmother's sake, even if it was only for a few days.

By the time two weeks had gone by the papaya tree was bare, the bamboo grove was no more than a pile of sticks and several generations of Florida mosquitoes had now been raised on California blood. More importantly, though, Otto had finally been put back together again.

For not knowing anything about auto repair at all when we left Eureka I had since become a veritable Toyota Corolla mechanic by the time we left Jensen Beach. When all the shop work had been finished, I decided to reassemble the old boy as far as I could before turning him over to a real mechanic. Before I knew it though, I had somehow managed to put him all back together myself (and with hardly any parts left over!). Even so, when the fateful moment came to start him up for the first time, I wasn't at all sure what to expect. Karen and my grandparents came out and stood by to watch while I held my breath, crossed my fingers and turned the key. As the engine cranked away with no hint of even wanting to start, I felt my spirit fading away faster than the battery was. We tried everything we could think of to adjust and inspect but it soon became clear that the old boy just wasn't going to do it. I was very disappointed, to say the least, and the thought of tearing him down again was more than I could bear.

With little else do to, Karen, Irving and I pushed our fallen mount down the gravel lane that was our street to the service station that lay at its far end, about a quarter of a mile away.

I was still hoping for a miracle as I watched the mechanic poke around under the hood, and after a few minutes he delivered. He pulled the distributor out of its hole in the engine, gave it a twist and then dropped it back in again. That was it. Otto jumped into life again on the very first turn of the key and sat there humming like a barber in a quartet. A simple misalignment was all that kept it from being a total success. I was extremely proud of myself right then.

More than proud, though, I found I was suddenly filled with a surge of elation. That old feeling of freedom once again came rushing up and slapped me in the head. I hadn't realized till just then how stifled I'd come to feel these last two weeks, living at my grandmother's with no car or money, and now that Otto was up and running again I knew it was time for us to beat feet and get the hay out of here. We packed up our meager possessions the very next day, said goodbye to my grand-folks and happily aimed Otto southward once more. It felt so good to be back on the road again with our mobility and freedom regained and we danced through every moment of it.

We decided to base ourselves about 40 miles away in West Palm Beach. It was the nearest city that had a substantial number of sailboats and job possibilities, both of which were crucial to the next step of our journey.

***

The revelry we enjoyed at our departure from Jensen Beach didn't last very long, however, for the stagnation we felt while there turned out to be only a precursor of the mood that came to dominate our entire stay here in Florida. The rosy flush on the face of our trip soon drained into a dull, ashen gray as the wheels of our momentum ground to a stop, due mostly to the general mismanagement of our time and money, and without the diversion of new discoveries this loss of movement began to eat away at our spirits. We began to feel trapped here and as time dragged on the road that would lead us out of this place became ever fuzzier in our minds, the ruts just that much deeper.

It was during this time, too, that we had to finally deal with the circumstances of our departure. We could no longer hide behind the imperative of daily survival now to keep us from confronting what we were both loath to do but knew we must.

Karen had by far the biggest job of it. She had a lot of "splainin" to do. She spoke several times to her family during these months trying to explain why she did what she did and to assuage their fears and doubts about this crazy idea of hers of running off to strange places with a strange man. As soon as she hung the phone up with them, however, it was my turn to help assuage her own feelings that welled up afterwards. It was mostly guilt in her case though, for although the one constant of our trip so far was the overwhelming feeling of "rightness" of both being together and of following our hearts on this adventure, she still had to do battle with the feelings that she had deserted her family and of the responsibility for how all their lives were changing now on account of what she was doing. Many were the hours I sat talking with her afterwards trying to help her keep a positive perspective on everything we were doing and to keep fresh the reasons why we'd left in the first place. Even so, the weight of her role in other people's lives rested heavy on her.

Much worse, though, were the times when she talked to Tom. She cringed at the thought of having to deal with him and the repercussions of having left him. At first he was in denial of the fact that she even had. He tried to convince her at first that he'd suddenly changed his mind about traveling with her and that now he wanted to come join us. We all knew that he didn't really, that he was just grasping for anything to that might keep her from actually leaving him. It was heartbreaking to see his desperation in trying to hold on to his only sweetheart and I shared with Karen many of the feelings of guilt in watching him go through it, especially when he started talking about killing himself if he had to go on without her. Karen had to do a lot of very delicate and painful talking to defuse this dangerous direction but she held fast to her guns and somehow managed him through it. When it had finally become clear to him that she wasn't going to let him join us, he relented some but still denied the truth of the situation to himself. He told her now with a noticeable sense of resignation that though he didn't understand why she'd left he'd wait for her just the same and that once she had gotten all this crazy travel stuff out of her system she could come back home to him. This was encouraging, if only slightly, for he was at least moving through the process. Unfortunately, that process seemed an excruciatingly slow one.

It didn't help our moods, either, that we stalled out in what was for us one of the worst places we'd been to so far. There seemed to be something uncomfortable or unpleasant about almost everything we did or saw while in Florida. The humidity was very high here and our clothes were always damp and sticky from sweat. It didn't matter if we wore fewer clothes either because it was always just as hot and steamy. It was the air itself. At times, I'd find myself gaping my mouth open like a fish, trying to force a yawn, because I felt like I wasn't getting any oxygen. The daily rainstorms didn't help clear the air either; in fact, they only made it worse, for as soon as the rain hit the hot streets it immediately vaporized into steam and, unlike back home, actually increased the humidity rather than diminished it.

The steaminess of the air was only one part of it, though. The land here was flat, scrubby and devoid of any features that might be considered at all aesthetically pleasing, and it seemed all the water we came across here was swampy and brackish. To be fair, I must say that the ocean was very pretty to look at, with its clear, warm water splashing up on the white, coconut tree-lined beaches. But even this proved somewhat less than comfortable as the sea was full of jellyfish and black, gooey blobs of tar bobbing about in it and even if I managed a swim without getting stung or stuck from either of these I always came out feeling stickier than when I went in. I don't really know why but my skin felt tacky as the water dried on it and the tiny bits of white seashell that comprised the beach sand here adhered to my legs as though they had been sprayed with glue. Mind you, it wasn't horrible; we actually went swimming fairly often while here. It just wasn't entirely comfortable.

By far, though, the worst of all for me were the mosquitoes. I quickly grew to hate them intensely, and that whiney little drone of theirs as they buzzed past my ears at night. Everywhere we went there they were and no matter how many screens we had on our windows they'd find us. While in Jensen Beach, the spray trucks would drive down my grandmother's street every few days, spraying left and right, but it only seemed to make them madder and hungrier, for I always got bitten much more after they passed by. Maybe they just wanted to get in one last meal before they went down for the count. At any rate, I found these little guys to be totally without merit and I killed them indiscriminately whenever I had the chance to. Karen, on the other hand, ever the compassionate one, refused to kill them at all and replied to my fits of entomological cursing with an ever so sweet "it's okay, they don't eat much". This as they drilled holes into her flesh, sucking her blood out. She'd just shoo them away.

It seemed there was no refuge for us anywhere here and though we drove all over that part of the state we never found anyplace that really felt just plain nice. After our idyllic springtime in California, our joyous summer in Portland and our beautiful New England autumn, I'm afraid winter here in Florida just wasn't quite cutting it for us.

***

It was an odd feeling that first day out from Jensen Beach to drive into a strange city arbitrarily chosen as our new home with no idea of where we were, where we were going or, for that matter, even where there was to go. We got there about midday and spent the afternoon driving around the city, taking inventory of anything that might be useful to us. We were primarily looking for a place to park ourselves at night but by evening time we hadn't succeeded and so headed back to the freeway where we knew of a nearby rest area that would do for the time being. We did however spot a large shopping mall while out scouting about that we thought could be a good place to hang out if we needed and also some showers down at the beach that we knew would come in handy. We of course kept an inventory of any restaurants we came across since we were to go out job shopping the next morning.

The rest area, it turned out, wasn't quite as trusty as we thought. Our old friends the mosquitoes were there in force to welcome us this first night back on the road. Not wanting to be an ungracious host, I felt obliged to stay up until the wee hours of the morning entertaining our unwelcomed guests by arming myself with a flashlight and a rolled-up newspaper and mercilessly annihilating any that foolishly dared come within striking distance. So maybe I'm not the best host but there is something in that dive bomber whine of theirs that just sends me into fits and there was no way I could sleep until I knew that every one of those bloodsucking little buzz-saws had been reduced to a red splat on my dashboard. Seeing my own blood spurt out of them at the moment of impact made me feel only that much more redeemed.

It was not until about 3 a.m. that I was convinced the last one had finally met his demise and I could go to sleep. In order to prevent troop reinforcements, however, we had to keep the windows rolled up for the rest of the night which made for a very hot, stuffy and, in my case, short night. Amazingly enough, Karen had managed to sleep through the whole ordeal, none the worse or wiser.

When morning came, we went straight down to the beach for our first morning shower before hitting the pavement in search of work. It must have been quite a sight, us standing there on the open beach like that, shampooing our hair and scrubbing our armpits as though we were in our own homes, because most of the people down there that morning just stood and stared at us while we did. We had our bathing suits on, of course, but you wouldn't have known it by the way everyone looked at us. The water was awfully cold so early in the morning but it felt divine to wash off yesterday's sticky sweat and feel clean again. We just called it "refreshing" and saw it as a good thing.

Even so, I found after my night of battling the mosquito Luftwaffe that I wasn't in much of a mood to look for work that day so we decided to play hooky instead and do something more fun. Karen's love of animals suggested that we go to the nearby zoo and my momentarily suspended sense of responsibility happily agreed so off we went on safari.

The zoo, of course, charged admission to get in which, of course, violated Rule #3 of our adopted travel code (no admission fees) but no adventurer worth his/her khaki shorts would let something so trivial as that stop them and we were adventurers so we followed the eight-foot high cyclone fence around to the backside of the compound and jumped over it with the help of an overhanging tree branch. We made our way back to the zoo proper and spent the better part of the afternoon enjoying an otherwise quiet day before returning to town to continue our quest for a place to call "home".

The fates were kinder to us that day than the day before and we ended up finding a wonderful place to park almost immediately that couldn't have been more perfect for us. At least as far as parking spaces go, that is.

It was a little one-way side street that doubled as a parking lot for the Norton Simon Art Gallery, which stood at its upper end. It was only a block long, albeit a very long block, and doublewide to allow for the diagonal parking stalls that lined its entire length on the right side as you approached the gallery. Forming a canopy above them was a row of large, bushy Ficus trees, which not only provided us with a nice, thick, green roof at night but also hid the multi-story apartment building that stood directly behind them.

Between the trees and the apartment building was a swimming pool and, far more importantly to us, a small pool house with bathrooms that remained unlocked day and night. This alone was worth a lot to us, for having to pee (or worse) in the middle of the night when you live in your car, in the city, can often be a challenge.

At the foot of the street where you entered this little parkway, ran the Intracoastal Waterway, a large, river-like body of sea water that runs down almost the entire length of the eastern U.S. seaboard. It proved to be an answered prayer in its own right, as well, for it provided us with a double-edged gift in the form of a steady sea breeze that both kept us cool on the hot, sticky sub-tropical nights and (much, much more importantly) served to keep the wind-shy mosquitoes away. It was very rare to be graced by their presence while here which alone qualified this as a four-star parking place, at least as far as I was concerned, and one to recommend to friends.

On the left side of the street, opposite the trees and the apartments, was a simple, green grass parkway, one block wide, that separated the two one-way lanes of the street. It became our playground when we needed to do some rassling, play football (later soccer) or to just stretch out on a sunny day. All told, we couldn't have asked for a better spot to park ourselves, particularly for being right smack in the middle of town.

With our chore for the day so easily accomplished we now found ourselves with some time to kill, so we went off to look for the shopping mall we'd spotted yesterday to check it out.

We found it easily and ended up spending the entire evening there watching the big television they had set out in the middle of the main walkway. When it started getting late and the mall shops began closing up, we retreated to a remote corner of the huge parking lot outside and whiled away a couple more hours sitting in the car playing cards under the neon moon of one of the big floodlights out there.

As soon as it got late enough to not be so obvious in what we were doing, we made our way back to the cover of the Ficus trees eager to try out our new home. With a little bit of shifting around we managed to clear a space big enough for Karen to recline the passenger side seat while I took the driver's side. It was the least favorite side because of the steering wheel but besides that it really wasn't too bad. I found being very tired helped my appreciation quite a bit.

I fell asleep quickly and with a sense of humble satisfaction as I reflected on our first full day here. All things considered, it had gone very well for us this day, our previous night notwithstanding, and it bode well in our otherwise vulnerable minds. It worked so well, in fact, and the Ficus trees were so welcoming, that the rudiments of that first day pretty much became our daily routine from then on, at least for a while anyway.

Indeed, so welcoming was this urban oasis that we felt comfortable enough sharing our relationship with one another, in the most personal of ways that people do, while parked here. As an enticement to help Karen quit smoking (her one vice that challenged me the most) I made a deal with her that if she would quit smoking for one month, I would give her a 30-minute massage for each day of that month. And, as so often happens with lover's massages, the sessions frequently became much more intimate afterwards. It was only just before we left our spot here for the last time, some months later, did we speak to a man who lived in the adjacent apartments and who confessed to us as having been aware of what we were doing during our stays here. We were a bit unnerved to think of just how aware. [Unfortunately for me, it turns out Karen had no problem quitting smoking. She just had a problem staying quit and, though she relentlessly held me to my end of the agreement, no matter the lateness of the hour, she promptly resumed her habit as soon as the month was over.]

Our first month here moved pretty quickly. We both found jobs the very next day at a restaurant called Lord Chumley's, which was conveniently right across the street from the mall. I was to start the next morning bussing tables and Karen the day after that as a waitress. Luckily for us, they were both day shifts, which was real nice because it allowed us to not only be together at work (just like back at Lazio's) but also to be together outside of work so we could go off and play or explore.

Fortunately, we also had that first weekend off together, too, and we spent it driving back up north to Cocoa Beach, about 60 miles away, to see what there was to see there. We were hoping to run into Capt. Nelson and Jeannie there (from the old TV show "I Dream of Jeannie) but alas, we didn't even find a Coke bottle on the beach that day, let alone a genie lamp.

Later that afternoon however, we did find out about a rocket launch that was scheduled for that very night from nearby Cape Canaveral. As the day began to grow dark, we excitedly made our way out there and found ourselves a parking place alongside the roadway a few miles south of the launch pad. Darkness had settled in when, several minutes later, we watched as it blasted off in a bright explosion of light and slowly lifted up into the evening sky. There was a thin layer of cloud partly covering the sky that night and when the rocket pierced though its thin veneer, the fire from its engines suddenly reflected clear across its top all the way to the horizon, lighting up the whole sky in a big flash that slowly faded as the spaceship made its way toward heaven.

Through a clearing in the clouds we watched it continue on as it flew off into the blackness of outer space, until it was nothing more than a little tiny star-like dot, indecipherable amongst all the real stars that were just now coming out. After all of the rocket movies and TV shows of my childhood, it was terribly thrilling for me to watch this, my first real rocket ship blasting off into outer space. Jeannie would have been fun but this was a good second best.

We camped in the car that night there in Cocoa Beach but had another buggy night. We had to move several times before finding a sleepable spot somewhere around 3 a.m. Duly inspired by last night's show, we went to visit the Kennedy Space Center the next morning, at least as much of it as we could visit for free. It wasn't very exciting though, so we went to the beach and collected seashells instead before heading back "home".

With our brief taste of excitement over now, our daily routine was quickly resumed. Work at Lord Chumley's during the day, TV in the mall until closing time, cards afterwards out in the hinterlands of the parking lot and then, finally, off to our sleeping spot 'neath the trees for the night. Though it did get a tad bit monotonous after a while, we seemed to have a pretty good time of it anyway. In spite of anything, we could usually find a way to laugh and have fun. We did, however, buy ourselves a Yahtzee game just the same, for at least a little variety [we justified its expense by calling it a reward for us finding work].

That very next Thursday was Thanksgiving Day and it found us on the northward highway once again to spend the holiday with my grandmother and Irving. On the way up we stopped at the Oakbrook Plaza so Karen could call home from the payphone there. Her mother, it turned out, was out of town for the holiday which disappointed Karen a lot but her dad (a.k.a. "Soda Pop"), her brothers, her sister Judy, and even Tom were all there. It was obvious to anyone who could see the expressions on her face and hear the excitement and joy in her voice as she talked to everyone in turn, that she was truly and deeply happy to be speaking to them all. She was glad Tom was there with the family and doubly happy when her sister told her that she had just gotten married the day before in a totally impromptu civil ceremony. Judy said she would wait until Karen came home to have a real ceremony so that she could be the bridesmaid. In fact, everyone there was doing very well with their lives, which pleased her greatly. Even Tom sounded better. I think perhaps that the other side of her happiness was as much relief as well. Relief that their lives were moving well despite the fact that she wasn't there to help them. I think it was a big load off her conscience. Still, she missed them all terribly.

We had plenty of time to spare that day so after hanging up with them we took a tour of the plaza. It was a small, ring-shaped mall with about a dozen shops circling an open courtyard. Down at the far end of the plaza was a large water fountain with flowerbeds and brick pathways and patios winding around it. Due to the holiday, the shops were all closed and the place was completely deserted. It was another hot, humid Florida day and as we walked around the courtyard checking out the stores through their windows, our gazes kept flashing over to the splashing fountain, beckoning to us with its gurgling gaiety. We didn't need much more coaxing than that and before we knew it we'd stripped down to our shorts and were splashing about in it like two happy sea otters. It was a simple stone fountain with water cascading out from its center column into a large circular pool at its base. Large enough that we could almost actually swim strokes in it. Once again, with the titillating abandon of truant school kids we frolicked and played in there for some time. We had a wonderfully fun time before finally climbing out and continuing on to my grandmother's for dinner.

We were back to work the next morning but things in that department were beginning to change. The day before Thanksgiving Karen had gotten a second job working nights as a bus person at a place called Ben's Steakhouse. Three days after Thanksgiving I got my second job at a place called Willoughby's but I only lasted a day there. I didn't like it very much.

After only three days at Ben's, though, scheduling conflicts forced Karen to have to choose between her two jobs and though Lord Chumley's was a fairly casual place to work the atmosphere there was a bit too dry for her blood so she opted in favor of the informal, family-style Ben's and left Lord Chumley's that following Monday, the very same day that I left Willoughby's.

It was unfortunate because not only did we not work together anymore but Ben's was about 20 miles away, which made our commutes to and from work considerably more complicated now. Since, obviously, only one person could have the car at a time, whoever had the later starting shift was now responsible for dropping off and picking up the other, all the while keeping to their own schedule. This often meant either very speedy drop-offs and/or very long waits. Many were the hours that I spent out back in Ben's parking lot napping, throwing pebbles at pieces of litter and listening to the radio while waiting for Karen to finish her shift. I didn't really mind too terribly, though, because I knew that if I wasn't sitting in the car here whiling away the hours I'd most likely just be sitting in it somewhere else.

In the end, though, it was worth the trouble, for Karen made some friends here that we went out with occasionally, which was a nice break for us. I rarely made outside friends at the places I worked at since I usually chose restaurants that were more formal and therefore with people that I couldn't relate to very much. Karen, on the other hand, usually picked places that were more family-like and always seemed to make friends at them quite easily. I'm not really sure why this was but it was unfortunate for me because it seemed Karen always had a much better time at work than I did.

A few days later Karen replaced her now available daytime slot with a bussing job at Holiday Inn in Riviera Beach, a few miles to the north of town. Now not only was she splitting her job sites farther apart, which made our transportation schedule even more tenuous, but she also had to show up for work at 7 o'clock in the morning every day.

Due to this tight scheduling, we often had too little time to easily change our work clothes in between jobs but having been so successful at changing drivers while flying down the freeway as we crossed the states, we saw no reason not to make the best use of our commute time in a similar fashion. Karen was usually the driver at these times and also the one with the more difficult chore as she couldn't change her top as easily as I could, at least not with any modesty anyway. When it looked like the coast was clear of traffic, she would throw the seat back all the way flat and then lay down and change out her bra and blouse while also managing the gas pedal. I sat in the passenger seat working the steering wheel and giving her throttle instructions while also keeping an eye out for any big trucks coming up behind us that would have a clear downward view into our seemingly driverless car, only to find a naked woman lying there. It was somewhat daunting for me as well trying to keep my mind focused on my duties while she lay there so enticingly exposed.

There were times, too, that I would get out a can of Sterno and a frying pan and cook up some pancakes there on the floor of the car for breakfast while she drove me to work.

We originally thought that the Holiday Inn might be a good place to work for the possibilities of using the connection to get work later at Holiday Inns around the world but the logistics just weren't working out and Karen was starting to get cranky from being so tired. We'd both been cranky lately anyway and this was the last thing we needed now. In fact, I wonder if maybe Karen didn't leave Lord Chumley's partly to get a little clear air between us. At any rate, Karen only lasted at Holiday Inn 12 days before quitting. We'd just have to get our future jobs some other way.

Our moods were growing fragile in all this shuffling about, particularly on the day that we'd quit Chumley's and Willoughby's. It was clear that we needed some balance, something to keep us on a positive track, so the day after our respective quittings we treated ourselves to a little picnic on the beach. After I got off work that day, we went and bought some cheese, wine, bread and apples and then went to the beach to watch the approach of the warm and balmy dusk.

We ate and drank and reminisced about home as the sky grew dark and on until the stars came out. It was still quite warm outside and with our spirits finally lifting nicely out of their grouchy shells, it seemed only fitting that we should baptize them with a swim in the nighttime sea. Leaving our clothes in a pile by our discarded wine bottle, we ran out into the surf and had a wonderful time frolicking together in the warm waves. It was a good thing that we hadn't yet learned that sharks, which are plentiful in Florida's waters, usually feed at night because I'm sure that would have changed our minds a little bit about what we were doing, but in this ignorance we found our bliss.

By the time we were done our spirits had really been enlivened and once again we felt the unburdened freedom and gaiety that was the very heart and purpose of this whole trip. As we emerged from the quietly lapping sea, we were challenged now to find a way to rinse the sand and sticky salt from our bodies. A quick look around gave us an excellent idea. We crept down the darkened and deserted beach, still naked, until we came to a nearby hotel. Hiding behind a small ridge of sand, we peeked over to spy a beautiful, big, blue-lagoon colored swimming pool blazing in the bright, gleaming lights of the hotel. There was no fence around it and not a soul to be seen anywhere near it.

It was exactly what we were hoping to find and so, with a quick nod of agreement, we launched ourselves from the dark side of the sand dune and streaked into the blazing incandescence of the hotel courtyard. Running like madmen, we made straight for the pool and dove in, made one crossing of its width, and then hurriedly jumped back out again. Before our ripples had a chance to make two laps of the pool, we had already disappeared back into the oblivion of night, with only two mysterious sets of wet footprints running off toward the sea to give any clue of our visit. It was a real nice night. A really real nice night.

***

One of the people that Karen had befriended at work was a young woman named Katherine. Actually, Karen had met her back at Lord Chumley's about a week after we'd been there, when Katherine was hired on as a fellow waitress. They became friends right off, which was very exciting news for me when I learned of it because Katherine was an extremely attractive woman and I had been enamored of her from her first day there.

About a week later, just before Karen left for Ben's, Katherine extended an invitation for us to come up and join her for a few days in the motel room she was renting, both to give us a break from the confines of car life and give her a break in the rent. We both happily accepted her kind offer (I think me the most happily) and moved in the following Friday,

December 1st. It was only one room but it was relatively large and it had two beds in it and an adjoining bathroom, which was all we needed.

Though she was originally from Louisville, Kentucky, she had actually come down to Florida from Dothan, Alabama where she had been living most recently. As befits Southern women, she possessed all the feminine grace and charm that they are so often known for. She stood at about 5 and a half feet tall, slender, with a body designed by God himself and a face that would break any man's heart. Her long, straight brown hair was cut into bangs in the front but fell down below her shoulders in the back, where she usually gathered it gently into a loose ponytail. Her voice was soft and her tone sincere. She had come down to Florida to work the restaurants for the season. At least I think that's what she wanted herself to believe.

She had just turned thirty, very much to her dismay, and was feeling the sharp pain that seems to be so common in women as they approach that dreaded number. Her pain, though, was not from the fear of losing her youth and beauty before she'd had a chance to marry and have kids. She actually had been married once before, had two kids living back home with their dad and had been divorced long enough to have had several dud boyfriends. Hers was just the fear of losing her beauty and youth, period. Leaving her kids and lost lovers behind, I think she came to Florida in search of that same mythical fountain that Ponce de Leon had come here to find so many years prior. The one that would forever keep her from getting old.

Unfortunately, that fountain proved just as elusive to her as it did to that old Spanish explorer and the frustration of not being able to stall time had given her serious stomach ulcers and probably aged her twice as fast as if she had just let it go. She went out on dates two of the three nights we stayed with her at the motel and both times she came home late at night afterwards and went straight to the toilet and threw up because of them. It was sad to see such a beautiful and warm person go through so much trauma just because some unfortunate little idea got stuck in her head that growing older is a bad thing.

We stayed with her there in the motel for three days and it worked out so well that when they drew to a close she proposed the idea that the three of us should go in on an apartment together. I almost wet my pants at the very thought of it. The thought of sharing an apartment with both Karen, whom I dearly loved, and Katherine, whom I dearly would have loved to have dearly loved, was almost more than I could bear.

She had since quit Lord Chumley's herself and had taken another job at the trendy Cork n' Cleaver restaurant, working nights as a cocktail waitress. She had a friend there, she told us, who knew of an available apartment in the building where he lived and thought we might consider it. She certainly had my yes vote to the idea and thankfully Karen agreed to it as well. We decided to go check it out the next day but since Karen had to work only Katherine and I actually went to look at it.

It was a two-bedroom upstairs apartment, nice and bright but a bit run down. Still it was affordable and better than the car so after talking it over briefly, we decided we would go ahead and take it. That night at work she mentioned it to her friend. It wasn't until then that he told us about the only catch to the deal. The owner, it turns out, was very conservative and would only rent it to a couple if they were married. Since there were three of us that were going to live there, this posed a small problem for us. It didn't take us long, though, to come up with a suitable cover story that we thought would work well enough. It was certainly worth a try, at any rate.

The next day Katherine and I went to visit the old man who owned the place. We explained to him that we were newly married and that we were interested in renting his dump of an apartment as our cozy little love nest (those may not have been our exact words). He looked at us a bit sideways when we said we were married. She was a little taller than me and, at 30, obviously older but he seemed to buy the story anyway. Since Karen wasn't there, we didn't bother bringing her up in the conversation, thinking that later on I would simply tell the old guy, should he ask, that she was my sister who'd come to visit for a while. I figured that it would explain our obvious closeness (God help us if he ever caught us making out!).

With that we signed the rental agreement and moved in immediately. I must confess that telling him Katherine was my new wife was without a doubt one of the most enjoyable lies I've ever told and probably the one I would most liked to have been true. I considered myself fortunate to have had the opportunity to visit with her these last few days, and now I was actually going to be living with her. It was a wonderful fantasy coming true for me there with the both of them. I was as much in love with Karen as I was in lust with Katherine (especially when she ran around the apartment in her underwear or her denim hot pants with her butt half out of them) and when Katherine mentioned one day that she wanted the three of us to get into a routine of going down to the beach every morning and doing exercises it was difficult to contain myself. Bikinis were made for women like her and the thought of watching her do toe touches sent me into shivers.

One day when Katherine complained of being a little tense, Karen and I hopped up on her bed and gave her a quick body rub. Karen had volunteered to me some time earlier that if I ever wanted to fool around with Katherine, it was perfectly okay with her just so long as it was strictly recreational and not because I found Karen lacking in any way. With that thought in my mind now it was a fun feeling I got sitting there on the bed rubbing Katherine's body, along with Karen, as my imagination proceeded to go much further than we did. I felt as if I were perpetually on the verge of a wet dream living with the two of them.

Christmas came only two weeks after we moved in and it found us in a mixed state of emotions. Katherine had gone home for the holidays, leaving Karen and me to ourselves. The absence of her bright personality there left a bit of a void in the character of the dreary little apartment, making it seem just a shade less alive there now. Karen, for her part, was feeling progressively more homesick as the big holiday drew closer and missed her family a lot. Making it worse, I had to work that night at Chumley's, leaving her all alone on Christmas night for the first time in her life and in such an unfortunate place.

Fortunately, Christmas morning, we got to drive back up to Oakbrook Plaza for our now traditional holiday fountain swim and Karen's call home. Both were eagerly anticipated and both were tremendously enjoyed. Karen talked to everyone in the family again and everyone was doing very well. The best news for Karen was that Tom was seeing a woman on a regular basis now. We'd heard a rumor about it earlier but now it was official. It was a great relief for her to know that he was healing and moving on.

Probably not as important but definitely more exciting was the news that her older brother, Mark, was going to be coming out to Florida in a couple of weeks to visit his kid sis! Karen was, of course, overjoyed. I, on the other hand, though happy for her, was a bit more uncertain. This was going to be my first test with the family and I knew that it was going to be an important one.

Nonetheless, we had a great day together. Karen had given me a very special present that morning for Christmas - my very own soccer ball! Soccer, of course, had been a very important part of our early relationship way back at CR, and it meant a lot to me to have this. She had written on it in permanent marker "Ya Sexy thing Ya," a line that she'd picked up and paraphrased from a song by Hot Chocolate that had become her special endearment to me.

We spent the rest of the day up at my grandmother's house before heading back to West Palm so I could go to work. My mother had sent a box of presents for us there, which was real nice and made it seem a little more like a real Christmas, but all in all the holiday still left something lacking.

Sadly, once the holidays were over, we got a call from Katherine that caused me great dismay. While home, she had gone into the hospital for treatment of her ulcers and had since decided to get back together with her ex-husband. She told us she wouldn't be coming back to Florida and apologized for leaving us with the apartment like that. She asked if we would send her things up to her but if we didn't want to take the trouble to just throw them away.

My heart was broken. Perhaps more accurately, my fantasy was broken. I was never going to get a chance to watch her do toe touches. I didn't get a photograph of her or even an opportunity to say a real goodbye, which made it all the worse.

On the other hand, though, it was probably just as well that she didn't come back, for if she had perhaps my wet dreams would have actually come true and messed things up with Karen and me. Crush or no, that was the one thing I least wanted to do. Sometimes desire, I think, is best left unrealized and simply kept as a fantasy for desires, when realized, tend to wither and dry. Fantasies, however, can remain with someone forever full and alive, as does mine with Katherine still.

***

With Katherine gone now, there was no reason for Karen and me to keep the apartment so we decided to give it up and move back into the car. It was a bit dicey moving out because in order to get our much-needed deposit back I had to somehow convince the old landlord that my wife of only three weeks had just left me and that now I was going to take my sister and leave at the end of the month, and this without giving but a week's notice. It was tough. I don't think he ever believed that Katherine and I were married in the first place, let alone that Karen was my sister, but I did it. At least enough to get us back most of our deposit, anyway.

It was sad for me to leave the apartment after only one month. I felt like I had missed something with Katherine leaving so abruptly. On the other hand, Karen and I were actually glad to be moving back into Otto. After living in him so long, it turned out that we were actually more comfortable now sleeping there than in a real bed. We had grown so accustomed to sleeping in the car that sleeping in a regular bed now gave us backaches.

It was good, too, to be parking back in our old spot again under the ficus trees. This may sound strange but there are very few places in this world where I felt as comfortable as I did under those trees. There was something about the way the early morning sun shone on their bright green leaves overhead, always the first thing I saw in the mornings as my sleepy eyes came into focus, and the way the cool night breeze made them sway back and forth so gently, singing to me their quiet lullabies as I fell into sleep each night.

I found it all very comforting in this place so far from my home. In the midst of all the unpleasantness that Florida was to me, this was my oasis. Maybe it was just the contrast from everything else but coming back to our parking stall at night felt like coming home. I somehow felt secure living there on that little side street with Karen.

I think, too, that since this was to be our last domestic base we knew we were on the edge of our adventure here and that soon we would be leaving it for some unknown, exotic destination which, though I found tremendously exciting, was still a little intimidating to me and perhaps made me cling just that much more to anything that gave me a sense of comfort and familiarity.

Once a month, while camped out here on our street, I would gaze up at the full moon. Seeing her bright, round face gave me comfort, too, knowing that no matter where in the world we ended up each month, when I looked up into the night sky she'd be there, too, keeping us company. Diana, the virgin goddess. Excitement and eagerness always returned to me as I wondered just where these places would be, where we'd be the next time she graced us with her visit. This became a monthly ritual for me, one that I maintained throughout the remainder of the trip. At least once every full moon I would stop and take stock of all that had happened since I'd seen her last and wonder about all that would happen before I would see her next. It gave me a wonderful perspective on the whole trip, gave it form, and helped to keep fresh in my heart the reason why we were here and just what it was that we were doing.

Four days after we moved out of the apartment, Karen's brother, Mark, showed up just as promised. A friend of his had come out here to Florida to visit with some family and Mark had come along for the ride with his girlfriend, ostensibly to visit his kid sis. In truth, I think he really came out on behalf of her family to size up this upstart that had so brazenly stolen his sister and then to report back on what he found.

It was touch and go at first whether or not I passed the admittance test but on the eve of their arrival the defining moment came. Standing in the parking lot at the rear of my car, Mark mentioned aloud that he had to pee. He unzipped himself right there, turned toward my car and began to pee on my rear tire. Somehow I knew, as perhaps only a man can, that this was the real test before me. The ritual of the peeing, that fraternal moment. Without missing a beat, I unzipped right along with him and together we washed my tire clean (in a manner of speaking anyway). I felt good afterwards. I knew I had done well. Later, when he bid us his goodbyes, he gave me a hug and I knew in that moment that I was family now.

It was a nice visit and it really picked Karen's spirits up a lot to see him again. Of course, it also reminded her once more of all the people and things that she'd left behind and now she was saddened to see him go. In fact, she confessed in her journal that if she hadn't felt so good being there with me she'd be back home in a heartbeat.

For my part I was glad not only to have been accepted but also to have met someone from her family and, more importantly, for them to have met me. It helped a lot to alleviate the guilt of leaving like we did, knowing that someone back home could say firsthand how truly happy we were together and that maybe I wasn't such a creep after all.

However happy we may have been together, though, it did little to dispel our ever-growing unhappiness at being here in Florida in the first place and the next several months proved to be the most challenging to both our senses of spirit and adventure.

***

Ever since Mark's departure, it seemed things began going downhill pretty fast. The seeds of discontent, the fine cracks in the porcelain had, of course, all found their birth within the first couple of weeks that we were here but they were few and relatively minor. It wasn't until now, though, that the seeds fully sprouted and the cracks grew until the pieces began to chip and fall. By the time our fourth month here in this miserable place drew to a close it seemed we were no closer to achieving our goals than when we'd arrived.

Actually, from a strictly numbers point of view, we had already achieved three of the four objectives we had set for ourselves while here. It's just that they were the easy three. The first one was simply finding work. Obviously, we'd done that easily enough. Our second objective was to get ourselves outfitted for international travel, which wasn't much of a chore either since our mode of travel literally allowed for nothing that couldn't fit into a small backpack. We had gotten our passports some time ago, as well as every shot the county health department could think of. Our third goal was to learn how to sail, which was only moderately more difficult. We'd signed up for a free Coast Guard Auxiliary class in boating back in January, just before moving out of the apartment, which although not a sailing class, per se, did introduce us to the general dynamics of boating, including nautical terminology, rope handling and safety, etc. We were satisfied that it was enough to get us started anyway.

It was really only the fourth, and final, objective that proved to be such an obstacle to our forward momentum. That one was to actually get ourselves on a sailboat going somewhere south.

In our casual approach to this trip and perhaps in our overconfidence, we'd put off looking for a boat too long. By the time we'd started the boating class we'd already been in Florida for two months and then made the mistake of waiting the several weeks until the class was over before making our first inquiry into finding us some crew positions. After the final class meeting, Karen and I waited behind and approached the old instructor to see if he could recommend us to anyone. Unfortunately, he told us that we were too late, that all the boats he knew of had already left. If we'd only come to him sooner, he said, he could have helped us. It gave me a sick feeling when he told us this, that our lassitude had stolen our chance for escape.

This disappointment, of course, only added fuel to our already burgeoning sense of gloom and despair and we started getting even crankier and grumpier with each other as the time went by. We took to spending a lot more time going to movies and hanging out in bars to help alleviate our darkening moods and to keep us from becoming contemptuous of each other. We looked for excuses to keep us from having to go back to our parking space too early so that we wouldn't have to sit there all evening with nothing to do but get more cranky. Many nights, usually after our visits to the bars or movies, we went to the local Denny's and just sat in there until the wee hours of the morning eating pancakes and hanging out until we were tired enough to go home and straight to sleep.

It became a vicious cycle for us. The more we tried to feel good about being in this place that we'd become so mired in, the more our funds dwindled that would pay for our escape from it.

Otherwise, we pretty much jumped right back into our old routine of life in the car with only a few changes. We had since found an RV park that was easy to sneak into and had hot showers, which was real nice, so we didn't have to take public ones with cold water anymore.

We were still spending most of our evenings and night times camped out in the mall's parking lot with our Yahtzee game and deck of cards, passing the hours away while cooking our dinner outside on a can of Sterno that I'd filched from the appetizer tray at work. "Dinner" in this case was usually nothing more than a can of collard greens or peas, primarily because we needed some greens to balance out the greasy stuff we normally got at work but also because Karen was gaining weight (which certainly didn't help her general mood any either).

We couldn't watch TV anymore in the mall itself since, while we were away on our brief respite in the apartment, they had taken the TV set down. Now, in order to watch *Mork and Mindy* (our favorite show), we had to go to the Greyhound Bus station back in town and watch it in one of the little pay TV booths they had there. It wasn't so bad, though. In fact, we looked forward to TV night, usually. It was a welcome break in our monotony.

We'd normally spend the early part of the evening loitering around in the public library across the street from the depot then, at the appointed hour, dash across the street and pack ourselves into a single booth and start dropping in our saved-up quarters. We had to sit on top of one another to get us both in there but we alternated every 10 or 15 minutes who had to be on the bottom so that the bottom guy wasn't totally squished. As uncomfortable as it generally was, we actually had a lot of fun on these nights with both of us doing the "dog-pile-on-a-chair" version of rassling or otherwise creating general havoc in the bus station's lobby.

In fact, despite the dreary, frustrating gloom that had become the predominant flavor of our environment we still managed to find time to have fun together. There was a small park just down from the library and bus station that we often visited and a marina just beyond that on the waterway. If we weren't at the beach swimming and collecting seashells, we were most likely here in the park either playing some one-on-one tackle soccer with my new ball or one-on-one tackle football, instead. Of course, both inevitably ended up a rassling match.

We were saddened one day, though, when in a mad race to climb up one of the pine trees there, we'd forgotten our beloved football, which we'd left unattended down on the grass below us. We thought nothing about it when we heard a group of teenage boys walk by below us several minute later, unaware of our presence, until we climbed back down to find the ball missing and the boys nowhere in sight. We both felt really bad; we'd had a lot of fun with that old ball. At least I had my soccer ball still.

Occasionally, we'd walk our daydreams across the street to the marina and stick them onto some of the big sailboats we saw there, pretending and hoping that soon they would be real events and not just dreams. We always checked the bulletin board there just in case someone happened to put up a notice that they were looking for an inexperienced, young couple with big dreams to travel around the world with them. Alas, we were always disappointed there. Still, the dreams were there and we knew that someday, somehow they would yet come true.

As it happened, that someday wasn't very far off, for as the winter of our discontent (if I may borrow the phase) slowly faded into spring, the fabric of our dreams did indeed begin to materialize. As befits the season, our resolve seemed to gel up and assert itself. Our sap began to rise, so to speak, and we knew it was time to finally get serious. Way past time, in fact.

Toward the end of February, I decided to quit Chumley's. I had become too accustomed to the place, which only helped to cloud the reason why I was there.

After very briefly trying out two other restaurants, Portofino in West Palm and Banana Boat in Boca Raton, respectively, I finally settled on the Buccaneer Yacht Club up in Riviera Beach. Though it was a relatively low-traffic, low-scale sort of joint, it was a place obviously frequented by boaters. And though they were mostly the old, martini-drinking, power boat crowd I figured it would at least be a step in the right direction. I knew by now that luck would ultimately play a big part in the success of our trip and I wanted to make sure that we were in a position to maximize our availability to any that might come our way. Besides, we only needed one break, one sailor with some extra room. Fortunately for us, my strategy proved perfect, for that is exactly what we found.

***

The Buccaneer Yacht Club was a little by-water type of place out in the middle of a residential neighborhood and not really near anything else of any particular interest. Although the restaurant had a nice outside patio right on the east bank of the Intra-coastal waterway where it broadens out into Lake Worth and was encircled on the other three sides with a two-story row of apartments that were in the process of being converted into condominiums, it was actually a fairly rundown, cheap-looking place. I think that twenty some years earlier it had actually been pretty nice but those days had since passed.

In truth, it wasn't so much a rundown look as it was an aging, fifties-style look. They just happen to be close relatives. The old carpeting and flimsy paneling, mixed with the low lighting and subdued atmosphere, just made it seem like it was rundown, I guess.

I was hired as a daytime dishwasher/busboy/custodian/fill-in waiter/errand boy. There were only about a dozen people working here, half of them day shift and the other half nights, and like you might expect to find in a dark little side pool of life's stream, most of them were slightly oddball characters that drifted in but never caught enough current to drift back out again.

Like most of the club's members, the owner of the joint was also an old, martini-drinking kind of guy, named Jack. He had a fondness for women and reminded me of the cheesy sort that you'd expect to find in a place like Florida or maybe Las Vegas. He seemed to be in it for the status but didn't quite have the class to pull it off. He seemed like a fifties holdover, too.

The manager of the place was a younger, friendly fellow but one teetering on the tight wire of alcoholism. Unfortunately for him, he was falling the wrong way. I would find his empty bottles hidden in various places around the restaurant in the mornings when I did my cleanup, and was under orders to report them to Jack. He only lasted another couple of weeks before he was replaced with a young and very pretty woman of Mayan blood named Muneca.

Moon, as she preferred to be called, had no experience at all in restaurant management and everyone knew that Jack only hired her for some potential south-of-the-border playtime. She was very nice though, and I think Jack was unsuccessful in his maneuverings. She and I sometimes sat and talked during the slow afternoons about life in her part of the world. Mostly I grilled her for any information she had to offer in the event that Karen and I ever made it out of this place. I was always keeping an ear open for good places to go and helpful hints just in case we did.

The daytime waitress was an older woman named Ruby. She was probably in her late forties I'd guess, still thin and lively. She was a fun one and had a good sense of life about her but it seemed qualified at the same time with perhaps just a hint of despair. I suppose, though, that when fifty is charging at you like a mad dog and you're still living alone, working as a lunch waitress in a dreary little restaurant, you have a pretty good reason for a dose of futility. In counterpoint to my inquiries to Moon, Ruby was usually grilling me for information on my current little bit of the world. She was fascinated when she found out that Karen and I lived in the car and wanted to know all of our tips and hints so that she, too, could live in her car.

I didn't get to know the others very well. The bartender was a gay man in his early fifties who used to wink at me and call me Buster Brown. I didn't really feel comfortable around him so I kept a healthy distance from him, and the daytime cook was a gruff old Navy cook. He never smiled but was never really nasty either, just a persona he maintained. At any rate, he wasn't the kind of guy you chum up to very easily, especially if you were some upstart 23-year-old Californian.

With this cast of characters as my only resource, it was difficult for me to understand just how this job was going to help us out any, but in lieu of any better ideas I stayed and kept my antennae up for anything that might come through this way. I just had to have some hope and patience. A few weeks into the job, however, the answer finally came, though it took a while longer before I could be certain of it.

* * *

This answer came in the form of man named Bruce. When I first saw him, he was sitting out on the patio having a friendly chat with Jack. They seemed to be conversing as peers so I figured him for a friend who had come to visit. As it turned out, I was wrong on both counts.

In actuality, he was a man who had just divorced his wife, quit his job, liquefied his assets and bought himself a 40-foot sloop in order to sail down to the island of Grenada, near the northern coast of South America. He was in his early forties so I suppose maybe it was a midlife crisis sort of thing. Anyway, before he'd left his home back in Connecticut, he had promised his now ex-wife that he would take her for a sail before he left the country and now found himself with three weeks to wait before she could make it down here to take him up on it.

In spite of the fact that the job he'd just quit was as president of his own electronics company he was on a very limited budget and couldn't really afford to sit around idly for three weeks so he decided that he'd take up a temporary job in the meantime. The Buccaneer, he thought, would do nicely and that's what he and Jack had actually been discussing outside earlier. Bruce must have done a good job selling the idea to Jack because he agreed to take him on as a daytime dishwasher working for minimum wage despite the fact that he already had a daytime dishwasher (me!) and didn't really need another one.

This meant, of course, that we'd be working together and though he and I had virtually nothing in common we got along and I got to know him pretty well. The moment I'd heard the particulars of his circumstances I got a strange feeling that this was the break Karen and I had been waiting for. It was just too unusual and too perfect to be anything else but a gift from whomever it was that was looking out for us. I mean, here we were, two wayward travelers in dire need of anything that would help us get on a sailboat going to South America, if only we could convince someone to take us on. Then from out of the blue comes this guy, sailing alone on his 40-foot boat (plenty of room for three) on his way to South America (Grenada, close enough), who just happens to get sidelined out front of the restaurant and land himself a job working right alongside me for the next three weeks! I felt it intuitively as much as anyone can that this guy was here to take us away. Whether he knew it or not.

And apparently he didn't, for a few days later, once I felt I'd gotten to know him well enough to broach the subject, I carefully mentioned to him what Karen and I were doing. I knew I had to be discreet and I prided myself for wording it in such a way as to not appear as though I was asking him for anything.

He was a very intelligent man, though, and pretty much knew exactly what I was after. He simply replied that he was sailing alone and made it clear that he was going to continue that way but said that he'd let us know if he heard of anything that might help us.

I have to admit; I was surprised at the certainty in his voice as he rebuffed my cloaked request and my own certainty took a slight back step when he did. It didn't negate my original feeling though, only knocked it off balance a bit. Still, I respected his position and didn't try anymore to plead our case to him. Besides, there was still plenty of time for things to develop. After all, a lot can happen in a week. I certainly knew that lesson well enough, and this time I had three of them!

In the meantime, Karen and I were covering our bases, just in case Bruce was a washout, and had actually gone out and posted 3x5 cards at all the local (and not so local) marina bulletin boards offering ourselves as crew. That we were a couple made things more difficult, we were told, and limited our chances. That we didn't have any sailing experience (our boating class notwithstanding) seemed to make it nearly impossible. Still, we were resolved now and not to be easily dismayed. Things were going to start moving soon and we could feel it.

It was only about a week later when I received a phone call that made our spirits soar. It was from a man down in Fort Lauderdale. He had seen one of our notices down there and wanted us to come down for an interview with him and his wife on their boat, the "Intrepid Dragon". We were ecstatic and the following Saturday we went down with wings on our feet. We strolled down the docks not believing that we were actually there to get work. When we finally arrived at the slip, we were flabbergasted at what we found there.

The "Intrepid Dragon" turned out to be a 90–foot long, wooden Chinese junk with red cloth sails and an entirely teakwood interior decorated throughout with all hand-carved dragons and figures. The owners were a couple in their thirties from Arizona and were preparing for a three-year cruise to the Mediterranean, back through the Panama Canal, over to Hawaii and then on to San Francisco. They had two young sons and wanted to find a couple that could handle the deck as well as take care of the kids.

What interested them too was the fact that on our card I'd offered myself as a photographer. As it happened, this guy was a publisher of some sort and had a full array of cameras onboard, video and still, to document their trip. It was near perfect for us. Actually, we would have jumped ship once we had gotten to the Mediterranean, but other than that it was absolutely ideal.

We were almost giddy now. The interview went very well, we thought, and when they said they'd give us a call in the next couple of days I just knew we had it bagged. Those two days took a year to come. In the meantime, we made haste in getting new clothes, tying up loose ends and otherwise making ourselves ready, both mentally and physically, for our big departure.

Monday, the day they were to call, came and went with no word. As Tuesday evening was drawing up with still not a peep, I took the chance of being pushy and gave them a call instead. The fellow apologized for not calling and then broke the horrible news that they had decided not to take on any crew just yet. We didn't get the job. Sorry.

Our spirits were both sorely, painfully dashed, but I took it particularly hard. It was right there in reach, that which we had so long hoped and wished for, and it was snatched from us just as our fingers came upon it. I was devastated because I knew that if we couldn't land this job that we were so ideal for, we most likely couldn't get any other. I was smart enough to know that they had to take on crew (because they didn't know how to sail very well) and they were only trying to spare our feelings by saying they weren't.

Karen had been so sure of our success that she had planned a Victory Picnic for us that night (complete with motel room) as a celebration. There certainly wasn't anything to celebrate now but we tried to make the best of it and had it anyway though I'm afraid it couldn't quite match the glory of our first picnic on the beach. The next day was no better so we decided to play hooky from work and drive over to the Gulf side of the state for something new. It didn't help though, and we returned early. I just couldn't shake the feeling of hopelessness that was fast gaining on me.

But Fate only lets you down when you try to second-guess it. Karen and I had been sitting with Bruce in the restaurant when I went to make the call to the people and he saw the greatness of our disappointment when it fell through. It must have moved him because when I returned to work after our day out driving he offered me a proposition. Having thought about it during our absence he decided that he could indeed use some help crossing the Gulf Stream on his way to the Bahamas. He had never done any blue water sailing before, he told us, and figured that the moral support, if nothing else, could be helpful after all. He said he would take us as far as the island of Nassau (in the middle of the Bahamas) under the provision that we could truthfully promise to him that we had enough money to take care of ourselves once we got there and this only to protect him from feeling guilty about leaving us there.

Well, we had plenty of money by now and I don't think I could have been more emphatic in my promise to him that we did. I felt like getting down and kissing his feet right then. Our day had finally come, after all, and my funny feeling about Bruce when he had first arrived had indeed proven itself true.

As miserable as I felt the moment before his offer, it was hard to believe the ecstasy I was feeling now. Life was good indeed. It wasn't a big wooden junk and it wasn't the Mediterranean but it was the whole world to us. It was finally happening. We were to leave in two weeks.

I quit my job that very day and since Karen had already quit hers a few days earlier, this meant that for the first time since arriving here we were actually free again. It felt wonderful to be inundated with pure unadulterated, joyous freedom again, to finally loosen the knots that had been cinching so tightly these past months and cast off the lines to our great adventure.

We went over to Skeeter and Chip's house (friends of Karen from Ben's) so that Chip could help me do some last-minute work on Otto. I had made plans with my grandmother to leave the old boy with her so that she could sell him for us and send on the money. After all we had gone through in that little car, it was a very sad thought for me leave him like that. I'd had many, many memorable times in him. It would be hard.

Though we were still supposed to be looking for other, more permanent, boat jobs in the meantime, we couldn't seem to muster up the incentive now and pretty much loafed our way throughout the remaining days, wallowing in the glory of our upcoming adventure.

We spent our last Friday and Saturday at my grandmother's house. Saturday night, Bruce called to confirm everything and on Sunday morning Karen and I caught the Greyhound bus for Miami, where we were to meet up with him.

He had told us that he probably wouldn't be there at the boat when we arrived so to just hop aboard and make ourselves at home. Since neither of us had ever seen his boat, he said he'd leave us a signal to let us know which one it was, though he neglected to say what that signal would be.

We somehow managed to not only get ourselves to Miami but also succeeded in finding our way through the crowded city bus system to the marina, with all of our bundles intact. I have to admit that I felt a bit uneasy as we walked down the marina dock looking for his boat. I was afraid of misidentifying his signal and climbing aboard someone else's boat by mistake. I needn't have worried, though, for there aren't too many things more noticeable on a sailboat than a pair of checkered slacks blowing in the wind from the top of the mast.

We boarded with confidence knowing that we had indeed found the right boat but now we weren't so sure of him (in truth, I was relieved to know he had a sense of humor). It was a supremely thrilling feeling I got that first time I climbed aboard "Spirit". It seemed a very appropriate name. We spent our first night aboard there in the marina. The next morning the three of us all went into downtown Miami to do some major grocery and supply shopping for the trip and then spent that night in the marina again.

Finally, on the following morning, after some last-minute purchasing (snorkels and masks at Sears), our long-awaited moment of reckoning arrived. Poised ever so roguishly on her gleaming white decks with a faraway look in our eyes, we cast off the docking lines and slowly motored away - right around the corner where we dropped anchor and spent the night.

So it wasn't a grand departure, but it was our departure and we were nonetheless thrilled by it. Our very first night out on the "tropical" sea, being gently rocked to sleep by the ocean currents. It was truly marvelous for me.

Before turning in for the night, I snuck outside and climbed into the dinghy that was tied to our stern, so I could take a pee. I didn't feel comfortable going inside in the head with such close quarters. Kneeling there on the side of the dinghy I was surprised to look down to see hundreds of little glowing sparkles in the water where I disturbed it. At first I thought it was my water that was doing it until I knelt down and ran my hand through the ocean water and saw a trail of glitter shine in its wake.

I had no idea what was causing it but I sat out there for some time afterwards, thoroughly enchanted, just running my hands back and forth through this fairy water, before climbing back inside. It was a good night and already a good trip. I slept that night with a happy heart.

BAHAMAS

The following morning, we weighed anchor and quietly slipped out of the harbor. Once again, as with our final visit back at the Summer Cottage, the serenity of the moment belied the tremendous excitement I felt inside. It was a poignant excitement really, a feeling that I decided I liked. I didn't just see a boat sailing off into the sea; rather, what I saw was a huge door slowly opening with two kids standing at its threshold, wondering what they were going to find behind it but knowing somehow in their hearts that it was going to be something good. I watched the skyscrapers of Miami shrink ever so slowly into the horizon behind us until the only thing that existed was the featureless gray sky, the deep blue sea and us.

Our first port of call was to be the island of Bimini, which was only about 40 miles from Miami. Almost immediately after losing sight of land we ran into the 10-15 foot seas that mark the currents of the Gulf Stream as it shoots past Florida on its way up from the Gulf of Mexico, past Ireland and on to the North Sea.

It was unnerving to see these liquid mountains racing up toward us with such seeming intent, enormous towers of water that seemed to defy gravity itself, certain that at any moment they would realize their violation of natural law and come crashing down on us, then only to have them instead lift us up so gently into the sky as they quietly rolled past and then set us back down just as gently, caring not a whit about us. It was right around this time, too, that I learned that peanut butter sandwiches don't mix very well with up and down oceans.

Nerves or no, this was Karen's and my first time out in the open sea and we were amazed at all we saw out here. The immense blueness of the water particularly captivated us both. It was so blue that it was as if we were sailing in a sea of indigo ink or blueberry soup, at least until we got closer and saw the sun's rays shining down through it for several feet before they disappeared into the depths far below us. Running my hands through the water that sped past us, I could see that it was in reality crystal clear as far down as I could see. It was only the depth of the sea itself that made it look so dark and thick.

It was almost 7 p.m. as we neared the channel coming into Bimini. The approach to the harbor was very narrow and Bruce had to line the boat up just right with it if we were to make it through in one piece. I was given the job of standing up forward on the bow and keeping a watch out for any shoals or coral heads that we might come across, just in case we missed a turn somewhere.

This would have been a relatively easy job normally but now as we headed into the channel we were met head-on with a steady parade of large swells coming at us and my ride up on the bow became more like a rodeo ride. As a swell reached us, it would shoot the bow straight up in the air. I had to bend my knees and clutch the bow railing to keep from being flung off the boat like a catapult shot and then, as it passed under us, the bow would suddenly plummet straight back down. It was literally like a roller coaster ride and I would have enjoyed it much more were it not for the horrible fear that seized me as we began our first plummet.

Standing high in the sky on the crest of that swell, I looked down into the trough at the bottom of it and was terrified to see that the ocean floor was only a few feet below it. There was no time to do anything about it except to clutch the railing with all my might and brace for what would be certain death as we smashed into millions of bits of flotsam on the bottom. The bow came falling fast but instead of crashing as I had feared, it merely swooshed down as though landing on a feather pillow.

My wits returned quickly after this momentary reprieve, thinking it must be a fluke, and I yelled back to Bruce that we had run out of water. To my great surprise, though, after checking his depth sounder he yelled back that we were well into 20 feet, not two, and he didn't know what I was talking about.

This was when I learned my second lesson of sea life for the day. Prior to today I had only known the silty, sandy California coastal waters that had visibilities of about two feet, and never from the deck of a boat. I'd never had a chance to learn that perceptions in clear water were all out of proportion to what they would be otherwise. As we came plummeting down our second swell, I tried to keep an open mind about this and only half froze in fear. Eventually I came to trust that, despite what my eyes were telling me, it must be true since we never did smack bottom.

Having now learned my clear-water-depth-perception lesson, I was soon enjoying my bucking bronco ride up on the bow until we finally turned out of the swells and into the harbor where we anchored for our two-day visit.

The next day, after Bruce cleared us with customs, Karen and I went ashore to explore the tiny island of Bimini. Though it's only a couple of hours away from Miami by motorboat, Bimini seemed worlds away to us. It was, after all, not only our first port of call but also our first exotic foreign land. It even sounded exotic. Romantic visions of pirates and shipwrecks swirled in my head as we walked through Alice Town (its only town) and out along the beaches.

It looked, however, just like Florida - low, flat, dry and barren. The people there were poor and their houses were old and dilapidated. The only apparent income came from supplying the sports fisherman that came over from the States. As if to compensate for its terrestrial shortcomings, however, the ocean was unbelievably beautiful. The water was clear and warm and looking out toward the horizon, it took on that wonderful azure blue that we've all seen so many times in the travel ads but never believed to be real.

We'd brought our masks and swim fins with us that day so after walking around for a while, we were eager to get out to the beach to try them out. We sat there at the edge of the water getting ourselves all fitted and adjusted and then slipped into the sea and slowly glided along the gradually sloping, white sand shore.

Unfortunately, that was all we saw - white sand, with just the occasional conch shell for accent. After about half an hour of splashing about, we made our way back to the boat for the remainder of the day. All in all, it wasn't terribly exciting but this was, nonetheless, our first "tropic isle" (though technically not tropical) and we went to bed (technically a bunk) that night satisfied.

I was eager the next day to hone my snorkeling skills but was too lazy to go back to the beach so I decided to go diving right off the boat there in the harbor. Although we were in about 25 feet of water, from the deck of the boat it looked closer to 10 feet and already having forgotten my clear-water-depth-perception lesson of only two days ago, I jumped in, put my mask on and stuck my head under the water. Once again my heart stopped in fear as I looked below me. The water was so clear and the sandy harbor floor so detailed that my mind read the 25 feet of water I was in as being air and I was immediately gripped with a profound, if absurd, fear of falling. Absurd or no, the terror I felt at the time was real enough and I was back in the boat in mere seconds.

A short while later, I decided to give it another go. I jumped in and just floated there for a few minutes this time, psyching myself up, before ducking my head under. Aside from a brief little catch of breath at the outset, things went well and I began to slowly swim around the boat. It gave me the creeps for some reason to see its dark underside floating above me, like a whale I thought.

116

As I was thinking this, I looked down just in time to see this monstrous stingray flying up from the depths of the harbor straight at me. I didn't leave myself any time to panic, though, for I literally shot out of that water like a Polaris missile, landing in the dinghy a few feet away. Again, coming from the murky waters of the Pacific Coast I wasn't accustomed to seeing living things in the water with me, particularly when those things are monstrous stingrays charging up at me.

Actually, it wasn't really monstrous; I just hadn't yet learned the old swim-mask-underwater-magnification lesson yet, nor was it actually charging me, only swimming by. Just the same, I decided to give snorkeling a rest for a while.

We had intended to stay in Bimini for only a couple of days but due to bad weather we ended up staying for a week. Bruce spent most of his nights in town, hanging out in the bars and looking for a permanent first mate (of the female kind). He confessed to us that, despite what he'd told us back in West Palm about sailing alone, his escape fantasy did, in fact, include having a "mate" (in both senses of the word) sail with him. Neither Karen nor I were much into drink and we needed to watch our money anyway so we mostly stayed onboard the boat at night, enjoying the privacy.

Not only that, but I still hadn't quite gotten the hang of rowing Bruce's wooden dinghy yet, especially in the high winds we'd been having ever since we'd gotten here. One day Karen and I had gone ashore on a grocery and ice run in town. Afterwards, I tried to row us back out to the boat but every time I took a stroke one or the other of the oars would pop out of its oarlock. By the time I could reload and resume rowing the strong headwinds had already blown us right back to shore. I was beginning to get very frustrated until finally, after several unsuccessful attempts, what looked to me to be the world's largest motor yacht pulled up alongside of us. Looking down at us from the lofty height of its deck, the mate hollered down and asked if we would like a tow. We gladly accepted both his offer and his towline.

It must have been quite a sight watching this huge boat pulling our tiny little dinghy across the harbor like that and we got a good chuckle when we got alongside "Spirit" and saw Bruce come flying out from below with a look of panic on his face before he realized that he wasn't actually being rammed as he apparently had thought. Once he saw what was going on it was his turn to laugh at us for being such weenies.

We finally left Bimini on Thursday and headed next for Gun Cay. We had good winds that day though and when we got to Gun Cay earlier than expected we decided to just keep going. Since there were no other islands close by, that night was our first one spent anchored out at sea.

Most of the Bahamian islands are on a large, shallow underwater bank and though you can be completely out of sight of dry land, if you look down you can see every shell and rock on the ground only a few feet below. This seemed really strange to me, particularly when we came up on an old and badly corroded shipwreck that was sitting perfectly upright on the sea floor only 20 feet or so deep.

From a distance, it looked like a specter out on the horizon and only got spookier looking as we came nearer and could make out the holes that perforated its diseased hulk. The old freighter had washed up onto the bank during some long-ago storm and was now waiting out eternity parked here all by itself in lonely witness of the passing of time.

I enjoyed sitting up near the bow as we passed over this shallow bank, watching my dangling feet skipping along the surface of the water and over the ground so clear below us. It reminded me of a day not so long ago, back at the little ramshackle house where this story really begins, when I had gone out back for a walk. I had been in a quiet, reflective mood that day as I walked barefooted alongside the creek there. Somewhere along the way I looked down and began to watch my feet as they carefully tramped through the cool, green grass beneath them. I didn't watch them as though they were my feet though. Rather, I watched them objectively as though I were watching a movie of someone else's feet as he walked across a patch of earth, narrating as he did about the particular place where his feet presently were.

For some reason this exercise really intrigued me. Feet on earth. Moving across it one step at a time. Reconnecting my body with each step to the source from which my body was made. It put my sense of self and my relationship to the planet into such a broader and more integrated perspective. It was as if my feet belonged more to the earth than they did to me and made me feel, paradoxically, more connected to the earth. After all, they were made and designed for the sole purpose (no pun intended) of doing just that, connecting us to the earth.

Karen and I had, at the time back then, only recently begun talking of world travel and as I walked along watching my feet below me, I began to wonder where, when all was said and done, these two guys will have been, what places in the world will they have walked through. In my mind, I named the movie "Feets"...Around the World."

Now, as I sat there on the gunwales dipping my tootsies in the sea and recalling this "movie," I decided that I was going to make sure to walk barefooted at least once in every country we visited just so that I could look down and see my feet walking in this new place and add this new scene to my movie. (I'm strange, I know, but when you're out in the middle of the ocean or off in the woods by yourself it's sometimes hard to put strangeness into context. It's easy to see how people who live alone can get so nutty after only a short period of time).

We dropped anchor that night at about 9 p.m. right there in the middle of the ocean. It was a warm, perfectly clear night and there were a gazillion stars out. I sat out in the dark for a long time that night, by myself, just sitting there watching them as though they were going to do something. I got a strange feeling inside when I realized we were in the Bermuda Triangle but it somehow seemed appropriate that night. Look as I did, though, I didn't see any strange green fogs or even one flying saucer and I eventually went down below to attempt some sleep. I say "attempt" because out at sea there is nothing to protect you from the swells and we were out at sea. All night long the boat yawed over to one side then after a moment's hesitation would swing over to the other and then back again to the first. Every time it did this, all the pots, pans, dishes and cans of food we had in the cupboards slid violently, crashing noisily into each other. Worse, though, was that Karen and I were doing the exact same thing with each other (though without all the racket, of course). It all made for a long, tiring night.

We sailed all the next day in light winds and eventually made it to Chub Cay in the Berry Islands at around 6 p.m., where we anchored for the night. Earlier that day, while leisurely bobbing on our way, Bruce had tossed out a fishing line just for the heck of it and we were happy to have caught us a big tuna with it a short time later. Unfortunately for Bruce though, Poseidon wasn't about to give up one of his kingdom for free and made off with a bag of Bruce's dirty laundry that he'd tied up in a net bag and had also tossed overboard in order to get an easy wash. After a couple of hours when he went to pull it in, he found that the line had broken somewhere along the way and he'd lost all of his spare clothing.

Shortly after arriving at our anchorage and getting the boat all squared away for the evening, Karen and I took the dinghy out for a leisurely row over to the island. On the way back to the boat, we stopped alongside a protruding piece of coral and watched the setting sun turn the sky into an eerie blaze of orange. I took a photo of "Spirit" silhouetted against it, a picture that would turn out to be a very fortuitous one for us a few months later. At the time, though, it was just a pretty picture taken at a quiet time.

We weighed anchor at seven o'clock the following morning and pointed our bow toward the island of Nassau, our next port of call. It was only one day's sail away and my emotions were becoming mixed as we got closer to it. I was excited at the thought of seeing a new place but this was tempered by the knowledge that it was to be the end of the line for us with Bruce. This was going to be our first foreign country as homeless vagabonds and I wasn't too sure how the game was played here or how we would fare with it.

Coming on late afternoon we started scanning the horizon for any sign of the island. It wasn't long before we were rewarded and, as its flat little head peeked up over the rim, my suddenly surging sense of adventure completely obscured my worries. Standing up at the bow, with the setting sun at our backs, I was once again the intrepid explorer making ready for landfall in this obscure and exotic pirate's land while the island of Nassau laid waiting before us, growing ever larger in the gathering pinks and oranges of the coming evening. We sailed into the harbor and dropped anchor right in front of the equally pink Sheraton's British Colonial Inn.

We thought it was a bit more interesting here than in Bimini. First of all, we were anchored right off the Sheraton's private beach and it was fun to sit there on the boat and watch all the people who were sitting on the beach watching us. Bruce usually took the dinghy ashore early in the day and then spent most his time there still searching for that elusive dream mate. This meant that Karen and I had to don our flippers and snorkels and swim ashore whenever we felt like exploring the island or sneaking some food and showers from the hotel. Sometimes we'd just lie about the hotel's beach or swimming pool like the other tourists and gloat to ourselves that we got to go home to a nice, big, pretty boat rather than an expensive, little hotel room.

It was also interesting for me that we had anchored only a short way from the island's cruise ship dock and I very much enjoyed sitting back and watching these grand ladies as they quietly paraded by us, so big and bright, only a couple hundred feet away.

Other than that, though, Nassau wasn't much better than Bimini, only larger. It had a small touristy section full of little shops and an open marketplace scattered around the cruise ship's landing dock, but otherwise was mostly just poor and dilapidated.

Karen and I started scouting around the island for our next job right away. There were a lot of boats there in the various marinas around Nassau which was encouraging, but after asking around we learned that virtually none of them were looking for crew and weren't likely to be anytime soon.

While out hunting that first day, we spotted the "Intrepid Dragon" anchored farther down the harbor and the thought came up to go over and see if they might have changed their minds about taking us on now that they could see that we'd made it this far very nicely without them, but my pride wouldn't allow it. Rumor had it that they had run aground while trying to leave Ft. Lauderdale and for some reason I enjoyed hearing that. That'll teach them not to take us, I gloated to myself.

One afternoon, four days after arriving, the three of us were sitting down below when all of a sudden the boat started shuddering violently, lasting for several seconds. Our eyes went big as we looked back and forth at one another in bewilderment before racing up top to see what the heck was going on.

What we saw was one of the blackest rain clouds I'd ever seen and it was heading straight for us. The low pressure that was advancing before it was so deep and so sudden that it had caused "Spirit" to literally shake in her boots when it hit us.

We could see the heavy curtain of rain that it was dragging beneath it and we immediately set about battening down the hatches and stowing any loose gear before it found us. It started raining only a few minutes later, slowly at first, and then suddenly, just as we were finishing up on deck, the sky opened up and unleashed a furious, raging torrent. The wind came up right behind it, blowing ferociously and turning the raindrops into stinging needles as they were driven sidelong into our faces.

Once everything had been secured on deck, we scurried down below and watched through the small doorway at all the water that was pouring from the sky, glad now to be out of it.

We watched, too, as many of the other boats in the anchorage began dragging their anchors in the fierce winds. Just then, Bruce shouted and I turned to see one of these boats coming right at us. We jumped back up on deck to fend him off. His course was going to bring him right off our stern, between us and our dinghy. Bruce yelled to me to hurry back and undo the dinghy's tether and then hand it off to the skipper of the other boat as he scooted past us so that he wouldn't get tangled in it. I had only just managed to untie it, with a couple of seconds to spare, when his bow slid past us only feet away. As he did, I tossed the line over to him and he took our dinghy away with him.

Just as I took a deep breath of relief, now that our crisis had been handled, Bruce realized that it was, in fact, us that had dragged past our nearly collided friend and not him past us! Not only that, but we were now coming up fast on yet another boat.

Karen and I quickly readied ourselves to fend us off from it while Bruce ran forward to let out more anchor line with the hopes that it might make the anchor grab hold better on the sandy bottom. After a few tense moments, it finally did take

123

hold but not before the three of us had to kick and shove the other boat away from us as it slid down alongside our hull.

Fortunately, his boat dragged back a few feet itself and got clear of us but then threatened to entangle his anchor line in our propeller, which caused some worry. When the wind had died down a little, though, we managed to pull up some on our anchor line and get completely clear of him.

In the meantime, several other boats had either been relocated or were adrift, many without their skippers on board, one of them banging dangerously up against a nearby cement wall. Within a half an hour of its dramatic arrival, the squall took its fury away just as quickly and left us once again under calm, sunny skies.

I was amused shortly after it was all over when I glanced over to the Sheraton and saw the hotel's patrons all sitting there in the restaurant casually nibbling at their lunches while blandly watching all this commotion outside through the restaurant's big picture windows as though watching a dull movie.

Two days later, as Karen and I were out canvassing the town looking for work, Bruce was out canvassing the town as well, still on his mate quest and though we returned unsuccessful in our pursuit, happily for Bruce his two-week search for a woman finally yielded success. Her name was April and she was there on vacation from her hairstylist job back home in Indiana somewhere. She had met Bruce while laying out that day, sunning herself, right there at the Sheraton's beach.

After a very short courtship (one day), Bruce invited her out for a week-long sail to a nearby chain of islands called the Exumas. She didn't want to pass up this possible dream vacation but, on the other hand, she wasn't entirely sure of this guy after such a short acquaintance so she agreed to go but only on the condition that Karen and I come along too, just in case. Bruce readily agreed to her terms and we, in turn, happily accepted his invitation for an extra week's worth of sailing and island hopping.

Since he had to bring April back here to Nassau afterwards, this wasn't really going to help Karen and me out very much as far as making any miles, but it was a new adventure and we weren't about to refuse an offer to go sail around the Bahamas for free. Our job search here wasn't proving very promising anyway and I think we were both eager for anything that would postpone the inevitable hustling we'd have to do if we wanted to find any boat work. Especially since we'd already been told that it was both illegal and difficult for us to work on shore, which severely reduced our options.

Whatever it was we were to do, though, we would need to do it soon as we returned from the Exumas, for we were already down to just a few hundred dollars and that wouldn't last us too very long once we became orphans.

Almost a week from when we'd first sailed into Nassau's harbor, we now were heading out of it toward some of the more eastern members of the Bahama Islands. We anchored out in the ocean again that night and had ourselves yet another tough night of rolling about in our beds while, again, all the cans and jars of food banged away in the cabinets. Waking up the next morning to a sunny, semi-tropical sea and then remembering for the first time of the day where we were and what we were doing made all the discomforts of the night fade away though.

We arrived at Normans Cay the next evening and found ourselves a beautiful little harbor to anchor in for the night. Karen and I could barely wait for morning to arrive so we could don our snorkels and fins and do some exploring. It was our first opportunity do any serious snorkeling and we set out first thing to see what we could find. We weren't disappointed, either.

The area near the boat actually wasn't very exciting and at first I thought that this was just going to be more of what we'd already seen back in Nassau and Bimini but later, on a solo excursion out toward the entrance to the harbor, I came upon what I thought must surely be the underwater version of the Garden of Eden. If that stingray back in Bimini took my breath away, this rivaled the feeling only this time it was awe, not fear, that caused it. Huge brain corals protruded several feet from the sea floor and several feet across, looking every bit like their name implies. Alongside these calciferous monoliths, and in such stark contrast to them, was the delicate lacework of the many-colored fan corals, gently swaying back and forth in the currents. All sorts of plants were mingled in amongst these, and several other types of coral unknown to me, and through all of this swam the prettiest fish I'd ever seen. Little, iridescent fish of literally all colors of the spectrum, swimming ever so calmly in and out of the crevasses and rock grottoes along the ocean floor.

I was so taken with the serenity and the beauty of the place that when I came upon another stingray, resting on the bottom directly below me, I wasn't even startled, let alone afraid. In fact, I even hovered over him for several minutes, watching him as thoughts of all those Cousteau films came to mind, and then swam down to within only a few feet of him so I could get a closer look. It was a wonderful place and Karen and I swam out here several times during our brief stay here just to see it all again.

It was a good thing we did, too, as it was to be the last thing we'd be able to explore during our visit here in the Bahamas, for in these past three days since leaving Nassau, several things had been finally resolved, by all parties, as to the upcoming nature of the trip.

For our part, Karen and I had begrudgingly decided that we were going to take what little money we had left and break our first, and foremost, rule of budget travel and catch an airline out. Rather than wearing our resources too thin in Nassau, looking for something we probably wouldn't be able to find, we decided instead now to fly straight down to the Virgin Islands in the Caribbean.

Months ago, back in Florida, I had overheard a conversation between two of the waitresses I worked with at Portofino restaurant. One of them had mentioned that she'd just come up from St. Thomas and that she'd been working in a restaurant there. Though I'd never even heard of the Virgin Islands before, I had made a mental note of her comment at the time with the thought that if she could find work there then certainly so could we. That conversation came back to me now and it seemed that this would be a good time to go and find out. Later, when we checked a map to see just where these islands were, we were surprised, and encouraged, to learn that not only were they relatively close but also that half of them were actually owned by the United States. That could only be good for us, we thought.

At the same time that we were coming to our decision, April was coming to her own. She had by now come to the conclusion that Bruce was a pretty nice guy after all and she now wanted to have some cruise time alone with him while she still had a few days left in her vacation.

Karen and I were eager to get moving now that we knew what our next course of action was to be and Bruce and April were just as eager to have some time alone so it was agreed that night that Norman's Cay would be where our paths would part. There was a small airstrip there on the island which, for some unknown reason, was visited daily by any number of small, private planes and it was now our plan to try and hitch a ride back to Nassau with one of them on the following day.

We all had our last breakfast together that next morning before Karen and I gathered up our things and said our goodbyes to April. She was going to stay on board while Bruce accompanied us on up to the airstrip.

Norman's Cay was a small, virtually uninhabited little bit of sand out in its own piece of the sea. The only buildings on the island were, oddly, those of a small resort complex of some sort though they were all closed up and empty now. It seemed a desolate place. After rowing us ashore, Bruce walked with us slowly up the brush-lined sand road to the airstrip, about a mile or so inland.

It was quiet and somewhat sad in mood as we made our way past the darkened, deserted buildings of the resort that abutted the tarmac of the single runway there. The emptiness of the island was certainly part of the reason for the solemnity but much more was the fact that Karen and I had, for the better part of a month now, enjoyed undreamt-of adventures with Bruce and had grown very fond of him. We had also become good friends with April by now and I found it sad to think that we were leaving them and our Bahamian adventures behind us. It had been safe and secure for us on "Spirit" and now we were going out into the big, uncertain world again, where we were unsure of what would become of us.

There was an open-air patio just outside one of the buildings and near the runway that we chose as our "lobby." We sat out there for about a half an hour visiting with Bruce this last time while waiting for a plane to come in. He wrote both of us a nice letter of recommendation to use in finding work in the future and gave it to us just before telling us that it was time for him to get back. We said our goodbyes to him as he turned and disappeared back down the road, not knowing if we'd ever see him again or not.

If it turned out that we couldn't catch a ride that day, we were to go back to the boat ourselves and the not knowing made the farewell a little easier to accept. In fact, after two planes had come and gone without taking us along it was beginning to look like a real possibility that we would be back onboard that night.

A couple of hours later, though, a third plane touched down and taxied to a stop. I approached the pilot as he made his way toward the office and asked him if he could give us lift back to Nassau. There seemed a hint of suspicion in his eyes as he gave us the once-over but I guess we looked safe enough, for he then agreed to take us. A few minutes later we were up in the air looking down at all the sparkling water that had so recently been our home.

[We learned later that after his sailing trip to South America Bruce moved to Indiana and was living with April. I felt very happy for them both when I heard. We never did see them again, however. I also heard, several years later, that Norman's Cay figured prominently in a big, Medellin cartel drug importing ring which confirmed my suspicions at the time that there was something unusual about an empty resort with an airstrip out in the middle of nothing. In retrospect, it's no wonder the pilot eyed us the way he did.]

Melancholies aside, we both found the flight thrilling, particularly Karen since this was the very first airplane she'd ever been in, plus it was only a small, four-seater, which gave our ride a certain sense of immediacy that you can't get from an airliner. It was fun, too, to see all the islands from such an entirely different vantage point than what we had become accustomed to and we had our faces plastered into the windows the whole way back to Nassau trying to see if we could recognize anything below us in the shimmering ocean.

In only a half an hour's time we were in the airport back at Nassau. Once there, we sadly discovered that there were no direct flights to the Virgin Islands at all from the Bahamas and that we would first have to fly back to Miami, then connect with a flight to Puerto Rico and finally switch over to yet another to take us on to St. Thomas, the main island of the U.S. Virgins. We reluctantly bought our tickets, for we had no choice, and spent the next several hours sitting around the airport until our departure time.

The flight back to Miami took only about 45 minutes and it was a real letdown for us to be back there. Nearly a whole month of exotic, tropical adventure completely undone in about five hours. A whole new world rewound in a mere fraction of time.

After all the beauty, romance and adventure that we had just lived through, it was hard for me to adjust to being back in busy, crowded, vulgar Miami so suddenly. Adding to the insult, we found out that the next flight to St. Thomas didn't leave until the following morning. It was now early evening so we stiffened our upper lips and settled in there at the airport as best we could, making our beds across its plastic chairs that night.

CARIBE

The flight from Miami to Puerto Rico was an unexciting one and it only reinforced our disdain for the blandness of airline travel. San Juan airport was only a little interesting because it was so different from any other airport I'd been in but otherwise, our two-hour layover there was mostly boring. The insecurity of not really knowing what we were doing added a slight uneasiness to the mood, especially since we now only had about $200 left between the two of us which ain't much for exploring a new world with.

It was a tiny little jet that took us from there on to St. Thomas, with only one row of seats on either side of the aisle. The luggage was just piled up in the back near the door as we got on.

Reading the back of my ticket jacket while waiting for takeoff, I noticed that the pilot had the right to jettison any luggage that he felt necessary should he, at any time, determine that the plane was too heavy. Since we each had only one small backpack apiece, I could afford to find this amusing as I imagined the horrified looks on the faces of those whose belongings were being chucked out of the jet's open doorway at 20,000 feet over the ocean. I have to admit that this did add a certain air of adventure to the flight (another pun unintended).

As we flew over St. Thomas, I could see that these islands were very different from the ones we'd just left. Where the Bahamas were low, flat, scrubby islands projecting modestly from an underwater shelf, these islands were actually the tops of underwater mountains which rose steeply out of the sea, tall and green with palm lined beaches, and coves and bays circling the many islands.

Any adventure to this flight, as it turned out, was purely in our imaginations and we landed at St. Thomas completely unscathed at one o'clock that afternoon. We got off the plane with absolutely no idea where we were going to stay, what we were going to do, or even where exactly on this island we were.

We did know that we were somewhere on the outskirts of town, though we had no idea just how far or in what direction. Since we'd already broken the "no flying" rule, it wasn't too hard for us to continue the trend by hiring a taxi into town, despite our desperate finances. We figured it would be a good way to orient ourselves along the way and to introduce ourselves to the island.

And, hell, since we were hiring a taxi, it was only another small step to decide then to spend our first night in a hotel, too, as neither one of us was all that eager to head off into the steep, brush-covered mountains to look for campsites, especially after spending last night in Miami Airport's wholly uncomfortable waiting lounge.

Earlier, while still on the plane, I had seen an ad for the Holiday Inn here on the island and, thinking it might be one of the cheaper places in town, I took a blind stab and had the taxi driver take us there. We needed to tell the driver something and it seemed as good a place as any. Since it was clear on the opposite side of town from where the airport was, it gave us a good chance to scope the place out on the way.

Driving through Charlotte Amalie, the islands main town, I can't say I was much impressed with the little bit we saw. Passing along the concrete quay at the edge of town, it appeared that the capital city of the Virgin Islands was little more than a row of bars and shops sitting next to an old 18th century fort-cum-museum.

Farther on down the harbor we noticed the only marina in town and were happy to see that it was attached to a big, pink Sheraton Inn, just like our old friend back at Nassau. I took special note of it as we passed by, for I had a feeling that we would be seeing a lot more of this place before we were done with this island and it turns out I wasn't wrong in thinking so.

We continued on through town and up the hill on the other side of it to where the Holiday Inn sat perched on the hillside, overlooking the entire harbor and city below. It was immediately apparent that, instead of being the roadside cheapie that I was expecting, it was actually one of the island's posher resorts, going by the name of Frenchman's Reef. Since we were already here and since I had to go inside to cash a traveler's check for the cabbie anyway, I asked about the rates just in case and was stricken dumb when I was told that their cheapest rate was $55 a night for a single. [By today's standards that would be a wonderful bargain but for those days it was an exorbitant price for one room for one night for one person.]

It was obvious we couldn't stay here so we had the cabbie take us back down into town. We were really in the dark now about where to go so I asked the driver if he knew of any cheap hotels nearby that he could recommend. "Oh sure," he said, no problem, he could fix us up. As we were heading back down the hill, he spotted a woman he knew walking down the road and stopped alongside her for a few minutes so that he could proposition her before continuing on our way.

He took us to a small hotel in the Estate Thomas section of town. Many years ago, these islands were all slave-based sugar plantations (estates) and Estate Thomas had been one such plantation. Now it was a fairly rundown suburb of Charlotte Amalie, but the price was right and it was within walking distance of downtown so we checked in and made ourselves at "home."

In actuality, I was feeling very much like a stranger in a strange land, not knowing anything about anything here, and so as soon as we got settled in (read, throwing our packs on the bed) we headed straight back out to explore more of our new town.

As we walked along the waterfront and on into town, I was startled to find that the unimpressive little street that we'd driven along earlier on our way to Frenchman's Reef, and that I had thought to be the main street of town, was actually only the waterfront road. Princes Street, the real main street, was a block farther up from the harbor's edge and was another world altogether, a much more charming and interesting one.

The buildings that ran along the upper side of Princes Street, the side nearest the center of the island, were the type that one usually thinks of in the Caribbean: two-storied plaster and stone buildings with iron-railed balconies, their once brightly painted pastel coats now peeling and faded. Inside these old buildings, though, and in stark contrast to their outside appearance, were glittering shops selling all types of duty-free gold and jewels, electronics, cameras, liquors and anything else they could unload to the many hundreds of cruise ship passengers that make their way through town on almost a daily basis.

The other side of street, the side nearest the harbor, was lined instead with several huge, old stone and mortar buildings that housed even more shops and most of the downtown restaurants. Three hundred years ago these old buildings were the warehouses where all the rum, sugar and molasses from the plantations was stored prior to shipment around the world.

Huge iron shutters and grates still protected the windows and doors that opened onto the dark, narrow walkways, called alleys, that separated one building from another. Barely more than eight feet across in places, these brick-paved alleys cut all the way down to the waterfront at the far end of the block and, in places, meandered around through the old buildings, creating little alcoves, some with fountains and hidden shops.

We liked it here a lot and, while walking back to our hotel room late that afternoon, we decided that it would be real nice to stay here for five or six weeks, instead of only the two weeks we had originally planned on. This would give us an opportunity to enjoy the place a little bit before running off again, as well as a chance to save up some badly needed travel bucks. We would have to cut short the South American leg of our trip but this idea didn't seem to really bother either of us very much. It was beginning to seem that the closer we got to South America the less interested in it we became, for some reason.

That evening, we walked up to a nearby grocery store and brought back some cheese, bread, apples and wine for a picnic dinner back at the hotel room and spent our very first night on a tropic isle watching local T.V.

Ever since our first picnic back on the beach in Florida, they'd taken on a special significance to us. It had been so wonderful that whenever we felt like we needed a lift or had to iron out any wrinkles in our relationship we would have ourselves a picnic and everything would be better afterwards. This evening was no exception.

After all this time, it was fun, too, playing house together again. We hadn't had a place to ourselves since our apartment with Katherine five months earlier.

First thing next morning, we went out and picked up a copy of the local newspaper and sat there on the curbside by the news rack while we went through the Help Wanted ads. We'd decided to take up some restaurant jobs first so we could get in some quick cash and free food and then start looking for boat work once we got ourselves better situated and prepared.

Most of the restaurant work listed in the paper was back at Frenchman's Reef so we returned to our room, got dressed up as best we could with the few clothes we had and hitched a ride on up the hill to try our luck. The Reef turned out to be far too strict for our tastes and their requirements for employment much too involved so we decided to return to town and see if we couldn't muster up something there first. If nothing turned up there then we could reconsider coming back here. We regrouped and opted for the strategy of just starting at one end of town and hitting every restaurant we came across on our way to the other side.

Well, the gods must have thought it a good idea too, because Karen was hired as a waitress at the very first place we stopped at and I was taken on as a busboy at the next. Both were in the old stone warehouses and were only a couple of alleys apart.

Karen's new job was working lunches at a smaller, informal place (of course) called Drake's Inn and wasn't to start there for another five days or so. My job, however, started the very next morning, also working lunches, at a much more formal (of course), ritzy French restaurant, called L'Escargot. They required the obligatory white shirt/black slacks uniform of the restaurant world, which meant I had some quick shopping to do all of a sudden. I didn't even have socks or shoes.

Since Karen had lots of time to prepare and so much less to prepare for, she didn't share my newly sprouted sense of urgency but I was so happy to know that things were working out that I really didn't care. We were going to eat and have money. Life was good. All we had to do now was figure out where to stay in the meantime.

We were fast realizing that our original thought of making a camp somewhere up on the hillside in the bushes was a bad one. The relentless, pernicious, ubiquitous mosquitoes were a large part of the reason but so too was the difficulty, let alone the inconvenience, we'd have of getting ourselves dressed up for work every day while hiding out under a palm tree. Not only that, but after experiencing our first tropical cloudburst, it was clear that anything not tied up in a tree, including us, would be immediately washed down the steep hillsides in the first few minutes of the daily (and nightly) deluges that occurred here with marked regularity.

All of this considered, plus the assurance of knowing that we had jobs now, made it pretty easy for us right then to decide to stay one more night at the hotel and deal with it all tomorrow. In fact, we pretty much had to so that I could get myself ready to start work the next day. I had slacks to hem.

Just to be certain of our thinking, Karen took all of our things back out to the airport the following day while I was at work and locked them up in a rental locker there so that she could be free to go off and explore the bushes near the college.

As if in direct answer to our concerns, it rained too hard all that day for her to even get past the campus and she spent most of the day holed up in one of the dorms instead. We discussed the situation later that afternoon when I got off work and decided that our only real option was to try and find a cheap room somewhere that we could rent on a short-term basis. The motel, even though relatively cheap, was still far too expensive to consider so we grabbed a phone book and started thumbing through the yellow pages to see what we could find.

There were many guest houses listed that served both as apartments and short-term vacation rentals and since the vacation season was coming to a close as we stood there, it was easy to find a vacancy at one of them, Ramsey's Guest House. We left straight away to go check it out. It was also in the Estate Thomas part of town, not very far from the hotel, but it was in the upper section of the old plantation along the side of the hill overlooking the town rather than down on the flat part where the hotel was.

We walked to the edge of town, a mile or so on, and then another mile up the winding side streets through the humble bungalows there before rounding a final curve to spot Ramsey's Guest House perched above us. It was a plain and fairly shabby looking concrete building, two stories high but looking much taller due to the steepness of the hill that it was adhered to.

Ramsey wanted $100 a week for the room, which was virtually all the money that we had left. This thought certainly added to the general discomfort we had about this whole renting idea in the first place but we had little choice at this point so we agreed to the terms and moved in that night. It was a consolation to us though, while lying in bed that night, to think about how ignorant we'd been about this place as we stepped off the jet, total strangers and nearly broke, and now, only two and a half days later, to have everything so well in hand and set up for us. It was reassuring to know that our travel strategy was not only workable but actually working. We slept well.

***

L'Escargot, it turns out, was not only one of the fanciest places in town but, due mainly to the cruise ship business, it was also one of the busiest, especially during lunch times. The turnover for bus help was very rapid here as few of the locals, which made up the primary work force, were able or willing to handle the extremely fast pace of the place. Added to this was that they (we) were responsible for as much of the table service as the waiters, if not more.

Since I had cut my restaurant teeth back at Lazio's where we'd often get several tour busses pull up at once, I had very little problem keeping up the pace and because of this I soon became very popular with the management. After only a few days, I was offered a dinner shift in addition to lunch and since we needed all the money we could get, I gratefully accepted even though it would mean working a minimum of 12 hours a day, six days a week. It wouldn't be but for a couple of weeks, I thought, I could handle that.

Dinners were much more relaxed and formal than the lunches were, which was nice. After the lunch crowd had gone, the dishes were washed and the tables reset for dinner, I had the fun of going outside and closing up the huge iron shutters over the 8-foot-tall windows that ran along the alley side of the restaurant, with the heavy metal clank of the swing arm. I'm not sure why I enjoyed that duty so much, perhaps because I could pretend to be closing the gates to the castle before the imminent attack of the barbarian hordes or shutting the storm cellar door as the fast-approaching killer tornado came whipping up. It was just too appealing to my vivid imagination and seemed so dramatic as I pulled the lever into its locked position. Ah, all was safe now.

Once done with this chore, I was free for about an hour before I had to be back to start dinner. This was the only hour I had during the day to see Karen and we often just met up either here or at Drake's or in one of the hidden alcoves of the alleys and sat for a while. If we were lucky, the daily thunderstorm would come by now so we could fully enjoy the overhead violence from our safe enclave. [It was actually pretty cool to be in the restaurant when they came over, too. All of a sudden the light reflecting off the adjacent stone building outside the windows would grow very dark only moments before the torrents began to fall in a mad rush to meet their demise on the ground. The thunder would crack directly over top of us at times and echo around inside our own stone walled once-upon-a-time warehouse. Seen against the warm colored stone walls and through fine crystal and china of the place settings, the storm's ferocity seemed all the greater, as did my enjoyment of it.]

Other than this mid-afternoon hour, the only other time Karen and I had off together was on Sunday of each week since it was the only day neither of us worked. We looked forward to them not only as our respite from work but also because it was our only opportunity to go and explore the island together. After all, there's not much purpose in going off to a tropic isle if you never get out to see any of it.

Unfortunately, the breakneck pace of my job, combined with the number of hours I spent there each day and the fact that I had to commute the several miles to get there every morning by foot, had me so worn by the time our first Sunday came along that I was not only too tired to move but I had come down with a cold as well. In fact, I was usually so spent by the time I finished work each night, usually around midnight, that I rarely had enough energy left in me to make the long hike home on my own. Even though, technically, they were still a taboo with us, I began taking taxicabs home after work. It only cost two bucks a ride and I felt I could justify it in this case. Even so, it had been too little, too late an effort to do any good and we spent that first Sunday sitting at home, resting and recuperating.

In contrast to my seemingly nonstop work schedule, Karen worked far fewer hours a day than I and had a lot more time on her hands with nothing much to fill it up. Since there were no busses on the island and nothing of any real interest within walking distance, there wasn't much alternative for Karen but to hang around the house.

It was dangerous, this idle time, because it gave her too much opportunity to think of home and she was getting more and more homesick as time went by. Her resolve to finish the trip was unquestioned and that wonderful feeling of "rightness" still tailed us endlessly as strong as ever, but homesickness never really goes away once it's been felt; it either festers or just gets buried.

At any rate, she remained true, and spent much of her free time getting to know our housemates. She became good friends during this time with the two youngest of Ramsey's five kids, Juna and Leona, who all lived upstairs from us. She grew particularly fond of Leona.

She also became pretty good friends with the three other people who shared our floor: Clarence, a man somewhere in his 60s or 70s who liked to spend his welfare money on booze; Harriet, his 90-year-old, infirm mother that lived with him; and George, a younger man who worked as a projectionist at the Sheraton Inn and who we rarely ever saw.

Actually, due to my hours, I rarely ever saw any of them, except for Clarence. He, on the other hand, I saw almost every day. He never worked and was always up watching T.V. when I came home at night. I'd usually sit with him for a few minutes and try to talk a while before heading off to my sweetie pie and bed.

I say "try" because Clarence usually talked in an incomprehensible, indefinable garble and he'd often go on rambling for a fairly long time. He made faces while he talked like this, with his eyes particularly, that were very interesting and, oddly enough, endearing to watch.

It wouldn't have been so bad sitting there with him while he garbled on, for he was a pleasant man, but every now and then he'd suddenly stop talking and look at me with an expectant look on his face. I felt awkward whenever he did this because I soon realized that it meant he'd just asked me a question, though I hadn't a clue as to what it was. He'd just sit there patiently for my reply. All I could really do was just say yes and smile. West Indian accents are very hard to understand anyway.

We both saw Clarence downtown a lot, too, usually on the first few nights after his monthly check came in as he went from bar to bar. He was a sweet and gentle old man and despite the fact that I seldom knew what he was saying to me I was quite fond of him.

I've always found it interesting to see the hidden sides of people that alcohol releases from them. The things we all repress are finally given a chance to show themselves and what usually comes out is violence, sadness, silliness, horniness or any of a host of other dubious qualities, but I've never seen before alcohol releasing gentleness.

That's what I seemed to see in Clarence's bloodshot eyes, oddly enough, and when he got drunk neither would he stagger nor fall around on people and things. He would just sit and get a lost look in his eyes as he began talking his incessant gibberish to anyone close enough to hear him, never loudly or aggressively, and no matter how drunk he got he always kept track of the one and two dollars he often borrowed from me and always paid me back. [We were both much saddened to leave him when we moved out of Ramsey's a month later. He gave us a nice, warm smile the day we left and said he'd miss us.]

***

It's perhaps important to say something here of the truer nature of our trip together. We'd set out almost a full year ago to have an adventure while traveling the world and we knew that true adventure is nothing if it's not uncomfortable. In fact, a certain amount of discomfort defines adventure. Otherwise it's just a trip. If our travels seem awkward or difficult, well, we saw them as challenges and memorable stories. The more we had the more interesting our tale, the more exciting, and certainly the more adventurous.

By seeing life in this way we converted what would normally be unfortunate circumstances, and therefore negative in nature, into positive ones that made life much more fun. It allowed us to rise above the discomfort and make friends with those forces that would otherwise threaten us. It's the things in life that challenge you that end up being the things you remember most and in time the very things that you revere. The two mottoes that we reminded each other of on a regular basis were "Oh well, it builds character" and "Someday we'll look back on this and laugh." They weren't just empty platitudes either. Though we usually uttered them lightly, we knew them to be true and, in fact, relied on them to keep things in perspective. Because of this, it seems that the times we were the most vulnerable and disadvantaged were the very times we had the most fun.

The entries from each of our journals of this time give good highlights to both of these aspects of our trip and a small insight to the quality of our relationship.

FROM MY JOURNAL:

It's now 10:10pm, Sunday, May 27, and I'm sitting in our one-room apartment in St. Thomas swatting mosquitoes and sweating bullets while Karen sits in the common living room watching T.V. with a foot full of sea urchin spines that she got while we were out snorkeling today. I've been working 12-13 hours a day, 6 days a week and I only get to see her for about one to two hours a day. Though the situation is uncomfortable I don't think we would have it any other way. We know it's only temporary and so see it as just another part of our experiences. It's these times we will look back on, oddly enough, with fond memories. There is something inside me that says I'm doing what I should be doing because despite all else it still feels right doing it. Even now I look back fondly on our stay in Florida even though at the time we were in a semi-miserable slump for several months.

FROM KAREN'S JOURNAL:

[12May79] Mark has been working day and night since Thursday so I haven't seen him much; boy, the guy's exhausted. I'll be glad to start work so I don't have to spend so much time doing nothing while Mark is working. Tomorrow is Sunday so my honey will be able to rest his weary bones and I'll be able to

see him and play with him. Markie's birthday is in one week and I can't think what to get him. I want to get him something special he can use. With no money it might be tough. He says to get him nothing but I want his birthday to be a real nice one.

[15May79] - It's Tuesday night, a little after 11:00pm. Markie is still at work; he's putting in a 13-hour day. Honey's going to be a pooped honey when he gets home. He's going to look 40 on his 24th birthday if he keeps up these hours! Even next Saturday on his birthday, he's scheduled to work a double. I hope he doesn't have to. He should have a real good birthday because he deserves it. He's a special guy and he's my best friend, which should give him full rights to a happy, happy birthday. I feel real "right" being with him; it just seems to fit right. I wish I could show him and tell him how much he means to me. Well, I guess he knows 'cause he's just that way. I guess it's our feet. Hee-hee. Well, I'm just sitting getting ready for bed and thinking about lots of stuff like Mark and home and stuff. Never could write down all that goes on in my head. It's hard to think about all the feelings I've got, let alone try to put them on paper. I'm feeling good and happy, though, thinking about all the people I love. I sure love lots of people! Boy, am I a lucky one! Started work yesterday. It seems okay. I work upstairs, sometimes by myself. I'm waitress, bartender (I've got my own little bar!), buskid and cashier. It was kinda hectic yesterday at first, couldn't remember everything I was supposed to be doing, but I did good. Today had somebody helping, Sandi, which made it simpler. It's a real relaxed place, can even drink on the job, not really supposed to but can, everybody seems real nice. My eyes are sagging so I'll say goodnight "goodnight." Honey is home! Hooray!

[26May79] - Hi. Mark had to work a double on his birthday but when he got off we had a picnic in our room. He liked his birthday, he said. I wrote him some poems. His mom called him *at work which was real nice for him. He misses her an awful lot. Well, my honey is now an old man of 24.*

For my birthday, Karen bought me a new toothbrush to replace the one I'd somehow lost a few days ago. She'd tied a single ribbon around it and presented it with these poems that she'd written for me on the backsides of some wrapping paper scraps.

The sun is happy
Shining on the mountains

The earth is happy
To be strong

The butterfly is happy
Dancing on the breeze

I am happy
To be with you

THE MOON IS OUR FRIEND

IT GIVES US SEASONS OF
                    LOVE
IT GIVES US SEASONS OF
                    GROWTH

WE LIVE BY THE MOON
WE LIVE WITH THE MOON

THE MOON IS OUR FRIEND

Like a fragrant flower
covered with morning
                dew
a friendship sparkles

Like a high mountain
looking up at the
                sky
a friendship endures

Our friendship is warm
Our friendship is lasting

Our friendship is love

A week later, when our second day off arrived, it was Karen's turn to be sick and she wasn't in much of a mood to go touring about so we once again stayed home and had a quiet day. Finally though, on our third go-round, we actually managed to both be well and to have a chance to see a little bit of where we were.

We had been eager to go to Coki Beach, over on the other side of the island, ever since we'd heard that it was a good spot for snorkeling, so we packed up our Sears masks and fins and hitched out to see for ourselves. It was a pretty little bay, with the palm trees, the white crescent-shaped beach and all, and after our hot, sticky trek from town, its swimming pool blue water was screaming to us. We wasted no time donning our fish faces and frog feet and made a beeline for the water. It was our first underwater safari since the glorious "gardens" of Norman's Cay and it was wonderful to be bobbing around under the water again with all the fishes and corals.

As is so often the case, however--particularly, it seems, in the tropics--things that look so beckoning on the outside too many times are only hiding their dark sides from view. Swimming along the rocks on one side of the bay Karen found this principle out when she inadvertently kicked one of the little black sea urchins that dotted the rocks and sea floor.

Looking much like baby porcupines, they're surrounded by dozens of long, black, needle-sharp spines, several inches long, that are made of soft mineral so that they break off in the flesh of any creature unfortunate enough to get too near.

Poor Karen limped out of the water with about ten or so of these needles embedded deeply in the bottom of her foot. We lay down on the beach so that I could try and get hold of at least some of the needles and pull them out but I had no success. Though she never cried out I know that it must have hurt tremendously. While we were there, an older, local man saw us and came over to offer advice. He commented on Karen's fortitude, saying that he'd known grown men to cry who had suffered this same misfortune.

He also told us that it was pointless to try and pull them out since they were too soft to grab hold of. There was nothing more we could do now but to go back home, so I helped Karen hobble on her one good foot back up to the road, where we hitched a ride back to town. Karen never whimpered nor complained even once the entire way back home and my admiration for her strength and resilience grew enormously that day.

In addition to the kindly old man on the beach, many people offered us a number of different folk remedies for urchin spines, ranging from pouring hot wax on the needles, letting it cool then pulling it off (presumably with the needles attached to it) to simply peeing on her foot and letting the acid dissolve the calciferous spines.

The most bizarre procedure suggested was to rub Vaseline on her foot and then heat it up with a lit match (I have no idea what this was supposed to do) and by far the most painful suggestion was to stomp around on her foot until the needles finally broke up internally and then pour some vinegar over it. Since these were literally needle sharp and, in a few cases at least an inch into her foot, this idea was understandably her least favorite. The easiest suggestion was to just do nothing and let her body dissolve them naturally.

That night, in spite of the warnings that it wouldn't work, I tried to pick some of them out anyway with a sewing needle and tweezers, but to no real avail. I did manage to pull out a couple of short ones but the rest were hopelessly embedded. Over the course of the next few days Karen tried, in desperation, virtually every suggestion given to her by everyone. It was a valiant, if painful, attempt and whether any of it had any true effect was hard to say.

By week's end her foot was mostly back to normal and I had somehow managed to get that Saturday off so we happily decided to give the beach another try. This time we went straight over to the other side of the island from town to Magen's Bay. It, too, was a small bay and supposedly was one of the worlds ten best beaches. Though it was indeed very nice, I'm not so sure I'd go so far as to say it was in the top 10. At any rate, snorkeling was much more enjoyable this time, sans the urchins. We swam out along the right side of the bay where the water stayed shallow enough for us to see the bottom, but was far enough away from the rest of the people on the beach.

A little yellow fish followed us all the way out there and I had a lot of fun playing with it. As I swam along, it would swim with me directly underneath my mask but as soon as I stopped and stood on the ground for any reason he'd immediately drop down and swim all around my toes. As soon as I resumed swimming, though, he would rush right back and pick up his spot about three inches below my nose. We went through this ritual several times and always it was the same.

By now we were fairly far out from the beach and we realized an opportune moment of privacy here. Standing there, chest deep in the warm, crystal clear water, Karen wrapped herself around me and we tasted of Eden's fruit together, witnessed only by the rocks, the beach, the open sea and, of course, my little yellow friend who was swimming all about, not at all sure where he was supposed to go now. It was a wonderful day and one we sorely needed.

The next day was our regular Sunday off. It was cloudy out and a quiet day for us. We took a slow walk down and around the Sheraton marina, looking at all the big pretty sailboats, and then over to the nearby cruise ship docks. None of the ships were in that day, though, save for the beaten, burnt-out hulk of the Angelina Lauro.

She was an elegant, old, Italian cruise ship that had caught fire and sunk right there in the harbor just before we had arrived at the island. She had since been raised up again off the harbor floor and was now tied up there at the end of the cruise ship dock where she sat waiting for her sad fate to be determined.

We went down and stood there looking at the charred remains of what had obviously been, once upon a time, a very nice ship and I wondered about all the people whose lives had shared some time with her before old man Neptune had tried to make her his own. Rumor had it that she was to be towed to Rotterdam and scrapped.

Mostly though, as we stood there looking at this barbequed rats' nest, our thoughts were, not too surprisingly, something more on the order of "Hmm, Rotterdam, eh." We began almost immediately to devise a plan on how we could stow away on this certifiable death ship and get ourselves a free ride to Europe with her. We'd come here late on some dark night, we figured, with containers of water and food and sneak up the huge docking lines that held her fast to shore. Then we'd

149

find ourselves a cabin that hadn't burned in the fire that we could set up as our own and then simply sit back and enjoy a quiet cruise to Holland. Simple. Of course, there would be danger but then that's what adventures are all about. We knew that if anything happened while under tow (and anything could) that they would simply cut the tow lines and let her go down to the sea. Our scheming was, of course, lighthearted but I think we were both prepared to consider it seriously if things ever got to the point where it became a viable option. Fortunately, they never did.

***

As our first month on St. Thomas drew to a close, we knew that it was now time to redirect our attention toward getting on a boat and away from the restaurant business. We had since changed our plans yet again and now we were foregoing South America altogether in lieu of a straight shot to Europe. I guess our hearts just weren't into all of the hardships that our style of travel would get us into down there. Our thoughts and hopes now were to get working passage on a cruising sailboat heading for the Mediterranean.

I promptly started asking around the restaurant and marina about any available cruising positions and was given back a devastating answer. It was one of those weird ironies of life that I discovered when I was told that the only month of the year that sailboats could make it east to Europe was the month of May, the very month that we'd just spent so casually here in our ignorance. We were crushed by this news. It messed up all of our plans, as fickle as they were, and left us without a clue as to what we were to do now.

A quick assessment of our options pretty much left us with only three to choose from: 1) we could either hang around here for another year working on charter boats and getting our experience built up, 2) break our first rule again and fly out, or 3) simply wait and see what else we could come up with.

We certainly didn't want to wait here for a whole year so that option was scratched off immediately and it wasn't critical that we leave right at this moment, either, so that eliminated option two as well. That left, like it or not, only option three. In the end, we decided to get ourselves work on one of the charter boats while waiting for our inspiration (or perhaps just some luck) to come to our rescue and take us away. We rationalized that it would give us chance to get at least a little sailing experience in and would save us a lot of money in room and board as well.

I had enough influence around L'Escargot by now to manage getting rid of my lunch shift, which freed up my days for boat hunting very nicely. Once I started thinking seriously about it, though, I realized that in order to make ourselves readily available to any prospective boat, we'd have to move out of Ramsey's first. With that thought, and much apprehension, we gave Ramsey our weeks' notice right away. This was a big gamble for us because if we didn't find something before our rent ran out we'd end up homeless. This put a lot of pressure on me to find something quick.

I began canvassing the Sheraton marina every day asking anyone and everyone I saw if they or anyone they knew was looking for crew. It was a discouraging process at first, hearing so many "no's" and seeing so many shaking heads. Within just a few days, though, people were starting to recognize me and to ask me how things were going in my search. It made me hopeful that something might come up and, in fact, it was only a few days before something did.

A sailboat crewman that I had gotten to know slightly mentioned one day that Paul Taylor over on the "Zorra" was possibly looking for some crew. I went straight over and arranged an interview with him for Karen and me later that same day. We crammed the next hour or so on all of our nautical lore so that we might sound like we actually had some experience but when the interview came with Paul and his wife, Paula, they asked us none of the questions we had primed ourselves for and the interview went badly for us. After only a few minutes, it was obvious we were dying and they decided to forego us.

C'est la vie, I thought, and vowed to keep looking. I think Karen, though, was beginning to look at old Angelina Lauro, sitting all alone over there, with a just bit more intent these days. In addition to pounding the boards of the dock, I had also written up some "crew available" index card notices to post at the various bulletin boards around the island, but they only blended in with all the other scraps of paper that were on them and we got no response. It was while considering this that my brilliant brainstorm struck.

Several days earlier, I'd had finally gotten my roll of Bahama film developed. Several of the pictures came out nicely but one in particular was very striking, I thought. It was the sunset picture that I'd taken of Bruce's boat, back at Chub Cay (remember).

Looking at all that white paper on the bulletin boards, I thought to myself *what we need is something that stands out on this board and will set us apart from all the other available crewers* and that's when the idea came and conked me in the head - a nice photo ad of a sailboat, silhouetted up against a brilliant, orange, Bahamian sunset and advertising its author as a photographer/deck hand! Not only would it stand out on the bulletin boards like a burning arrow but it would say more about us than any notice ever could. I was excited and set about in haste to work it up.

The idea worked fabulously, better than I could ever have hoped for, and it became the turning point of our stay here. The surprise, though, was that it ended up working in a way that I could not have guessed.

The photo lab where I had gone to have the prints developed was way over at the far end of the island, too far to walk. The day they were ready, I went out to hitch a ride to go pick them up but, although there was plenty of traffic going out that way, for some reason or another I couldn't convince any of them to pull over and give me a ride. After about a half an hour, I lost patience, gave up and went home.

The next day I went out and gave it another shot. This time I got a ride quickly but the driver was only going a little way and I was let off about midway to the lab. I started to walk the 1/4 mile or so toward the intersection where I was to turn off and was just coming up on it when a car passed me from behind. When I saw that it was turning down my road, I impulsively stuck my index finger out (locals don't use their thumbs) even though the car was already heading away from me. I didn't think for a minute that the driver would even see me let alone stop but to my astonishment, the car immediately pulled over.

I was surprised again as I ran up to it and saw that it was a late model BMW (neither common nor cheap here in the islands) but even more so when I found out that this kind person was an attractive woman, probably in her early thirties. I thought this must be my lucky day as I hopped in, but I had no idea just how fortuitous this ride was to be for us.

As it happened, she was, quite coincidentally, headed for the very same photo lab as me to pick up some pictures of her own. She told me she'd be happy to give me a ride all the way back to town afterwards, too, if I wanted. This ride just kept getting better.

On the way to the lab, I had the opportunity to tell her of my great idea and the horribly romantic story of Karen and me running off to travel around the world with little more than our good intentions. I told of our disappointment in finding a cruising sailboat and that we were now looking for local charter work. She didn't say much during the drive there, except to ask me a question here and there. She mostly just let me ramble on with my dreamy stories.

On our way back to Charlotte Amalie, though, she offered to me her own story. Her name was Marti and she and her husband, Charlie lived on their 70-foot sailboat there in the Sheraton's marina. This got my attention and a small pang of excitement began to burble in me but I said nothing and waited for her to continue.

They had been charter boat skippers for the past several years here in the Virgins, she went on, but they had just recently given it up in order to start a charter brokerage business instead and were currently in the process of contacting all of their charter boat skipper friends for the listing. In fact, she had come to the photo lab today to work on the pictures for their new brochure.

Boy, I thought, my lucky ball was really rolling today. This ride had become absolutely unbelievable and, just to wrap it all up in a nice bow, as we neared town, she said that she would ask Charlie if he knew of anyone that could use some help. She gave me the name and slip number of their boat, "Cordonazo," and told me to come by and check back with her there in a couple of days. I climbed out of her car, thanking her and the stars profusely, then beat feet straight home to tell Karen the good news.

Two days later, as instructed, I eagerly went down to the marina and looked her up. She told me that she had asked Charlie as promised but that, unfortunately, he didn't know of any available crewing positions.

Before I could get too disappointed, however, she surprised me yet again by offering me work right there on "Cordonazo" instead. It seemed that in the intervening days since I'd last spoken to Marti, one of the two fellows that had been working on their boat was suddenly called back to the States and had to leave. I'd be taking his place.

Even though it was only dockside repair I was thrilled for the job and I accepted without a moment's hesitation. And as if all that she had done for us already wasn't enough, a few days later, she even paid me $25 to use my photograph on the cover of their new brochure - my very first freelance photo job!

I didn't have any spare copies on hand so I walked on over to the marina office, took down our crew notice (which did look pretty sharp up on those bulletin boards, I might add), snipped off the ad portion from the photo and handed it over to her. All in all, a very profitable photo it proved to be.

Meanwhile, back in town, our last day at Ramsey's had come and gone and our fears of being homeless were now fully realized. With nowhere else to put our meager belongings, I took them down to L'Escargot and stored them in one of the lockers they keep there for employees. For that first night out we stayed in one of the upstairs booths at Drakes Inn (I told you they were casual here). We had to wait until the place emptied out, at around 2 a.m., before it was quiet enough to actually get to sleep up there but under the circumstances we didn't mind that so much.

We tried a different tack the following night and attempted to stay up all night in one or more of the bars around town but, try as I did, I couldn't keep awake so we gave up somewhere in the wee hours of the morning and shuffled back toward the marina.

On the way, we came across an old shed right on the edge of the harbor and decided to just spend the rest of the night there on a couple of benches we found in there.

This "shed" was actually nothing more than two rusty tin walls and a roof that leaked like crazy all over us during the thunderstorm that passed through. In the morning, much to our dismay, we learned that our beds were actually fish cutting tables used by the local fishermen and, in addition to paying our rent to the mosquitoes that night in blood, we took with

155

us as souvenirs of our visit, the stench of dead fish throughout the entire next day as well as a large following of gnats that clouded around us whenever we stopped moving for more than a moment. It was a novel night, to be sure, but we chose to just cherish it as a memory and never attempted to relive it.

On the plus side, though, it was now Sunday again, our beloved weekend! We had plans that day to take the ferry over to the neighboring island of St. Johns and go do some exploring. We made one quick circuit down the docks just in case someone wanted to hire us and since no one did we then thumbed out to the ferry docks at Redhook, right next to the photo lab.

St. Johns was the next big island over from St. Thomas and only a few miles away. With the exception of the one small town there, it's a mostly uninhabited island that has since become a national park. We'd gone there the past Sunday with the thought of renting a car and driving around the island but we had both forgotten our driver's licenses so we couldn't hire one. I was suffering that day from a strange recurring bout of extreme lethargy and literally couldn't find the energy to walk anywhere, so we just turned around and went back home. Even then, Karen had to get behind and push me up the hill to Ramsey's because I simply didn't have the strength to walk it on my own.

This time, however, I had both energy and a driver's license. It was fun to be driving again, to feel that I once again was in control of my mobility. It's not a large island, though, and our range was severely limited but we had a wonderful time anyway, driving out to the ends of the island to see what was there. We had heard that there were some petroglyphs on the island here, odd shapes and figures carved into the sides of boulders by some unknown ancient people. We wanted to go see them but they were only accessible by taking a three-mile hike down some foot trail and we didn't have the time to go down there that day.

We stopped for a while along the roadway up along the top of the mountain to take in the tremendous view of Drake's Passage down below and as I looked out at all the sailboats traversing up and down this waterway that ran between the American and British Virgins Islands, I envied the people on them. I told myself that one day soon, that would be us out there.

[It was, in fact, only a few weeks later that we were indeed out there on just such a boat, sailing up that very passage and, as we did, I stood on the deck and picked out the spot on this mountain where we were now parked. I tried to imagine seeing myself up here looking down at me on this boat now. It gave me a great sense of self-satisfaction when I did.]

On the way back down, we stopped at the ruins of one of the long-abandoned sugar plantations that was open to sightseers. There was hardly anybody there so we played around in the old windmill there for a while before running off to examine the overgrown remains of the slave quarters. It was my first real ruin and it gave me a somber feeling to see it now, to think about all of the lives that came through here and that now it was essentially just a great big terrarium.

We took the ferry back to St. Thomas late that afternoon and made our way to the marina. We tried to sleep that night on the wooden benches of an open-sided tour bus that was parked near the cruise ship docks but the mosquitoes chased us out after only a few minutes so we wandered out onto the marina's docks where they wouldn't follow us and tried to sleep right there in the middle of the cement dock. Later, when the floating bar "Kon Tiki" came in for the night we snuck aboard after everyone had left and spent the rest of the night sleeping on its wooden benches, instead.

All in all, it was yet another miserable night. We spent the next two nights back in the upstairs booths of Drake's again. At least it was dry and mosquito-free, if noisy. It was fast becoming clear that this situation wasn't working at all well for us. Karen was starting to drop things at work and customers were beginning to stare. We knew that we'd have to find someplace new to rent and I started asking around work if anyone knew of anything.

As it happened, one of my managers, Robin, did indeed know someone who had a room for let. She was an older woman, Ethel, who was looking to rent out her spare bedroom. Her house was quite conveniently only a few blocks from downtown so Karen and I went straight on over that afternoon and closed the deal. We moved in immediately.

It was the ideal situation for us. It was far easier now for us to get us to work, for one thing, and it was a much more casual arrangement than at Ramsey's since she wasn't in the business like he was, just an old lady looking to make some extra income off her otherwise unused room. She also agreed to rent it by the week which would allow us to cut our losses much shorter should we have to leave in a hurry.

It was a two-bed, two-bath, single-story house and much better tended than most of the places we'd seen on the island. Like all the shops out on the street, it had no front door, only an iron gate, which made the place seem so wonderfully tropical to me and a bit more fun. The down side was that it also allowed completely unrestricted mosquito travel throughout, which made it all seem so horribly tropical and much less fun. It was always very hot inside, too, and our only defense for both these maladies was a noisy electric fan that came with our room.

Mosquitoes, we'd learned, don't like turbulent air so at night when we got into bed we'd set the fan to blow right at us all night long. This system worked fairly well and kept us relatively cool and mosquito-free all in one shot.

After only two days, however, I decided that I needed to fix the obnoxious noise coming from the fan motor and in the process permanently broke the thing. Neither Karen nor I were very happy with me that night as we were devoured by the famished mosquitoes in the sweltering tropic heat of midsummer. Covering ourselves with the bed sheet to keep the buggers off only steamed us up until we eventually had to throw it back off to cool down and allowed the next wave of bloodsuckers their turn at us.

We ended staying here at Ethel's for only one week and it was during this week that we celebrated Karen's 21st birthday. For the gala event, I had gone to the market earlier that day and had come back with the now traditional birthday picnic. There were grapes and plums and apples and cheese and wine and bread. It was a feast fit for a queen and we enjoyed it tremendously, as we did all of our picnics. Afterwards, I presented her with a T-shirt on which I'd had printed her favorite nickname (Toad, oddly enough) and also a home-made coupon that was good for four one-hour body rubs from her favorite honey.

It was a humble celebration but she was very happy with it and that made me very happy, too, for I loved her then like no other before, or since. Later, after retiring to our sweltering room, we officially completed the ceremonies.

For as uncomfortable as the tropics inherently are, they seem to have a hidden appeal to them that is hard to explain. There is something very sultry about sitting in an open bar, late at night, with the ceiling fans blowing a balmy wind down your neck while you drink your margaritas, sweating like a pig anyway, and listening to Jimmy Buffet on the jukebox croon about the sailing life. Or watching the electrical explosions and torrential showers of a thunderstorm as it passes over your head. Along with the sultriness, and probably because of it, is the steamy sexiness that the tropics have become so well known for. Making love in the tropics seems more intense for some reason, though I think it's because you start out as hot and sweaty as you would normally end up afterwards anywhere else.

***

The very next morning following Karen's birthday, I was walking down the docks with Marti when we ran into her friend, Paul Taylor, from the boat "Zorra," the same fellow Karen and I had so miserably interviewed with almost three weeks ago. Marti knew that he had just signed a last-minute charter and was looking to muster up a quick crew. Wanting to help Karen and me get on a boat, she seized the opportunity and took it upon herself to convince him, right then and there, to hire us.

I had only been working for her and Charlie for a couple of weeks now and she hadn't even met Karen yet, but that didn't stop her from telling Paul that we were the best workers she had ever had, and she was adamant in her insistence that he take us on. She literally told him that he HAD to hire us. Poor Paul had little choice, for Marti had really put him on the spot, with me standing right there, so he sheepishly agreed to take us on.

I was beginning to get embarrassed as she went on and it was just a bit awkward considering my past meeting with him but, by the same token, I also felt somewhat redeemed by it. Embarrassment segued immediately into excitement, though, with the thought that we were soon going to be sailing the tropical isles in a big, beautiful sailboat and getting paid for it to boot. Marti truly was an angel to me. I raced straight into town from there to tell Karen the good news.

We both quit our jobs, effective immediately, since we were to start the very next day. Ethel wasn't home that day so we packed our things up and left her a note of thanks and goodbye. We weren't particularly close to her and our rent was paid up through the week but for some reason I felt a little bit guilty about just disappearing that way. Maybe it was because Robin, the manager who'd referred us to her in the first place, was off-island for a few weeks and had told me before he left that he didn't want to come back and find me gone. They were grooming me for management there at the restaurant and I think that's why he'd gotten us the room in the first place.

At any rate, no promises were made and so none were broken and any feelings of guilt dwindled away the moment we climbed aboard our new home later that same afternoon.

Yacht "Zorra" was a 73-foot Morgan yawl and, true to the meaning of her name, at least that which Paul shared with us, she was indeed a beautiful lady. At almost twice the size of Bruce's boat, we were taken by the spaciousness of what we found below. There was plenty of room with Paul and his wife, Paula, in the aft stateroom, Karen and me in forecastle (the bow) and up to six guests in the middle staterooms. We didn't have time to sit and admire, though, because the charter was to start the day after next and we not only had a lot to prepare for, but also a lot to learn about sailing a boat, especially one this big.

This reality hit me all of a sudden. We had only been working guests on "Spirit" and since Bruce had rigged her for singlehanded sailing, this meant that there had been virtually nothing for us to do the whole time we were sailing with him. Now, standing here on "Zorra's" deck looking at all the many lines and winches and the much larger sizes of everything, I could easily see that we were scarcely prepared to act as a real life sailing crew. No wonder we had failed our first interview.

Actually, I was the only one that really needed to know anything about handling the boat since my position on board was that of mate whereas Karen's duties were primarily down below, helping with food prep and seeing to the guests. She was no meek woman, though, and didn't want to spend her whole time down below and since I had a lot of experience in kitchens and domestic situations we opted to share our duties equally between us rather than specializing. It allowed us to work together much more closely and gave each of us a chance to enjoy the whole experience.

Paul and Paula were, for their part, very patient in teaching us all the things that we needed to know and when the day of our charter came I felt fairly confident that we were going to get through it okay. That morning, after shining all the brass fixtures down below, provisioning up with a week's worth of groceries and supplies and literally learning all the ropes of the boat, we welcomed our first group of charterers aboard.

They were three older couples and all from Ohio. This was not only their first trip to the Caribbean, but also their first time on a sailing boat and since our jobs, besides washing dishes and cranking the sails up and down, were to see to virtually every need of these guests, Karen and I knew we had a big challenge ahead of us.

Validating our concerns, that first charter did indeed get off to a rough start. Though it was a calm, sunny day, within the first half hour out of Charlotte Amalie one of the women became seasick. [It was also when I first learned that one of the less glamorous of my newly acquired duties was manning the bucket.] She never felt very good after that and within only a couple of days she and her husband decided to call it quits. We put them ashore on the island of Tortola in the British Virgins so that they could fly back home.

As we made our way over to the island of Virgin Gorda the following day, one of the remaining men aboard lost the last of his three hats overboard. He was bald and already sunburned on top so we had little choice but to swing the old girl around in a big circle and try to grab the hat with the boat hook as we swept past it.

The first pass, with Paula up on the bow manning the hook, was unsuccessful. She couldn't snag it before it drifted by so we came around again to give it another try but this attempt, too, failed.

I was back toward the stern this whole time, standing next to Paul, who was manning the helm, as this poor man's cap came bobbing past us for the second time. My thoughts were that we'd try once again but Paul interrupted them when he asked if I had anything in my pockets. I thought it a very curious question, all things considered, but patted each of them down anyway before telling him with some perplexity that they were empty. At this, Paul looked at me straight and said, flatly, "Jump in and get it, grab the dinghy and pull yourself in."

Now, rule of the sea says the captain is god so I didn't argue with him. Without another thought, I quickly flung myself over the side and landed right next to the wayward cap. In one swooping motion, I grabbed it and threw it on my head so that my hands would be free to catch the dinghy when it came trailing by. To my surprise, though, the little boat sped past me, right in front of my face, even as the water cleared from my eyes to watch it.

Normally, we keep a long tether on the dinghy when we're at sail and then switch over to a short one when anchored. Apparently, I'd forgotten to switch back to the long one this last time and I now found myself floating alone in the brine because of it as Zorra floated away from me.

Though I was not a good enough to swimmer to have made it to the nearest island, I knew I was at least good enough to stay afloat until Zorra came back for me, but I must say that it was a very peculiar feeling to be in the middle of the ocean like that, treading water while watching my boat sail away from me. Being only inches above the water's surface, the world looked so big and far away and I couldn't help but feel abandoned and vulnerable.

They, of course, circled back and, as they slowly bobbed their way toward me, I thought how truly scary it must be to survive the sinking of a boat, to not have anybody to turn around and get you. This time I did manage to grab the dinghy all right as they came past, and I pulled myself back up to the boat with no problem.

All in all, I thought it was a fun adventure for an afternoon. The man got his treasured hat back and his friends got a lot of snapshots of that crazy deckhand who jumped overboard to save it. We got some pretty good tips, too, once the charter ended.

We ended up working two more charters after this first one. Aside from manning the sails and anchor, some of my other duties were setting up barbeque picnics on the beach, climbing coconut trees for fresh coconuts and ferrying the guests to and from the shore whenever they had a mind to go island exploring. Karen and I both, however, taught the guests how to snorkel at the beginning of the charters and then accompanied them on their daily snorkel trips afterwards. It was probably a good thing that none of them knew that we'd only snorkeled a half a dozen times ourselves and not always with the best of results. Our abilities were tested, too.

About halfway through our third charter, Karen and I had taken the guests out to swim around the caves at Norman Island. There was no beach there so we had to jump in straight from the dinghy itself. After gearing up there in the boat, we all slid over the side and toured around the underwater caves, swimming amongst all the fishes.

The unfortunate part of dinghy dives, though, is that it's a whole lot easier getting out than it is getting back in. Normally this doesn't pose much of a problem for most people but in this case, one of our guests was a very overweight woman and when we were all ready to load up and go, she couldn't get herself back into the dinghy, try as she might. In fact, she could barely get any of her out of the water at all.

After several failed attempts, we saw the need to organize. We told her to kick her flippers with all her might and to try and shoot herself out of the water as much as possible. When she did, Karen and the woman's husband got behind her and started shoving on the poor woman's ample butt, each with one hand to a cheek and one to hold onto the dinghy with. I had to swim over to the opposite side of the dinghy and hang on to it as a counterweight to keep it from flipping over.

The strategy worked, though only barely, and the woman finally rolled into the little dinghy like the carcass of an old walrus. It was a three-stooge's affair to be sure and we had a good laugh about it afterwards (Karen and I, that is, not the woman).

We had a wonderful time during the three charters that we worked for Paul and Paula. Even more so as we began to learn more about sailing, the islands and chartering. There was a vitality to life, a sense of adventure that filled me the whole time we were here in the Virgin Islands but most particularly while we were sailing through these islands, having our beach barbeques, snorkeling the coral reefs, swimming the warm water, or just listening to the breeze in the sails as we cruised from cove to cove.

It was an atmosphere where my dreams of the world fit so perfectly with where we were and what we were doing. Perhaps it was just a sense of freedom. A healthy, natural kind of freedom, though, that one feels when one embraces life, not the guilty kind of freedom that comes when one merely runs away from it.

***

When our final charter had come to an end, so did our employment on Zorra and with the charter business pretty much over for the season, we now found ourselves once again in Charlotte Amalie wondering what we were to do next. This time, though, we were feeling much better about it than before because we now had the satisfaction and self-confidence from knowing that we were no longer the hapless dock rats begging for any tidbit of a chance to get on a boat. In fact, Marti was now acting like our personal agent and sending us a seemingly constant supply of skippers who were looking for crew.

It was such a great turnabout for us who only a month earlier had been so desperate to get on any boat at all and were now turning jobs down for the slightest of reasons. We both knew that it was time for us to leave the islands and get on with our trip but even so, we did entertain the thought of sticking around a while longer and taking advantage of some of these new offers that were ours for the taking. One offer was so good that we actually did take it though in the end it didn't work out.

It was an offer for the both of us to work on a 95-ft. motor yacht, called Pelorus Jack, that was by far one of the busiest charter dive boats in the islands, sailing 50 weeks out of the year. We were to be the second tier of crew. Me as second mate, helping the first mate prepare for the dives and Karen as a galley assistant, helping to prepare the meals.

Aside from getting to go scuba diving every day and having year-round work, it also paid extremely well. If we stayed for a year working on this boat, we would end up with more money and experience than we could ever need. It was too good to pass up even if it did mean hanging around the islands a whole lot longer than we really wanted to.

The skipper (who looked uncannily like the golfer Jack Nicklaus, I thought) motored us out to tour the boat and meet the other crew. It all went well and in the end we accepted the positions. It felt really good to be able to get such high-grade work so easily now and it was hard not to gloat about it to ourselves.

It wasn't a problem we'd have to deal with for very long, though, because the very next day after giving us the jobs, the skipper came back and apologetically reneged on them. He explained that his current crew were a couple that were saving their money up in order to buy their own boat and when they heard that we had been hired they threatened to mutiny rather than split the tips two more ways. He had little choice now but to give up on his idea of expanding his crew beyond the two of them.

We were only slightly disappointed, actually, and got over it quickly. We had already formulated a plan, prior to his offer, to try and get ourselves working passage on a freighter that was due into port in a few weeks and so were really only looking for temporary work anyway until it showed up.

We'd heard, in the days immediately following our departure from Zorra, that there was an office on the island that handled the few freighters that visited here throughout the year. We found out from them about the next ship due to come in that continued on to Europe. We figured that if we couldn't get ourselves working passage on it, then we would try to get paid passage--if it wasn't too expensive, of course. We were still against flying although, by this time, we certainly had enough money to afford it.

In the meantime, Karen went back to work at Drake's but this time as a part-time, sidewalk barker. Since the restaurant was located down one of the narrow little alleys, and therefore out of view from all the tourists, they usually had someone out on the street to lure people in. It didn't pay much but she liked it a lot and seemed to be very good at it. At least the restaurant was happy with it (probably just to keep her out of the place). I started back up with Marti doing casual maintenance work on Cordonazo while we waited for something to happen.

Ever since we'd left Zorra, of course, we had been homeless again. As darkness had descended upon us that first night out, it was with some apprehension that we set about trying to find someplace to stay. Our abilities to find suitable alternate sleeping accommodations had failed us so miserably before and we had no reason to think they would be any better this time. But things were a little different this time, albeit not much. Remembering that Charlie kept his VW van unlocked in the parking lot of the Sheraton, we decided to spend that first night in there.

As soon as the likelihood of his still using it that day had diminished to a reasonable point, we crept inside and spent the night in relative comfort. We had to get up early the next morning, though, to be sure he didn't find us.

In the end, after thinking of all the things he and Marty had done for us and of how awkward it would be if he had found us camping out in his car, we realized the value wasn't worth the risk and decided not to do it again. We spent our second night ashore back in the bars and on park benches.

Reliving that experience was more than enough encouragement for us to figure something else out. Fortunately, Karen came through for us on our third day. She'd managed to convince her friend Sandi, from Drakes, to let us move in with her temporarily.

Actually, moving *up* with Sandi would be more accurate as she was renting a little shack way up on the mountainside above town. It was so small that there literally wasn't room inside it for more than one person to lie down so Karen and I set up a spare mattress and frame out in her front yard and slept there.

We had to mosquito treat our faces each night and stay fully dressed but it really wasn't so bad. After all, we got to sleep in a real bed and we were able to lie out there and watch the stars and the moon overhead as we drifted to sleep.

As it turned out, we weren't there for very long anyway, for within the week we would be leaving not only Sandi's little shack but the entire Caribbean altogether and in a way that neither of us could ever have dreamed.

***

On the morning of our fifth day up at Sandi's we woke to the usual warm, sunny, dewless morning. I didn't have much of anything to do that day but Karen was scheduled to wait tables at Drake's so we got ourselves ready for the long walk back down into town.

As we wound down the snaky road, we came around a turn and into a wonderful view of St. Thomas Harbor lying far below us. The several cruise ships and the scores of sailboats that were anchored out there was a view that I had seen often and, in truth, didn't really awe me much anymore. On this particular morning, however, there was something unusual about it. Right in the middle of the harbor, sitting majestically in the morning sun, was a huge, black-hulled cruise ship that I had never seen before. It was much larger than any of the others that we'd come to know so well over these past several months. It was a pretty picture but I gave it no more thought as we continued on down into town.

Within a few minutes of reaching town we learned that this big, pretty ship anchored out in the harbor was in fact the Queen Elizabeth II, at the time the largest luxury liner in the world and England's maritime pride and joy. This still didn't mean much to me right then other than accounting for the dramatic increase in tourists that were all marching about outside on the street, not to mention the bang-up business that Drake's was doing that day.

In fact, I was sitting in Drake's with Karen later that afternoon when another waitress came over and casually mentioned to us that a couple of old ladies at one of her tables, passengers off the ship, had suggested to her that she should try to get a job onboard, as they seemed to need the help. Only then did it finally dong in my thick head. I mean, here we were, desperately searching for a cheap way to get ourselves to Europe when, anchored only a couple of blocks away from where we sat, was an immense English ship that would, sooner or later, have to go back to England. A whole great big shipful of opportunity just waiting for us.

Karen and I excitedly discussed this new revelation and, with a sinister gleam now brewing in our eyes, scurried down to the waterfront as soon as she finished her lunch shift, a short while later.

On our way down Princes Street, we spotted a couple of guys walking up ahead of us that were obviously crew members from the ship on shore leave. We realized a good opportunity to glean some free information here so Karen and I raced up ahead to them and started chatting them up about the possibility of us finding work onboard while I caught up to them.

They let some air out of our newly inflated sense of excitement, as the four of us continued on toward the waterfront, by telling us that only British subjects could work on board and that we were pretty much out of luck with that idea.

We weren't about to give up quite so easily however so, having nothing to lose at this point and feeling perhaps just a little bit cocky anyway, I blurted out, "Well, how about stowing away then?"

They both laughed at my brazenness and after a moment admitted that, though there were plenty of places onboard where someone could hide, there was no way we'd be able to sneak onboard to find them. They explained that, due to the many terrorist threats against her, the Queen Elizabeth II had the tightest security of any cruise ship in the world and finding a way to slip past it would be near impossible.

Before parting company, they did offer to us that if we were serious we might try to sneak aboard by pretending to be crew members who had gone on shore leave and had forgotten their boarding passes to get back on.

Oddly enough, I found some encouragement in this. As ludicrous an idea as this was, two Californians trying to pass themselves off to an English security guard as being British, they had left us on a positive note, which in my warped mind kept open a hint of possibility, blinding me to the true absurdity of their suggestion.

When we got to the waterfront, we began to seriously scope out the situation. I felt like a spy (for the first time of what would turn out to be many more to come) as we slyly scrutinized all that was going on around us.

Because of the ship's large size, she had to anchor well out in the middle harbor and use her launches to ferry passengers back and forth from the island. There were three of these launches in operation at all times - one departing for the ship with a full load, one in the process of loading up and one empty, newly arrived and awaiting its turn. Likewise, three officers were in charge of coordinating them, checking passes and handling their docking lines.

One of these officers was off on his own, tying up the most recent arrival. I wanted to get a second opinion on what the other crewmen had told us, just to be sure, so we went over to talk with him. Being an officer, we hoped he might know something the other guys didn't.

We approached him just as he finished tying up the launch. He was a smallish fellow, dark-haired, and bedecked in his starched black and white uniform. He looked more French to me than English and reminded me of Napoleon as we came up to him with our questions and hopes.

His answer to my first was, alas, the very same as that we'd been given by his fellow shipmates - only British subjects could work on board. His reaction to my second question was no different either. As soon as he quit chuckling, he told us that, though a person could hide well enough if onboard, one would never be able to get past security to get onboard.

We were obviously disappointed to hear this a second time but he was a friendly chap and, taking his less than encouraging answers in stride, we stayed and chatted with him for a while as he shared with us stories of life onboard. He seemed to particularly enjoy telling us of some of the stupid things tourists do and say; the woman, for example, who'd asked if the crew all slept on board while at sea.

[Little did he know, or we for that matter, the tip that he was passing on to us just then by sharing these tales or of its magnitude. A tip that would prove to come in extremely handy in only a few short (nay, very LONG) days.]

After about 15 minutes or so, it was time now for him to start loading up his boat so Karen and I left Napoleon there at the quayside and regrouped across the street to discuss the situation. It was time, we knew, to come to a decision on what we were to do next, a very big decision and one that pretty much needed to be made right now.

So far no one had told us that it was absolutely impossible to stow away on the old girl, only that it was difficult to get on. This was a once in a lifetime chance, we knew, to fulfill Karen's lifelong dream of stowing away on a big ship. It wasn't a freighter and I wasn't her dog, nor was it going to Africa but it was the closest she would ever get to it and it sure beat the hell out of Angelina Lauro. We knew we had to try. After only a half a moment's thought, we agreed to give it a go.

I of course knew that it would never really happen but I wanted to enjoy the fantasy with her. Just being able to write in my journal, "Got caught trying to sneak on the QEII today" was more than just about anybody else in the world could say and in truth I knew that it would be enough.

In many ways our fate was sealed at that precise moment for it was, indeed, at that precise moment that life seemed to develop its own momentum and instead of us guiding and controlling it, it was all we could do to just keep up and hang on. The adrenalin rush kicked in immediately as we realized our time to act was very short. Thinking was now a luxury that we found we could no longer afford, as the last boat left the quay at 5:30 p.m., only an hour away. If we were actually going to go through with this, then we had a lot to do.

We raced back to Drakes and told Sandi of our proposed audacity. We asked if we didn't return by evening to hold any belongings we left behind until we could send for them. We went back outside and hailed a taxi to take us up to her little shack so we could pack but not before stopping at a sidewalk trash bin there on Princes Street to fish out a couple of plastic shopping bags to use for our "luggage." We made sure to get ones that had plastic handles and with the store's name on them so that we would look suitably touristy.

We made good time and got back to Sandi's in only a few minutes. With the lingering idea that we would be pretending to be wayward crew members, we dressed somewhat grungily then stuffed our bags with all those things we felt to be essential and cabbed back down the hill, frantically practicing our English accents the whole way.

There was a large crowd of passengers boarding the first launch when we arrived back at the quay and we were disappointed when we saw that the boarding officer was checking everyone's passes very thoroughly as they climbed aboard past him. We stayed and watched for a while just to make sure there wasn't a weak spot in the security anywhere but after several minutes we saw none and fell back into the crowd so as not to be noticed.

With the moment now at hand, the realization of the absurdity of posing as crew finally dawned on us and it was obvious that we would have to scrap that idea. In its place, we took our cue from our recent conversation with Napoleon and decided to use instead a brand-new angle that was a little closer to the truth: we decided to simply pretend to be stupid tourists. We figured it was a lot easier for us to pretend stupid than it was to pretend British.

While we were standing there waiting and hoping for something to change, we noticed three more crewmen nearby waiting for their turn to board. We decided to better use this idle time and go over to see if we could add any new info to our hatching scheme. By now we were committed to the stowing away idea so I didn't even bother to ask them about work possibilities and just asked them straightaway if they could offer us any advice on stowing away.

My question caught them a little by surprise but I think they admired its honesty and began to muse about how it might be done. They agreed that the "wayward crew" ruse was no good and that we were much better off with the "stupid tourist" one. They didn't really have much more to offer than that, though, so we thanked them and slipped back into the anonymity of the gathering throng to practice our stupid look.

As I did so, I now realized that if we were to b.s. our way past the guard, we'd have to know things that a passenger would know because it was the only way the guard would be able to check our story. The more believable it was, the more likely he'd let us pass.

With this thought in mind, I scanned around the waiting crowd there at the waterfront for a likely source of some passenger lore. Over by the railing I saw a man standing alone as he gazed out at the harbor. *He oughta do,* I thought, so I made my way over and struck up a conversation with him.

We had a nice friendly talk for several minutes about scuba diving, California and other such general topics. All the while, using my best espionage techniques, I found out things like where the ship was headed, where it had just been, ports of call and a few other miscellaneous tidbits. Armed now with this new intelligence I returned to Karen, feeling only a tiny bit more confident about what we were doing than before, but right then every tiny bit helped. After all, it's only a tiny little key that can open the biggest door and we certainly had a mighty big one in front of us now.

We followed as the waiting crowd moved from one full launch to the next empty one, hoping that the security would be more lax than the one before but, alas, it wasn't. We tried the next one and then the next but it was the same each time.

It was beginning to look pretty bleak for us. It was now well after 5 p.m. and there were only a few more launches to go before the last one left. It was clear that even though there were now only two officers regulating the crowd, security was indeed very strict on this ship and we had all but resigned ourselves from this short-lived adventure.

Finally, having loitered around there for more than half an hour, we left the dwindling crowd and retreated across the street that separates the waterfront from the old warehouses, and from where we could keep a slightly more distant eye on things. As the last launch pulled up and was tied off, our hopes of wild adventure had practically vanished. It was in that very last moment, however, that everything suddenly changed.

The fear of being left ashore must be a particularly frightening one for cruise ship passengers, as most of them had returned to the ship well before the last of the launches were to leave. This meant that as the third from the last launch prepared to head back to the ship, the second from the last was only half full and the final one, the one nearest to us, was virtually empty.

As the forward-most officer was untying the departing launch and casting it off, our friend Napoleon, the rear-most officer, decided to take advantage of the break in the crowd and cop a quick sit-down break alongside launch #2. He was casually glancing around the harbor when we recognized the moment we had been waiting for and as soon as he turned his head away from us, toward the departing lead boat, Karen seized the moment and in a voice so firm and sure that I obeyed without a moment's thought, said, "Run!"

And run we did. Right into the middle of the street, which is as far as we got before Napoleon swung his head back over in our direction. We froze in our tracks, hearts thumping, standing there with our plastic-bag "suitcases" hanging at our sides while the cars of town came zipping past on either side of us.

We couldn't have made ourselves much more obvious, short of shooting off some fireworks, and I thought our adventure for the day had screeched to a halt as fast as we just had. How he could have missed seeing us is beyond me but that's just what he did and only a few moments later he again turned his head away from us. Again, Karen said, "Run!" Again, we ran.

Karen was in the lead and leapt aboard the last boat about 1/3 of a second before me. As I was flying through the door, I saw Napoleon in my peripheral vision turning his gaze back toward the rear boat and, of course, us. It was so close that if he'd known just where to look as his head turned around he would have seen my trailing foot in that moment before it disappeared inside the door.

We landed inside the launch as though dropped from the sky itself, which probably startled the few passengers that had already boarded and were quietly sitting there. We had to do an immediate change of pace as the surge of adrenalin that had brought us here now had nowhere to spend itself. We quickly parked ourselves on the nearest bench and tried to look cool and suave despite our rapidly racing hearts and sudden apprehensions of getting caught. I looked around at the other passengers in there as casually as I could to get a sense of the situation and as I did, I quickly realized our woeful appearance.

In our haste and misguided notions of pretending to be crew members I now found myself in high society wearing some old, blotchy brown corduroy pants, a pair of black cotton Chinese shoes and a green T-shirt with the name and likeness of "Zorra" written across it. I hadn't shaved in several days, either, and my flyaway hair was long past time for a cutting.

Karen, for her part, wasn't much better. She'd simply come as she was, wearing a gray, smock-like sundress with her own black cotton shoes. She wasn't wearing any stockings or tights and so had nothing to hide her "hairy little legs" from anyone who cared to look.

Making things worse for her, the plastic bag she had fished out of the trash bin earlier to carry her things in had a big wad of chewing gum stuck to the bottom of it and she hadn't realized this until after she had set it on her lap several times. Now she had little polka dots of chewing gum all over her front that began collecting dirt and gunk.

All in all, there was no way of hiding the fact that only seconds ago we were little more than dock rats. Whatever apprehensions I had upon landing inside this little boat were nothing compared to those that I was feeling now as I considered all of this, taking my only consolation in the thought that, Karen's dress notwithstanding, we were at least clean, if not pretty.

As I mentioned earlier, though, thinking was a luxury we could ill afford and there were much more important things we needed to address at the moment. We'd never considered the notion that we just might actually pull this off and we had no real plan beyond getting ourselves onboard (whatever plan that was). Once it became clear that they weren't coming to haul us away, we immediately had to start preparing for our next obstacle - getting on the ship itself.

We'd been told by the crewmen earlier that they checked passes here, too, and that now became our new, immediate focal point. We started practicing our B.S. in earnest, for it was clear that we no longer had the option of choosing our moments. They were now cast for us and we had to be ready for them.

Five-thirty arrived only minutes later and we nervously sat as our boat was made ready for departure. We still weren't secure in our knowledge of their boarding procedures and were fearing that the officer in charge might still come back and check our passes, retroactively, when they came to loose us from the quay. And God help us if it were Napoleon.

To our good fortune they not only didn't check for passes but Napoleon decided, thankfully, to catch his ride back in the other launch instead of ours. Regrettably, though, our attention was so consumed with our rehearsing and our still utter disbelief, that it didn't allow us to savor the thrill of watching us pull away from Charlotte Amalie that last time. That would've been nice.

We agreed, while on our way out, that should the miraculous happen and we actually make it onto the ship, we would do best to just walk on in any random direction as though we knew exactly where we were going. We realized that this would probably be the single most vulnerable time for us and roaming the halls with our plastic bags in hand and blank looks on our faces wouldn't be a good thing to do.

My nerves frayed more and more as the launch got closer. I continued to rehearse my lines right up until we came alongside the old Queenie, trying to think of every nuance that would make our story believable. Finally, the security officer that rode over in the launch with us opened up the hatchway to the boarding ladder that had been suspended down the side of the big ship. She looked monstrous to me, seeing her up that close, and I tried hard to still my heart as the first passengers queued up to begin their climb out.

We waited anxiously while the officers that were standing on the boarding platform steadied our boat and tied it off before preparing to help the passengers off. We held back a little bit in the queue, just far enough to see what they were going to do. If they were going to check passes, I wanted to see the procedure so we could ready ourselves for bluffing through it. At the same time, we didn't want to hold back too far as it would just give us that much more time to worry and fret. Best to just hop in and get it done with, one way or the other.

We slowly shuffled up to the hatchway. I watched carefully as the first passengers stepped onto the ladder of the ship. My heart was still pounding on my rib bones as I waited to see if they got checked or not and I think it skipped several beats when I saw them walk straight on through, unchecked, and up the steps of the ladder to disappear into the side of the ship. All that worrying, fretting and rehearsing had been for nothing and a minute later we ourselves climbed up the steps free and clear. Before we had time for any of it to even register, we found ourselves actually standing there on the world's largest luxury liner. Two dock rats in high style.

QUEEN ELIZABETH, THE SECOND

DAY ONE:

As we'd previously decided, we immediately took off walking down the first hallway we came to as though we had done it many times before. We needed now to get our bearings quickly and to erase the extreme anxiety that I felt must certainly be plastered all over our faces. Our thought was to get outside to the upper deck and to devise our next strategy from there. We figured that was where most of the passengers would be, plus it would give us a chance to look back at St. Thomas and help to register in our racing hearts and brains just what all was happening now.

Several yards down the hallway we found a map of the ship up on the wall and we began studying it voraciously. We noticed that the bow was where the crews' quarters were and we made a mental note to ourselves to stay as far away from there as possible.

It appeared that there was no direct route to the upper outside decks, only a circuitous, roundabout one that meandered up and through several different rooms, decks and stairways. We picked out a route that we thought would get us up there the most directly and then tried to memorize it as best as we could. We walked on a bit and then a bit more, trying to replay the map in our minds and correlating with what we saw around us, but somehow it wasn't working and we didn't seem to be getting any nearer the top decks at all. A moment later, we rounded a corner, sure that this was the one that would lead us out, but instead we ran right smack into our worst fear.

We had somehow managed to find ourselves right in the middle of the main thoroughfare of the crews' quarters, the very place that we had only minutes earlier determined was the absolute most dangerous place for us to be and we were now completely surrounded by dozens of uniformed crew members walking every which way around us! There was a wall map there, too, and we bee-lined over to it to find our way out - fast.

Oddly enough, it was because of this misguided direction that the very success of our trip was forged. Directions in life are not always as we think they would be. Standing there lost and confused (not to mention more than a little nervous), who should we run into but the two of the three very crew members that had given us our stowaway tips only a half an hour earlier!

They obviously knew what we had just done but before we could become too mortified by being "busted", rather than turning us in, they instead quickly spirited us out of the crowd. We'd managed to do what they didn't think could be done and it turned out they were impressed.

They were relatively low-level workers with not much to lose if they got caught helping us, which is almost certainly why they offered to sneak us down into their room. We scurried down the corridors behind them, deep into the bowels of the crew's section of the ship, before coming at last to their small, plain room. We sat with them for a while and told them all about our adventure so far. They were delighted to hear it and kindly offered to stow our bags for us while onboard then gave us a quick rundown on everything we'd need to know about surviving on the ship.

Their names were John and Perry and they were angels as far as we were concerned. They told us that meals were assigned seating only but that there was a Midnight Banquet every night open to any who happened to be up and interested. They told us that the disco was the best place for us to hide out in since it was dark and full of young people. They told us we could stay out on the deck at night, after the bars and casino had closed, when everyone else was in bed. They were more than kind to us and at substantial risk to themselves. We were very touched by their help and concern and though we accepted their offer to stow our unneeded things we told them that we wouldn't stay or visit with them in their room for fear of getting them in trouble. Assured that we would see them around the ship, we snuck back out and finally made our way topside to get our last look at the island while we still could.

It struck me at the time that the odds of John and Perry finding the two of us out of the almost 2000 passengers and 1000 crew onboard and in only our first 10 minutes was so incredibly low that I couldn't help but feel there was a greater power at work here. I looked up and said a silent thanks to David once again because I was sure now that he truly must be looking after his kid sis.

The ship didn't seem in any hurry to weigh anchor and after standing there at the rail for a while, looking out at the town that had been such a fond home to us these past three months, we finally got antsy and went back down below to the disco for what would turn out to be our first of many, many visits there. Indeed, it became our virtual home while onboard.

We were sitting here at a table in the disco about 30 minutes later when I turned and looked out the big, full-length window directly behind me to the ocean below and noticed to my surprise that we were actually moving. I can't say the thrill that flooded me right then as I watched the water slip by, for it was only in that moment that I fully realized our success. This was really happening. Against all odds, and in spite of ourselves, we had somehow pulled this caper off and were now actually, unbelievably, sailing away into our fates.

We wanted to say goodbye to St. Thomas so we raced back upstairs and out onto the deck. It was dusk now and the moon was nearly full as we slowly crept out of the harbor for the open sea, the warm tropical breeze coming to see us off. It was one of those magical moments that we had found so many of on this trip. It was August 9, almost a year to the day that Karen and I had sped down the highway as we left Humboldt County.   It too had been a warm, clear night, a major departure, a magical moment. It seemed appropriate that this night should be so similar. We watched it all sink into the evening sea before going back inside.

The first of the two separate dinner seatings came up shortly after returning inside and we immediately saw the need to be gone for a while. Those passengers that weren't in the restaurant eating their dinners at the first sitting were back in their rooms dressing in their formal dinner attire in preparation for the second. The bars were now virtually empty and we were quick to note that this would severely compromise our ability to blend. After a moment's thought, though, we came up with the simplest and most obvious solution - we simply ducked into a couple of nearby bathrooms and locked ourselves into a toilet stall.

We figured this would be the safest place for us anyway since if anyone should just happen to recognize the same pair of feet dangling below the stall door after a couple of hours and if they just happened to feel inspired to say anything about it we could just rub our belly and say with a grimace something like, "Ooh, I don't think ocean travel agrees with me." It wasn't too much to rely on, I know, but it seemed a whole lot better than the alternatives.

Our first thought, of course, had been to go jump into a lifeboat but the chance of getting caught climbing in and out of one of them was far greater and there was absolutely no way of talking our way out of it if we ever did. Besides, who wants to spend their cruise of a lifetime crammed into a little lifeboat?

We had agreed to stay in the restrooms for at least an hour so I settled into my toilet stall as best as I could. I put the lid down, took a seat, leaned over and put my head on the toilet paper roll, which was very conveniently right at shoulder level, and attempted to take a vertical nap.

When my closest guess to an hour was up, I re-emerged from my stall. Karen was nowhere to be seen and I must admit that I felt a little bit vulnerable and awkward out there all by myself for the first time since boarding. Neither of us had a watch so we couldn't very well coordinate our times together and I had no idea when she would be coming out nor any way to tell her that I already had. In fact, for all I knew, she may have already come out herself and gone off for a walk. Maybe she'd even been caught and dragged off to the brig, screaming and shouting. I would have no way to know.

In the meantime, I had no choice but to sit there outside the bathroom door and wait, feeling more self-conscious than ever since I now had no crowd to hide in. There was a big map of the world hanging on the wall there beside me so I managed to preoccupy myself for a while by studying it. It excited me, as I gazed at all those exotic sounding places, to know that soon they would all be real memories and stamps in my passport instead of just dreams and the thought that I would be realizing those dreams with my own little Karen pleased me more than anything else. Needless to say, I was overjoyed when she came out from her bathroom about ten minutes later.

From there we headed back down the short hallway to the disco (officially known as the Theater Bar, presumably because it adjoins the ship's movie theater) and found ourselves a table near one of the big windows that served as the outer wall here and that ran along the entire length of the disco/bar. Every time I looked out and saw the ocean washing past the ship's black-painted hull I was filled with the same tremendous thrill and vitality for life that I had felt the first time I'd glanced out of it as we left port. *I can't believe this is actually happening!* kept playing in my mind every time I turned to look at something else.

185

We sat there through the night, constantly overwhelmed at the thought of what we were doing. There were still so many things to figure out, though, which always brought us back to reality. We had actually done unbelievably well in our first two hours onboard - we had managed to figure out where to eat, where to hide and where to stow our "luggage" but now our next challenge was to figure out our sleeping arrangements.

The plan we came up with was simple enough: we would stay up in the disco until it closed around 4 a.m. and then spend the remaining three hours of darkness sitting outside in a couple of deck chairs until the other passengers began to reappear. Once the pool area had filled up with enough people to blend into we would then grab a couple of lounge chairs and sleep all day by the pool.

The only part of our plan that bothered me was our vulnerability during the in-between hours of 4 a.m.-7 a.m., when virtually every guest was in their room. Should anyone from the ship question us, while roaming the halls and decks at five o'clock in the morning, I felt it would be really nice to have a name and a room number handy just in case we had to finesse our way out of it.

I mentioned this to Karen as we sat there going down our list of concerns so she could keep her ears open for any helpful hints. We both agreed, too, that we couldn't afford to tell anybody about what we doing, not even friendly passengers. They might, we reasoned, resent the fact that they were paying several hundreds of dollars to do the exact same thing we were doing for free.

In light of all the wonderful things that had happened to us already, I shouldn't have been at all surprised by what happened next. Within minutes of having discussed all of this with Karen, the man sitting at the table next to us leaned over and asked me if he could use our table candle to light his cigarette. Without looking up I replied, "Sure" and handed it over to him. As I did, he got his first good look at me and blurted out, "Hey, aren't you guy I was talking to back in St. Thomas?" Before I could tell myself not to, I looked up at him and sure enough, out of those 2000 passengers onboard, I just happened to be sitting right next to the only one who could possibly recognize me as not being one of them.

I was in a real pickle now, for I'd just agreed not to tell a soul about what we were doing for fear of resentful passengers and yet I couldn't deny that I was indeed the same fellow who only a few hours ago was obviously not a passenger. I struggled quickly for an answer but we both knew that he had me dead cold. I had no choice at this point but to confirm his suspicions and hope he was an open-minded fellow.

As it turned out, he was more than open-minded. He had correctly deduced our situation before I could say anything, which made things somewhat easier for me to then tell him the rest of the story. When I was done, he admitted, much to my relief, that he thought what we were doing was just wonderful. If there was anything he could do to help, he said, we had but to ask.

Yet another "I can't believe this" ran through my mind and I remembered the one immediate obstacle we still had pending and that I had only just finished discussing with Karen.

"Actually," I replied, carefully, "there is something you might be able to help us with." I then mentioned to him our problem of having no name or room number to use in case of emergencies. "No problem at all," he quickly replied without even thinking, "you can use mine. And, hey, if they don't believe you, just bring them down to the room and I'll vouch for you."

The kindness of strangers, I have found, is often the kindest of all. We very thankfully accepted his offer.

He told us his name was Chet and then introduced us to Valerie, his date that night. She had been right there at the table with Chet this whole time we had been talking but hadn't really been a part of our conversation as the music was sufficiently loud to drown out anything we had said. She was unaware of all that had just been discovered, which suited us just fine. In this case, we thought the fewer that knew our secret, the better.

We hadn't been onboard more than four hours and already we had every single one of our initial problems solved for us and had four new friends to boot. A very auspicious beginning, to be sure.

Shortly after midnight we eagerly, though nervously, made our way to the Tables of the World Restaurant where the Midnight Banquet was served. Tables of Food might have been a better name for it that night, though, because that's just what we found there. Big tables. Lots of food. One whole table of nothing but fresh fruits and vegetables, one whole table of only meats and cheeses, a table of breads and rolls, but the best table for me was the one lined edge to edge with cakes, pastries and other assorted desserts. It was an absolute feast in its own right but for two dedicated foragers like ourselves it was a double bonanza. Not only was it unlimited but it was also free!

We ate as much as we could since we didn't expect to be eating much between now and the next night's banquet. Once our bellies were filled we then started squashing the little loaves of bread flat and slipping them down our pants for later. It was unfortunate that we couldn't get more down there than we did but we didn't want to blow our cover just for the sake of a loaf of bread, so we contented ourselves with what we could shove down there comfortably and discreetly.

When our busmen came over to take our drink orders, we were awkwardly surprised to see that they were none other than John and Perry. We had to play sophisticated and cool to them as we ordered our beverages, to pretend to airs of the well-to-do, when in fact what we truly felt like doing was getting down on the floor and groveling at their feet in total supplication for all the help they'd already given us. But they played the game back to us, pretending they'd never seen us before while slipping in an occasional wink or a knowing smile. It was fun to them. It was life and death to us. Or so it felt at the time, but we weren't there to punish ourselves. We were there to have an adventure and we were going to enjoy it.

And we certainly did. Amongst all the fears and insecurities we were going through, and to a large degree because of them, we were having the time of our lives. After our big meal, we contentedly retreated back to the disco to finish out our night by hearing "Born to be Alive" and "I Will Survive" two or three more times before the night ended. When it closed around four o'clock that morning, we did indeed go out on deck to sit and wait out the coming of the sun. We were joined shortly after by John, Perry and another worker who were now out doing their nightly clean-up duties. We all sat out there for a long time talking before they finally got up and went on with their work.

DAY TWO:

We stayed out there and watched the sun come up over the sea a couple of hours later, as the early morning joggers were coming out to run their circles around the ship. Once the poolside had filled up sufficiently we changed into our shorts and went out to try and get some sleep. I was still so pumped from this whole adventure, though, that I couldn't even nap. I just lay there in my lounge chair feeling as inconspicuous as a spot lit billboard in a desert night, despite the fact that no one seemed to care one whit about us the entire time we were out there.

Surprisingly, changing in and out of our shorts turned out to be an unexpected challenge. Not the actual changing, really, but where to stash our change of clothes when not using them. Obviously, we didn't have a stateroom to keep them in like everyone else and we couldn't go down to John and Perry's room anymore. We could've gone to Chet's, I'm sure, but we didn't want to impose ourselves on him every time we wanted to change our pants. Put to the task, though, we came up with a system that, although not very convenient, at least worked well enough otherwise.

Just inside from the upper swimming pool were changing rooms for any of the bathers that might need one. Going inside the men's room to change into my shorts that first day, I looked around for any place that I could stash my regular clothes while out at the pool. I scouted around for a few minutes, checking out the individual dressing stalls for hiding places, but found no place that would work.

Finally, looking under the sink, I found a small board about a foot and a half square that was used for access to the drainpipe inside the wall. I pulled the board out and saw that if I folded my clothes up real skinny there was ample space along either side of the pipe to stack them in. I went back out to the hallway to tell Karen of my exciting discovery and to have her check the women's dressing room to see if she had one of these handy trapdoors, too, but she came back out a moment later and said she wasn't so lucky. We had little choice now but to keep both of our things in mine which made things a lot more difficult, not to mention more dangerous, too.

As the doors into the changing rooms were visible all up and down the hallway there, it was important that we not be too obvious about what we were doing.

Normally, as our system soon developed, Karen would tell me what it was she wanted me to get and, while she stood guard outside in the hallway, I would slip into the men's room, grab her clothes, pop back out and hand them over. She would then slip into the women's room while I waited outside, change into her new clothes, bring her old ones back out and hand them off to me. With her once again keeping vigil for me, I would then duck back into the men's room, stack her clothes up on her side of the drainpipe, replace the board and come back out after changing my own clothes. Each time we did one of these pass-offs, we'd both instinctively look up and down the hallway with furtive glances while clutching our clothes close to our chests.

By the way we were acting, you'd think we were passing over national secrets to foreign agents, which, in truth, was actually pretty close to the way I was feeling at the time. So much for being inconspicuous.

At any rate, it all worked very well regardless of our surreptitious self-consciousness. Only once did someone come in unexpectedly on me. I had just that moment put the cover board back in place when he suddenly walked in but I hadn't yet gotten up off the floor from under the sink. Thinking as fast as I could, I quickly began patting around the floor with my hands as though I was looking for a dropped contact lens. It worked. He smiled sympathetically to me as he passed straight through the dressing room and out the rear door, which had somehow not been considered in our surreptitious planning. He was only taking a shortcut, thank God, through to someplace else. Only a moment earlier, though, or a moment longer and it wouldn't have been nearly so easy. I quickly left myself. Lot of good my door guard, Karen, was.

While I was laying out at the pool that day, in my unsuccessful attempt at sleep, I realized that if I was to pass myself off as a richy while on board, I needed to do some serious image work on myself. I pulled out the little brochure that Perry had given us down in his room yesterday and checked to see what kind of facilities this ship had that I might be able to use.

I found where the men's shop was and went up and bought me a tan woolen sweater and a new shirt to cover up the scroungy t-shirt I had been wearing since our arrival. They didn't have much of a selection there and the only shirt I could find in my size was a white, short-sleeved sport shirt with blue pinstriped squares on it. It looked horrible with my spotty brown pants but I had no alternative in the matter and bought it anyway. Once it cooled down enough at night to put the sweater on it would be mostly covered anyway, I reasoned.

Shortly afterwards I went down to the barbershop, too, and got myself a badly-needed haircut. It looked pretty goofy when it was done but at least it was better than before and I know I felt a lot more comfortable about being in public now. In fact, I felt so much better that I finally allowed myself to relax a little bit and take a stroll out along the deck just like a regular person, showing off my new duds. I stopped at the starboard rail, near the lifeboats, and gazed out for several minutes at the sunny blue sea, finally allowing myself the frame of mind to reflect on all that was happening to us.

It must have been this quiet reflection that caused me to lower my guard so dangerously as I did next. A fellow standing at the rail next to me broke into my reflection and started chatting with me about something to do with Puerto Rico. Without thinking I replied, "Yeah, I've never been there myself." As the words fell from my mouth, I realized with horror my grievous error - San Juan had been the port of call for the ship only the day before yesterday! San Juan, as in the capital of Puerto Rico. As a supposed passenger, that would necessarily mean that I was there, too.

As my brain suddenly clicked into emergency mode, I recovered enough of my wits to stammer in meek addendum, "Well, I mean... I was there of course, but... I didn't go ashore. I was too tired and didn't feel like dealing with another tourist trap."

I cringed inside as soon as I said this, for I knew it was a lame excuse and that he had to know that I was lying to him. I didn't dare look up at him, though, to verify it for fear he'd see the neon light that was blinking "Bald-Faced Lie" across my face.

To my great relief (and disbelief), he not only bought this story but he actually empathized with it and admitted to me that he was sorry that he'd gone ashore there. Boy, was I lucky or what? Not wanting to push it, I offered him a courteous word and then quietly slipped away and disappeared back into the shadows of the big ship. I would have to be much more careful, I scolded myself. Such a casual little slip of the tongue like that could give this whole thing away and land us in the brig.

At four o'clock that afternoon when the Theatre Bar opened back up we wandered in and settled ourselves in for the night. We took our places at our now usual table in the back of the room, with the big windows to our backs and the small wooden dance floor directly before us. To help us through our lack of sleep our drink of choice was Coca Cola, which we supplemented with some diet pills that Karen somehow had managed to convince a doctor back in West Palm Beach to prescribe for her.

As we sat there sucking down our Cokes, listening to Donna Summer's "Hot Stuff" start off the night's disco countdown once again, Chet's friend Valerie, from the night before, spotted us and came over with her friend and shipboard roommate, Helen. She introduced us all then leaned closer and confided to us that Chet had done what we'd hoped he wouldn't do. He had told her all about us and our adventure. Yet two more members of our little club that was growing in spite of ourselves and much faster than we were at all comfortable with.

Valerie's meeting, however, turned out to be much more fortuitous than we could've hoped. She, like Chet, John and Perry before her, thought what we were doing was terribly romantic and adventurous and she, too, offered us any help she could provide. We thanked her and warned her that we just might take her up on her offer. They left for dinner after visiting with us for a while and we went off to go lock ourselves into the toilet stalls.

I was really looking forward to attempting some sleep while in the stall tonight. I nestled up to the toilet paper roll and was just relaxing into it when I discovered that the only way to dry your hands in this restroom was with an air dryer which just happened to be mounted on the opposite side of the stall wall from where my head was now propped. As if this wasn't bad enough in itself, the damn thing was broken and common wisdom dictates that when something doesn't work you bang it several times, hard, just for good measure. I didn't sleep much.

Returning to the disco afterwards, we ran into Val and Helen again with their dates for the night and they invited us to join them at their table. We had to accept but it was a little strange sitting there with them at first, for the two men that they were with that night just happened to be a couple of uniformed officers of the ship and Karen and I weren't at all sure that was where we really wanted to sit.

Valerie's date was a tallish, blonde Irishman named Ken. The man escorting Helen was a shorter, darker Englishman named Graham. We soon learned that our apprehensions about dining with the two officers were mostly misdirected, for Ken was nothing more than one of the ship's travel agents onboard and Graham worked as an engineer. On this ship those positions just happened to be officer level. In fact, introducing us to Ken turned out to be the single biggest help anybody could have given us, though none of us knew this at the time.

Despite the relative neutrality of their positions onboard, we obviously didn't want to volunteer our secret to either Ken or Graham and had asked Valerie and Helen to keep a tight lip on it, too. As the night wore on, though, we began feeling much more comfortable with our new friends and began getting more daring in asking our "rhetorical" questions to Ken and Graham. Questions like "How easy would it be for someone to sneak off this ship, supposing they wanted to, of course?" We tried real hard to keep an innocent look on our faces and a neutral tone to our voice as we did but I doubt we did a very good job. Either way, by the night's end the relationship with our newfound friends had grown comfortable enough that our story had somehow managed to find its way out into the conversation.

At the risk of sounding monotonous here, and as unbelievable as it may seem, once they learned the truth, they too offered us all the help they could give. This was fast becoming entirely unbelievable. We had been on this ship just slightly more than 24 hours at this point and in spite of our vow to not tell a soul about what we were doing we now found ourselves with not only seven confidants but with seven accomplices too!

We spent the rest of the night there with the four of them, leaving only for our midnight foray into the banquet. After the disco closed, Karen and I went back outside into the warm, quiet night and sat up once again in the deck chairs until morning.

DAY THREE:

Once the sun was up we resumed our daily activity of lounging poolside and trying to catch up on all the sleep we weren't getting.

Either I was still too wired from adrenalin or the effects of the diet pills and colas were longer lasting than I thought because sleep wasn't even close to happening. Thinking our chances would be better if we got out of the public view, plus just to disappear for a while, we arranged with Val and Helen to let us use their room for a couple of hours that afternoon while they were out at the pool. We ducked in at 3:30 p.m. and though it was indeed nice to be out of sight and unguarded, I still couldn't fall asleep and after three hours of futile effort we finally slipped back out so the ladies could come back and get themselves ready for dinner.

That night we were back in the disco again as usual. It was different tonight though, as this was to be the last night of the Caribbean cruise. Tomorrow morning we were going to be in New York City's harbor. Many things that we'd come to appreciate and depend on were soon going to disappear. The Midnight Banquet was going, our friendships with Chet, Val and Helen were going, as was, of course, all their help. Because of all this, a certain degree of our sense of security was going to be leaving as well.

We had learned earlier that the ship would be sailing on to Southampton, England following the termination of the Caribbean cruise there in New York. It was our plan now to somehow stay onboard during the switch over to the Trans-Atlantic cruise and continue on to England.

We knew that the Caribbean cruise passengers would be disembarking the next morning upon our arrival (Sunday) and that later that same afternoon the Trans-Atlantic passengers would then board just prior to the ship's leaving in the early evening. We had also been told by Kenny that there would be 166 other passengers remaining onboard for the Trans-Atlantic crossing to keep us company. We were really happy to hear that, to know that we weren't going to be alone.

What we didn't know, however, was what we were going to do with ourselves during that critical time between the two cruises. On a ship designed to carry nearly 3000 people, 166 passengers was next to nothing, and even they would be mostly holed up in their rooms since the ship would be almost entirely shut down during the transition. We would have to find a way to remain unnoticed on a virtually deserted ship for the several hours between the two cruises while the crew scurried all about us cleaning and preparing for the new passengers.

We didn't have a clue as to where we would be the least noticed nor what we were to do during this time, and there seemed a good potential for us to get caught here.

We had tried to find out before what would happen to us if we ever did get caught but nobody really knew since no one had ever stowed away before, or at least had ever been caught. One story had it that if caught on the way to New York we would be taken off and arrested. If, on the other hand, we got caught on the way to England then it was anybody's guess as to what they would do. Either way, it wasn't a very fun thought at the moment and we tried to ignore it so that we could enjoy this last night with our friends as much as we could.

DAY FOUR:

When the morning came, we said our sad and thankful goodbyes to Chet, Valerie and Helen as they made their way off the ship. As soon as they had gone, we went back down and took up a couple of seats in the huge Double Down lounge to begin our long wait. We played cards and read for as long as we could but after a couple of hours we started feeling too conspicuous sitting out there all by ourselves and decided to retreat back to the ever-dependable toilet stalls again.

We knew that the Trans-Atlantic crowd was due to board later that afternoon so we synchronized our re-emergence times as best as we could and locked ourselves in the toilets near the big wall map again. We had a lot of time left to kill in there and I really wanted to take advantage of it to catch up on my sleep as much as I could, so I fluffed up my toilet paper roll and tried to nod off.

In the five and a half hours that we were in there I got maybe two hours of vertical sleep, which did help some though not much. At least I didn't have to deal with that damned air blower this time since everyone was gone. Our plan worked very well though and we made the transition unscathed with no one the wiser about our status.

Once the ship was loaded and underway, we crawled out of our stalls to see New York Harbor gliding past the big windows of the ship. I remembered just then an old mission that had never been resolved and I immediately set about to accomplish it with renewed vigor.

Wanting to get to a better vantage point, I made my way up to the big windows just outside from the dining room, where all the new passengers were lining up to get their dinnertime seating assignments. I nudged past them as I took up a position and began scanning the horizon back and forth, looking. I knew she was out there somewhere and I was going to find her this time.

It was a big harbor and for several minutes my searching went unanswered. Then, off in the distance, looking past a few nearby islands, I finally saw her, standing tall and proud. Yes, it was finally her.

My first attempts to see the Statue of Liberty had been thwarted all those many months and miles ago by the vagaries of the New York City freeway system, as Karen and I made our way through town on our way south to Florida, but this time she was right here, right in front of me. It was a meager thrill, to be sure, but as I stood there watching her float by, I had the pleasure of knowing that one more item had just been checked off my list of things to see before I die. It wasn't the best shot of her and she was only visible for a few minutes before she was gone but it was enough. I was content.

I was even more content, though, to be escaping from New York unshackled. We'd just passed a crucial leg of this adventure here and I was exceedingly relieved by it. The New York - Southampton cruise had a completely different feel to it than the Caribbean loop cruise. In addition to our friends and our beloved Midnight Banquet, we lost another old friend, the sun. The weather turned cold and gray while in New York and the clouds followed us all the way to England, ruining our plans of spending the daytimes out at the pool since it was now cold and completely deserted outside. The people, too, were different. This wasn't a party cruise any longer with young people drinking and cavorting down in the tropics. This crowd was older and stodgier, I thought.

The disco, however, was just the same and when "Born to be Alive" came on I felt the old familiar place come back alive, too. We saw Kenny in there and that was good, too, though he gave us a scare when he then told us about the stowaway search they were going to have that night. It was usual practice the first night out of port, he told us, and nothing to be too alarmed about. Despite this, he, in his kindness, offered to put us up in his room that night anyway just to make sure that we didn't somehow get caught in it. We gladly accepted his offer and agreed to meet him there in the bar at 3:30 a.m. to go up to his cabin.

The disco was fairly uneventful and boring that night so we eagerly awaited our meeting with Kenny. Happily, he showed up right on time but then surprised us by informing us that the stowaway search had already been conducted and concluded. That was good news for us. He said that we were still more than welcome to come spend the night anyway and so were soon on our way. Rather than taking us to his room, though, he took us instead to one he knew about that was closer and safer to get to.

Karen and I made ourselves comfortable down on the floor while Kenny settled into the cabin's only bed. We had such a good time lying there joking and laughing and carrying on with each other that we didn't get more than 45 minutes of sleep before it was time for Ken to get up and off to work.

DAY FIVE:

We spent much of that morning just milling about the ship. The weather was too cold outside for most everybody, which meant we couldn't stay out there very long without being noticed. There were only a handful of inside chaise lounges on the ship so when we did manage to find a couple of empty ones to crash in we likewise couldn't sleep but for a short time before having to get up and move to a new location. Two people, we thought, snoring away in stuporous oblivion for hours on end probably wouldn't help our efforts very much in blending into the crowd.

In fact, it was becoming increasingly harder to feel like we were blending in at all since not only were we having to wear our awful clothes while everyone else was dressing to the nines but we were having to wear them every single day and night. I alternated wearing just my new shirt by itself and with wearing it under my new sweater for a little variety. It wasn't much but it was probably good enough for me. After all, the disco was dark and guys seem able to get away with lackluster wardrobes easier than women.

Karen, on the other hand, had a much harder time of it, it seemed. To spice up her ensemble a bit, she'd bought some black tights a couple of days ago from the ship's store to hide her furry legs and now this day she went and picked herself up a knitted shawl to try to add at least a hint of some style to her gunny sack dress. I thought she looked pretty snazzy myself but then to look at me I don't think that was much of a consolation to her.

Later that day we were caught off guard when an announcement broke over the ship's intercom that all passengers were to return to their rooms immediately and begin preparations for the mandatory lifeboat evacuation drill. We hadn't been forewarned of this little exercise and as the color slowly returned to our faces we realized that we had no other choice but to head for our toilets pronto. Not at all sure what to expect from this, we locked ourselves into our respective stalls and hoped for the best.

I waited until I was reasonably sure that enough time had passed for them to have finished the drill and returned to normal life but I crept out cautiously anyway, just in case they hadn't.

Sometime later Karen finally came out, too. She didn't have such an easy time of hiding out, however, and ended up having a close call with one of the maintenance people who had come in to clean the bathroom she was holed up in.

The woman asked her suspiciously why she wasn't up in her room with everyone else going through the drill. Karen adlibbed as innocently as she could that she'd been on the previous cruise and had already gone through the drill once before and didn't feel like going through it again. Either Karen's story was sufficiently convincing or else the cleaning lady didn't really care much after all, for she accepted the explanation. Karen promptly made a hasty retreat to another bathroom nonetheless.

Other than for this brief incident our days soon became fairly routine. With the start of the Trans-Atlantic cruise, the movie theater started showing movies twice a day. We were usually pretty eager to make ourselves scarce after roaming around the ship all morning so we began going to the afternoon showing so that we could hide in the dark theater. My thought was that we could catch a quick nap in there during the afternoon and then return later for the night showing to actually watch the movie.

Unfortunately for my dreams of sleep, though, I found the movies to be such a wonderful escape from the daily mental overload that I usually put myself through that I usually sat through both showings with nary a wink nor a nod throughout.

When we came out of the theater this first night, after watching "Agatha," we were happily surprised to find that a tray of small submarine sandwiches had been set up right outside the exit door nearest to the disco. We eagerly scooped up as many as we thought we could get away with and took them back to our usual table and gobbled them down. When no one was looking, we went back and reloaded two or three more times. It was such a treat for us that we ended up doing this just about every night afterward.

In fact, since the Midnight Banquet's demise two nights ago our diet options had taken a major downturn. With a little effort though we found alternatives that worked well enough for us. They weren't tables laden to overflowing with cakes and pies but they were food.

For breakfast, we usually headed up to the little shop and bought ourselves a couple of Baby Ruth candy bars to tide us over till "lunch." It was the only food onboard that a passenger could actually buy. "Lunches," however, were a little bit riskier.

At around 4 p.m. when the Theater Bar opened, we'd go in and head for the nearest table. After ordering ourselves each a coke, we'd set upon the bowl of peanuts on the table like Yogi and Boo Boo on a springtime picnic basket. We devoured it in minutes and as soon as we were finished we simply got up and moved to a new table and ravaged its bowl of peanuts as well.

We went from table to table like this until we'd either had our fill or we ran out of peanuts, whichever came first. Since we were usually the only ones in the bar at this hour, it was hard to be discreet about it but nobody seemed to notice or care. It was much to our good fortune, during this part of the cruise, that neither of us were very big eaters.

By the time our midday meal was wrapping up, the Theater Bar was generally transforming itself once again into the disco so we usually lingered around until the place got going and then we'd move back to our usual table back in the shadows, against the windows.

If the daytimes were becoming routine, the night times soon moved in to take up the slack. That night after the movie and a couple of hours in the toilet stalls, Kenny came into the disco and joined us at our table. While we sat there talking with him, the greatest threat to this entire trip came casually walking into the disco.

My heart froze solid when I looked over and recognized our old friend Napoleon slowly making his way down the hallway in our direction, looking around the room as he did. He was the only person on board now that could identify us for what we were and that would care enough to do anything about it. In fact, Kenny had already told us that Napoleon was a high-ranking security officer whose very job it was, in part anyway, to keep a look out for stowaways. No wonder he had laughed so when I'd asked back on the waterfront in Charlotte Amalie about stowing away and why he was so sure it couldn't be done. It was his job to make sure it couldn't. Of all the people for me to pick to ask.

As he came nearer and as much as I wanted to watch him to see what he was up to, I had to force myself to look away. I knew one brief moment of eye contact could jeopardize our whole adventure and possibly our entire trip.

Looking intently now over at Karen and Kenny, I watched him as best I could with my peripheral vision as he continued ever closer to us. When he'd gotten between us and the dance floor, about 15 feet away, I saw him stop and look over in our direction. He stood there for several moments holding his gaze. Though I couldn't tell for certain that he was in fact even looking at us, I couldn't help but think that he had just recognized us and was standing there trying to figure out from where.

It was a monumental effort on my part that kept me from looking back, for my survival instinct was yelling at me right then to grab Karen and get ready to run. After another moment, though, Napoleon turned around again and continued on his stroll as before, leaving the room a few minutes later.

We didn't know then, nor do we to this day, just what was going on in his mind. We didn't know if he had, in fact, recognized us but couldn't remember from where or whether perhaps he had recognized us and knew from where but saw us with Kenny and, remembering the pleasant conversation we'd had with him earlier, simply decided to look the other way. Perhaps he was just looking out the window. We'll never know.

This was the first time we'd crossed paths with Napoleon in the five nights that we'd now been onboard and we felt relieved that with only four more to go we probably wouldn't run into him again. We were way wrong in that thinking, as it soon became apparent.

3:30 a.m. brought the close of another successful day in our adventure, close call notwithstanding, and we crawled back into our toilet stalls for a couple of hours of whatever rest we could find.

DAY SIX:

Candy bars, peanuts and roaming the halls once again punctuated our day. We had a brief break in the "monotony" of our shipboard life that afternoon while we were sitting in the bar. The captain of the ship had come in with some other passengers and had taken a table right next to us. We eavesdropped on their conversation and got a good chuckle to ourselves when we heard him brag to his guests about how well he gets to know all of his passengers on each cruise. We considered going up to him and introducing ourselves just for the fun of it but then thought better of it.

Our disco routine was starting to get a little boring, too, so this night we decided to be a bit bolder. We had gone to great pains since coming aboard to make sure that we blended into shadows or disappeared into crowds and other than our brief encounter with Napoleon the night before, we really hadn't run into anything close to being scary. So rather than sitting at our usual table in the back of the room against the window we sat instead on a small sofa just off from the dance floor, out in the lights and the crowd. We reasoned that we could at least afford one night of being seen.

I guess for all of our trouble we took to remain unseen, our subtle deceptions weren't subtle enough, though, for only a little while later the DJ came down from the raised stage at the back of the dance floor where he emceed from and sat down next to us. "You know, I see you two in here every night," he said to us. "Don't you want to see any of the other shows?"

He caught us off guard but not ill prepared. We had already devised a cover story to explain our oddness here. We were newlyweds from California, you see, which we knew would explain both our less than appropriate appearance and our youth, and this cruise was a honeymoon gift from our parents, hence our awkwardness at being on board. This trip wasn't our idea but we had to take it.

With the confidence of having what I thought was a perfect cover story, I replied no, we really loved disco and were very much enjoying ourselves here.

"Well, is there something I can play for you then?" he asked in his Scottish accent. It put me on the spot for a moment because in truth Karen and I hated disco music for the most part and we didn't want to hear any of it. Anything but "Born to be alive" again, I thought, but answered instead that we really liked this one particular song that he played every so often called "Are Friends Electric" by Tubeway Army. "Great," he replied, and then left us to go back up to his music.

Fortunately, in our naïveté and ignorance we didn't realize then the test we had just passed. As we found out all too soon, the DJ not only played records but he also watched the crowd for any irregularities and if he found any he then reported them to the security staff. Had we known what was at stake we might not have been so cool and collected.

It also hadn't dawned on me right then the reason for his asking us our request. It became all too obvious though when he put on the record we'd asked for and the entire dance floor, which had been packed edge to edge, completely emptied before our eyes. He looked over at us and waved. His intention had been to get us out on the floor to dance.

It wasn't to give us room, though, that all the other dancers left. It was because the song we'd chosen as our favorite was a loud syntho-techno punk song and the only one the DJ had that was absolutely undanceable. Its only saving grace, for the moment anyway, was that it was his favorite song, too, and that maybe we had somehow endeared ourselves to him by choosing it. There was no way in hell, though, we were going to get out there on the floor all by ourselves to try. It's not at all a good way to remain unnoticed. We just smiled and waved back.

Kenny came in later with some really good news for us. He had been searching around on our behalf and had found an honest-to-god bathroom for us five decks down, in the rear section of the ship. We were a real project for Kenny and sometimes it seemed he did nothing all day except try and think of ways to help us more. I began to think he must have a crush on Karen. Either that or perhaps just a boring life in need of a thrill. At any rate, we went down a little later to check it out.

Sure, enough, it was a small bathroom all right, with nothing more in it than a bathtub and a toilet but it seemed like heaven to us. It was unaffiliated with any of the guest rooms in particular and was for the use of any passenger who may have tired of the showers that came with their rooms. To us, though, it was a virtual suite where we could be alone together at night, safely locked in. Where we could stretch out and actually sleep laying down.

I found that this room, too, had a removable cover board. This one, though, was a big one that came down along the entire side of the bathtub to hide its undersides from view. Underneath the tub, we found, was a much better place to stash our clothes, which we still had stacked up along the drainpipe in the Men's room upstairs. Kenny had done good. We couldn't wait to try it out.

We did have to wait, though, but once the disco closed that night we ran down to our new room, eager to have a go with it. Going in the darkened room I reached over to flip the light switch on but instead of finding just one switch I found three. In the dark I couldn't see what the difference was so I picked one and flipped it. Immediately a bright green light went on in the hallway just outside the door. Realizing just then that it was actually the steward's call signal and fearing that it may also have rung a bell of some sort in the steward's station, we quickly left and made a wild dash back up the stairs right next to the bathroom.

We hid at the top of the stairwell for several minutes while peering down to see if anyone came. When nobody did, we slowly and cautiously crept back down. Once back inside I felt much more confident about flipping the second switch now that I knew what the first one did. As soon as I did though, to our horror, a big red light flashed on this time, right next to the green one that was still on. I had flipped the stewardess' call switch!

Again we high-tailed it up the stairs, but this time we didn't stop to see if anyone came to check it or not. We were too nervous now to feel comfortable in there so we begrudgingly trudged off once again to our ever-faithful toilet stalls.

DAY SEVEN:

Our seventh day started out virtually identical to the sixth. It was another gray and dreary day outside with nothing much to do inside. As the evening drew to a close and the night's activities began, the thought of spending another night there in the disco listening to the same old music all over again didn't help excite us much either.

Perhaps to offset this or maybe just feeling a bit emboldened now that we were "friends" with the D.J., we decided to follow our previous night's example and actually dare to sit out under the lights again next to the dance floor. This time we chose the sofa on the opposite side of the dance floor from where the D.J. was set up with the pass-through hallway and our normal table at our backs. We made ourselves comfortable and settled in for the long night, relishing this new change of pace we were so lavishly allowing ourselves. Dangerously allowing ourselves, as it soon turned out.

Being a person who has always enjoyed watching other people, I was pleased with our new seats for the vantage it gave me in pursuing my favorite hobby. In the many nights now that we'd been visiting this place, I'd come to know (in my own mind anyway) most of the people that came in here. Tonight, however, I noticed a young man out on the dance floor that I hadn't seen before. He looked slightly different than everyone else there, for some reason, but I couldn't quite figure out just why. His dress appeared a little too informal and his manner perhaps a bit too rough, I thought. Also, he was dancing with unusual abandon and seemed to be having too good a time with it. After an hour or so, this young man, obviously worn out from his exertions, took a break and sat himself on the opposite end of the small sofa from where we were sitting.

Within a few minutes, as I sat there watching the dancers, I noticed two of the darkly uniformed security officers quietly enter the disco from the door just off to our right and immediately adjacent to the dance floor in front of us. I watched with increasing apprehension as they began to move over in our direction and then with outright fear when I looked behind us and saw two more security officers coming in from the rear entrance to the bar and heading down the hallway towards us as well. Fear then moved into paralytic near panic when I then saw Napoleon following close behind them.

I quickly looked away (somewhere in the vicinity of my shoes) so as not to make any eye contact and warned Karen to do the same. Moments later, the entire backside of our sofa was lined with these five officers as they moved in to surround this poor young fellow that was sitting, as we now realized, far too close to us.

It was again extremely difficult not to look up as the officers questioned the young man, especially since literally everyone else in the disco was standing there watching the whole encounter. It would have been the normal thing for a person to do in our situation but when I did look up briefly I saw to my compounding horror in a nearby mirror that Napoleon was standing directly behind us, only a couple of feet away.

We didn't know what this guy had done and we were both sorry that he'd been caught but we were also at the same time tremendously relieved that it was him they had come for and not us. Despite this I had a strong lingering fear that Napoleon, still hovering right behind us, would take advantage of this moment to finally allay his suspicions of us, point and say "and take them, too!"

Fortunately, my fear went unrealized and Napoleon and the others hauled the hapless fellow away. Alicia Bridges' song "I Love the Night Life" came on shortly afterwards, for the second or third time that night, but we decided right then that the night life was just a bit too dangerous for us. We promptly retreated back to our usual table in the shadows, vowing that we would not again sit out in the open like this. This was twice now that we'd come across Napoleon, our one great threat, and this time it had been far too close for comfort.

Our nerves were just a little rattled afterwards so we were only too happy to accept Kenny's kind offer, a while later, to again put us up for the night with him.

He was taking us to his own room this time, which was a little bit dicier than the room he took us to before as his was way up in the very bow of the ship, not far from John and Perry's and much farther into enemy territory. It meant dire consequences for him and his job should we get caught trying to get there and because of this our sneaking down the rat's maze of hallways to his room took on an air of urgency and danger.

I felt like a foreign agent being smuggled out of East Germany as Kenny quietly led us down into the warren of crisscrossing hallways where all the crew cabins were, acting as lookout. Stopping at each intersection, he slowly peered one eye around the corners, making sure all was clear before hurriedly waving us on past him. He was walking faster than I'd ever seen anyone walk before and we were practically running to keep up with him as we meandered around and down the maze of hallways toward his room, not saying a word to each other the whole time until we finally made our target and were safely locked in. Mission complete. Whew!

If the trip down was a tense ordeal it was well worth the price, for once inside, we found out just how truly nice Kenny was. Not content to just give us a safe room to sleep in, it turns out he'd preceded us down here before meeting us in the disco and had prepared and laid out for our welcome a tray of bread, fruits and cheese. He then took our drink order and went back up to the galley, returning a few minutes later with our first introduction to real English tea (an introduction that, by the way, soon grew into a very popular daily tradition with us for the remainder of our travels). After delivering our teas, Kenny surprised us again by saying he was going to go back up to the disco for a while since it was still relatively early (1 a.m.). Before leaving, though, he told us to make ourselves "at home" and insisted that we even take his bed for the night. We protested that he was being too kind but he would have none of it and insisted again. He pointed out the towels and soap he'd set out for us as well so that we could take a shower, something we hadn't been able to do since leaving Zorra two weeks ago. [Actually, now that I think about it, I'm not so sure it was really us he was thinking about.]

It was absolutely divine to have hot water pouring over us again and to be eating something other than peanuts. In fact, with the bread, cheese and fruit it was much like one of our now-beloved picnics and I took great comfort in this. It may have been two weeks since we'd last had a shower but it was far longer since we'd been able to have one together and we didn't let this rare opportunity get away.

Afterwards, we made ourselves a comfy nest on the floor for our bed and went to sleep. In spite of Ken's insistence, and because of his over-abundant kindness, we couldn't bring ourselves to take his only bed and leave him the floor to sleep on as he'd instructed us. He was fairly angry with us when he returned a couple of hours later and found us down on the floor anyway. He confessed to me later, with a bit of a suggestive wink, that it was because he had wanted us to have a "proper night together" at least once while onboard. The inference being the kind of night a couple would have together.

DAY EIGHT:

Returning to the world above later that morning (actually only about four hours later) was as anxious as the trip down had been the night before. Kenny was leading our commando mission again, once again hurrying ahead of us and signaling us along when all was clear.

We made it out of there without incident and were soon back into our usual daytime world. Any anxieties we may have felt that morning were, as it turned out, only a taste of what was to come later that evening and the following day. It was the beginning of what would prove to be the most stressful part of the entire cruise.

This was Thursday. We'd been onboard now for a week and only had one more day to go before we were to arrive at Southampton, England. Even though we had been assured that sneaking off the ship would be relatively easy, it still hung over us as we went about our day.

We saw that "California Suite" was to be the movie for the day and we brightened up quite a bit in anticipation of it. We had been gone from home now for almost exactly a year and homesickness had since become a regular part of our daily mood. It would do us a world of good, we knew, to be able to see a little bit of home again for its own sake but also to help take some of the stress away from us and give us rest from the public view. We ran into Graham a little while later, who iced our cake by offering to let us use his room that afternoon if we wanted. We did in fact want to, very much, and arranged to meet with him after the movie got out.

Sneaking into crew quarters during the daytime wasn't nearly as treacherous as it was at night and Graham's room wasn't as far away as Ken's so we made it there easily. We were very grateful of Graham's offer, for getting any kind of sleep at all was a big thrill for us but getting lie-down sleep was virtual heaven. Unfortunately, it seemed that whenever we did manage to actually find the time and place for sleep, what with all the adrenaline, diet pills, and now tea surging through our bodies at any given moment, not to mention unnatural positions or the revelry with our hosts, it was usually very difficult to get ourselves calmed down enough to actually fall asleep for any appreciable time. Surprisingly, looking alert and awake every day, after getting minimal, if any, sleep, turned out to be one of the biggest challenges we had to deal with throughout this whole adventure.

We were sitting with Kenny in the bar later that afternoon, talking, when the ship's Social Director came walking through the bar in our direction. Kenny saw him coming and couldn't resist the opportunity to have a little fun so he called him over to our table and, with just a touch of devilish grin, introduced us to him. The Director gave us his professional, yet pleasant, smile and asked the obvious question, "And are we enjoying our cruise?" Summoning up as much sincerity as we could while struggling to quickly deglaze our eyes, we smiled back and assured him that we were having a great time indeed. Kenny gave us another of his mischievous little winks before leaning over to him a little closer and saying in an almost whispered aside, "Oh, I'm sure they'll be back." "That's wonderful!" the Director replied before politely bidding us farewell. It was all we could do to keep from laughing before he got out of earshot and it did wonders for us when we finally did. Kenny lived for these moments, I think.

When dinnertime arrived, Karen and I retired to our usual toilet stalls for what would turn out to be our very last time. Had we known this at the time maybe we would've had a little ceremony or something, for we certainly had developed a relationship with the place by now. On the other hand, though, maybe not.

We returned to the disco about an hour or so later and took up our places. A few moments later, I went up to the bar to order our first round of Cokes for the day. The bartender was at the opposite end of the bar and as I stood there waiting for him to work his way back toward my end, I saw in my peripheral vision someone come up alongside of me and stop, apparently to wait for the bartender as well. Since the person was standing unusually close to me, I instinctively swung my head around and found, to my sheer terror, my nose pointing directly into Napoleon's ear not three feet away.

My heart flipped over and nearly died in the panic that engulfed it right then. I was stupefied for a brief moment and didn't know what to do. Pulling myself together once again with a quick dose of adrenaline, and thinking as quickly as a person with no blood supply to the brain can, I stepped back from the bar a few paces, just far enough to put me into the open hallway just behind us.

Looking down to the far end, towards the bow of the ship and in the opposite direction from Napoleon, I waved as though I had just seen someone I knew down there and then turned and walked off in that direction, hoping that Napoleon would think my friend had pre-empted my bar order. As I made my way down the hallway I thanked my lucky stars that it hadn't been his nose I'd met instead.

Though I will never know for sure, I'm as certain as I can be that his actions were deliberate and that he was just playing with us. Standing as close as he did to me and then not turning around to face me when he couldn't have helped but see me turn and look straight into the side of his head strikes me as being just too contrived to be normal. At any rate, I'm glad he didn't turn around and look at me, for the jig would certainly have been up right then and there if he'd only gotten the briefest glimpse of the horror in my initial expression.

I circled around the ship and came back to the disco from the opposite side. Napoleon was gone, thank God, so I returned to our table, where Karen was still patiently waiting for her drink.

When the second showing of the movie came up, we opted to make ourselves scarce by going to see it again. There was still the hope of catching a nap in the dark theater but it never happened. It was just too exciting to see the California coast again. When it was over, we scooped up a couple handfuls of baby submarine sandwiches, as was our routine by now, and went off to devour them.

The disco was in full swing and, remembering our close encounter of the night before as well as our vow to not go out into the light again, we retired to our regular table. Kenny had told us earlier that the young fellow nabbed the night before was a non-officer crew member and that his only crime was having been in an off-limits area for such crewmen. Only passengers and officers, it seems, were allowed in any of the public spaces.

We'd been afraid that the man had been a fellow stowaway and we were relieved to find out he wasn't. Somehow it made me feel a tad bit more confident that we were safe as stowaways and that we just might pull this caper off.

Feeling safer and being safer, though, are two different things and in spite of our attempts to remain in the obscurity of the shadows our safety was once again imperiled when later that night another young man entered the disco and headed our way. He too seemed ill placed in there, much like the guy from the night before. He made his way over to our table and then leaned down toward us as he introduced himself to us under his breath. He admitted to us in an unmistakable British accent that he was, in fact, a common crewman, that he wasn't allowed in here, but that this was his last night onboard and he wanted to enjoy it just this once while he had the chance.

When he then asked if he could sit with us, I almost told him no. I wanted to tell him that I fully understood his feelings, and was sympathetic to them even, but that we actually had much more to lose and fear than him. I couldn't bring myself to do it to him though, and I agreed to let him join us.

He sat down and quickly asked another favor. Would I go up to the bar and get him a couple of drinks since he couldn't risk being seen there. I didn't want to encourage this guy but at the same time I felt sorry for him so I took his money and got him a couple of beers.

As soon as I returned though, I did the only thing I could think of to discourage him from befriending us by turning my back to him and engaging in a very "intimate" conversation with Karen, who was sitting on the opposite side of me from him, effectively ignoring him. If I didn't have the heart to get rid of him, we at least had to distance ourselves from him, for it would certainly look bad for us if we were found two nights in a row fraternizing with illegals.

Since he was there to have fun and we obviously weren't very, he finally got up after 15 minutes or so, thanked us, grabbed his remaining beer and left to go mingle in the crowd. We both breathed a big sigh of relief. Our plan worked.

Our faith in our guardian angels was once again renewed when, not five minutes later, the whole contingent of security officers from the night before came streaming in once again, circled their victim and then escorted him out. Had they been only that much sooner, Karen and I would have found ourselves literally with our backs against the wall facing five black suited security officers, one of whom was the dreaded Napoleon himself. It would have been certain death for us, as I was sure Napoleon was suspicious of us at this point. In fact, all night long afterwards, he cruised in and out of the disco, strolling by in front of us ever more slowly each time and often glancing over in our direction as he did so. I could only watch him peripherally, of course, and each time it was all I could do to not look back.

We were nervous, for even though we hadn't been with the fellow when he'd been caught, whoever had squealed on him had to have spotted him while he was still in our company, only those minutes earlier, very much like the incident the night before. There seemed to be an unfortunate pattern developing and we were afraid our guilt by association, if not our true guilt, would give us away.

In the end, I'm certain that it was only due to our naïveté that we were saved, for it soon became obvious to us that it was the D.J. who had ratted on these poor guys, the same D.J. who'd approached us as well only a couple of nights earlier to check us out, too. Had we known at the time what he was doing we might not have been so comfortable with him and had we not had the same taste in music as he did he might not have been so forgiving of our out-of-place-ness.

As it was, we emerged relatively unscathed from the ordeal but our fun for the day wasn't over just yet. A few hours later when the disco closed for the night we headed down for our first and long-delayed night in the "Bathroom of the Steward's Bell."

We had just gotten ourselves situated inside when we heard voices out in the hallway coming our way. We quickly shut the light off, locked the door and quit breathing while we nervously waited there in the dark to see where they were going. We were reasonably certain that it wasn't somebody out to take a bath since it was somewhere in the vicinity of 4:30 in the morning, but then one never knows about people.

The two voices came closer and we could hear that they were the voices of a young couple. They came around the corner of the hallway and stopped in the little service alcove just outside of our door. We sat there on the floor of the bathroom listening to their quiet conversation through the crack under the door. It soon became apparent that they were crew members and that this was a young lovers rendezvous that we were eavesdropping on.

Though not particularly dangerous to us as it were, we still feared that if they for any reason got spooked, or perhaps simply decided to further their relations a bit more seriously, they might try to duck in our bathroom, only to find it locked. We set about reviewing our options, just in case they did try to come in, only to realize that we had none. We had no choice but to continue to sit there and hold our breath in the dark.

It was an extremely long 10 minutes before they finally left us and returned back down the same hallway they had come from. After waiting a few minutes to let my heart settle down a bit, I eagerly climbed into the bathtub for the night while Karen made herself a nest on the fluffy bathroom rug, and we both went right to sleep.

DAY NINE:

I woke early that morning from a surprisingly comfortable couple of hours' sleep in the tub. When I did, I realized yet another perk of living the high-style bathroom life. We could have a bath! I doffed my clothes and tossed them over the side toward Karen, then reached up and turned the water on.

Karen was awake by the time it was full so I invited her to join me. She undressed and hopped in. We lay together in the steaming hot water and had ourselves a nice, long soak together. As soothing as it was though, this was to be our last day aboard Queenie and it was hard to not be concerned about our upcoming fate. It's really too bad, too, for not only was this the first bath that we ever had together but it would also prove to be the last (and only) bath we would ever share with each other, though we certainly didn't know it at the time. Maybe we could have savored it a little bit more. Then again, who's to say, for there were many, many important things for us to think about this day. How we were going to get off this old lady was not the least of them.

We had asked Ken and Graham earlier about disembarking with the passengers but they told us that it would be almost impossible to sneak off with them. Ken explained to us that in order to avoid paying an extra day's docking fee the ship usually came into port around midnight and that the following morning an Immigrations and a Customs agent would actually come onboard and set up a little station right at the exit gangway where they would then check disembarking passengers off from a computerized ship's roster, stamp their passports and admit them to the country straight from the ship. Since we were not on the ship's roster, we obviously couldn't be scratched off it.

Ken and Graham both agreed that sneaking off with the crew was by far the best option. They told us that once the ship was securely docked upon arrival in Southampton, any crew member whose work was done was free to get off the ship directly and go home that night. Shortly before docking, this off-duty crew normally started forming a large mob near the large cargo door on the starboard side of the ship. Once the ship was safely tied up, they said, the door was opened and the crew was allowed to simply walk off. Though proper procedure called for I.D.'s to be shown on the way out, we were assured that they never bothered with it. It sounded almost too easy yet they seemed very certain about it so we took them at their word.

Several hours before our docking in Southampton, however, we were to make our first actual port call in the city of Cherbourg, France for a quick cargo stop. We were due to arrive late that afternoon and after seven days at sea with nothing to look at but ocean, the thought of making landfall was tremendously thrilling for me. Not only from the break in the monotony of sea travel but also, and more so, because there was a remote possibility that, if we found the conditions favorable, we might try to sneak off here instead of waiting until Southampton.

The thought of making landfall bore home to me how close we were to the end of this adventure, that by the end of this day it would be over. One way or the other it would be over. My body seethed electricity at the thought, no, the thrill, of it. At least as much as my sadly worn body was able to conduct it. Elation was once again mixed with apprehension but this time it also had a good-sized dose of fatigue as well as a certain sense of resignation from knowing that our fates were really out of our hands at this point, that whether we made it off successfully or not was not for us to determine.

The "Boys from Brazil" was playing at the theatre that afternoon. We went not only to remove ourselves from the public view for a while but I think, too, to help give us a diversion from all these thoughts of what was to become of us at the end of this day. As soon as the movie was over, we raced straight up to the passengers' observation deck at the bow of the ship so we would be there for the first glimpse of land as it stuck its nose up out of the sea.

We were not alone in our yen for dirt, for we found many people already gathering there, apparently with the same idea as us (although certainly for a different reason).

The electricity was still coursing through me as I stood there, straining my eyes at the far horizon for any hint of land, just as I did back in the Bahamas on Spirit as we approached Nassau, and the romance of it all was once again not lost on me. It was easy for us to forget the true extent of our adventure while out alone on the open sea. The rest of the world so easily fades away into vague abstraction when you no longer have it to hold your life up against for reference.

Now, with the thought that we would very soon be entering our first port in Europe, the full impact of what we were doing, of what we had done, began to meet up with me and snap me out of this abstraction, reminding me that, in the greater perspective, we were indeed on a grand adventure.

It wasn't long before we heard the shouting and people began pointing to a spot just off the starboard bow. Excitement raced through us all as the first bit of land was spotted far off on the horizon. The weather was cool and clear that day so we could all easily see the little brown speck that would soon grow up out of the sea to become the mighty France.

As our first introduction to Europe, the port of Cherbourg seemed terribly exotic to me as we slowly pulled up some time later and made fast to what seemed to me an ancient dock. Memories of all those old movies that I had watched throughout my life from the era of the great ocean liners, movies of war, intrigue and espionage, welled up in me as I looked down on all those little Frenchmen running around the docks in their funny, little uniforms, loading and unloading cargo while Karen and I surreptitiously watched from the ship's rails, wondering if we might be able to slip off the ship here somehow or, if not, at least hoping to pick up any clues that might come in handy later in Southampton.

It was soon apparent to us, however, that we wouldn't be getting off here, as we were only in port for a short time and there were no other people getting off or on that we might hide amongst, which suited me fine. Somehow it all seemed just a little too strange and alien to me and I was glad we weren't going to try to get off here.

We soon left port and turned our bow toward the far side of the channel and sailed on for England. It was fast approaching evening by now. Karen and I said adieu to Cherbourg and went back inside, where we met up with Kenny a bit later in the Theater bar. He was excited because he had gotten hold of a couple of Service Questionnaires and thought it would be real fun for us to fill them out. It was.

We complimented them on the comfort of their bathmats and the length of their tubs (but complained that their toilet paper wasn't fluffy enough). Once again Kenny helped keep the trip fun at a time when it could very easily have been not. After our laugh, we turned our questionnaires in and retired to our bathroom to wait out the dinner hour that had since arrived, but we were once again too charged up by now to get any kind of real rest.

We came out after dinner was over and met up with John and Perry who had brought out with them our belongings that they'd been storing for us down in their room. We wouldn't be seeing them anymore after this and we thanked them profusely for all the help they had given us, but it still didn't seem to be enough for all that they had done for us. Without them we would have been goners from the very beginning.

We met Ken in the disco at about 8 p.m. and arranged to meet him there again at 11 p.m. to get ready for our big escape. He had agreed to act as lookout for us as the ship pulled in and docked, while we hid out down in our bathroom waiting for his coded knock to let us know it was time to go. The bathroom was conveniently just down the hall from the cargo door that we would be exiting (escaping) through and the plan was for Ken to wait until the door had been open before coming and letting us know so that we wouldn't have to risk being spotted while we stood there waiting. We could just walk right out.

Before he left us just then, though, Ken betrayed his heart's secret when he suddenly and very sweetly asked Karen if she would dance just once with him. He knew that this was the last opportunity he would have before we were to depart and he didn't want to let it get away.

I had suspected for a while now that he'd had a secret crush on her and that was why he'd really been so nice to us this whole time. I could tell now by his gentle insistence when she briefly hesitated in her answer and by the beseeching look on his face that indeed he did. Karen never was much into dancing and she didn't really want to go out there but there was no way she could deny him this simple favor, the only one he ever asked us for, and so she gladly granted it for him. They had only that single dance together before he excused himself and left us there in the disco to enjoy, appropriately, Donna Summer's "Last Dance" when it came on a short while later.

All the building excitement must have emboldened us that night, for we actually decided to forego the disco (at least for a while) and see another show. I had heard that there was a hypnotist show down in the Queens Lounge so we went on down to see it. I'd always been interested in such things and I enjoyed the show. There was no movie that night so afterwards we returned to the disco. I thanked God we weren't going to have to hear those songs much longer (though by now we were actually becoming pretty big Tubeway Army fans).

The excitement was building minute by minute as the clock crept toward 11 p.m. At about 10:30 I started seeing lights on shore going past the windows as we approached Southampton, and I was afraid that the ship had arrived early and that we were going to miss our chance. I was becoming antsy waiting. When 11:00 arrived and Ken didn't, I became outright worried. Then 11:05, 11:10, 11:15. The lights outside were moving awfully slow now; we were getting very close. Finally, I couldn't wait any longer and decided to go looking for him. Karen waited there in the disco in case he showed up and I took off to do a loop around the ship. Going all the way around and then down to five deck to check our bathroom, I couldn't find him anywhere. I was half-running the whole way around for fear that he had shown up at the disco while I was gone, but as I came in the front door of the disco I found my biggest fear standing before me instead.

Just a few feet inside the room facing the very door I'd just walked through was our beloved Napoleon. I couldn't believe it. The first four days of our cruise we hadn't seen hide nor hair of this guy and then all of a sudden he was a daily occurrence. Out of all these people onboard I didn't think we'd ever run into him. And to run into him now of all times.

My first instinct was to turn and run back out the way I came in but I realized that a man stopping in his tracks at seeing a security officer, turning white as a ghost and then running out of the room would probably seem a bit obvious. Not having the luxury of time to consider any other options, I had no choice but to continue on and try not to get close enough for him to smell the fear that was shooting out of my pores like water from a fireboat on parade.

My only available path through the room took me right smack in front of him. Gritting my teeth and trying to pretend to be normal, I made my way past, making sure not to look anywhere near him. I was so anxious as I walked by him that I was sure his heart started pounding faster from my adrenaline, but I didn't stop to verify it. Walking straight on I found Karen and Ken waiting for me at the far side of the room and we quickly left to go take up our positions in the bathroom.

We sat in there for several minutes waiting for Ken to come back and signal us to move. We removed our bags from under the tub and set them on the floor next to where we sat. It was a very tense few moments then. There was nothing to do but sit and think and nothing to think about except whether or not we were going to actually make it off okay.

We split up our $1200 worth of travelers checks between the two of us just in case the worst of all possibilities happened and only one of us got caught and hauled in. We still didn't know just what would be done with a stowaway at this stage of the game, so we had to make allowances for all possibilities.

After some consideration, we agreed that the uncaught one would wait there in England for the other's release. It was possible that, being Cunard's responsibility, they would simply let us go with a slap on the wrist in order to avoid the embarrassment of admitting to such a breach in their security. Since we had money and passports, we thought that might be likely but, on the other hand, they could just as easily opt to send us back to New York and have us arrested. Either way, it would have made it extremely difficult for the free one because they wouldn't have any way of knowing what had actually become of the other. Neither scenario much appealed to us at that moment.

We finally heard footsteps coming our way. I jumped when Kenny gave us the coded knock on the door that was our signal. We came out to meet him and then followed him back toward the cargo door. He had that same sense of urgency in his walk that he'd had two nights ago when he snuck us into his room, and my heart was in my throat as we trotted behind him, struggling to keep up.

If, for any reason, this plan became unworkable our only other alternative was to go out and jump off the back of the ship into the harbor, ostensibly to swim ashore. Ken had said that if it came to that he would take our things ashore for us later when he could get away but the fact of the matter was that we most likely would be dead. The ship was so big that the concussion of hitting the water from that height would most likely have knocked us out, the height of the pilings was so great that we would never have been able to climb out if somehow we didn't get knocked out, and even if miracles happened and we did get out of the water alive we would've had a real tough time explaining to the security guard at the exit gate from the docks why we were soaking wet and one step away from death. We were really rooting for Plan A at this point.

It was only a short distance to the staging area and I was surprised to find when we got there that the door hadn't been opened yet and there was a crowd of about 20-30 people gathered there waiting. Our whole plan had been set up to avoid having to stand around in view of the guards and trying to blend in, but that's exactly what we now found ourselves having to do.

We didn't have a chance to ask Kenny, though, why he had called us out so early, as he had already quietly wished us goodbye and slipped away as soon as we'd joined the group. We were now on our own again, standing there alone in this crowd, hoping beyond hope that we looked like limeys. Being a person of small stature and of obvious European ancestry I felt pretty good about blending in, despite my being several shades of tan darker than anyone else there (save for Karen, of course) but I winced as I looked around the room and noticed that not only was Karen the only woman in the whole crowd but for some reason she had chosen to wear her bright purple shirt that night. I often wondered about her but now I worried about her as well.

As more people slowly drifted in, Karen and I were glancing back and forth about the room, busy casing out the place. A large throng of people was gathering now, many of them with their arms full of bags of souvenirs, waiting for the two guards posted at either side of the door to finally open it and let us all out. I was a little relieved to see someone there with a very large pink stuffed elephant. The more distractions the better I was thinking.

After a few moments' thought, we decided our best hope was to use our small size to its greatest advantage and simply fall in between two big thugs and slip out unnoticed through the big door with them. In order to avoid getting caught together we also agreed to put a few feet between us so if one didn't make it the other one might. I didn't at all like the thought of splitting up with her. It was only the support that we got from each other that made this trip possible from the very beginning and it frightened me to think that we might get separated now and in this way. I looked over at her and she returned a nervous smile. It was the same one that had gotten me through so many other tense situations this past year and I immediately felt better from it.

For all the trying situations we had been in together, the one thing that always kept us going was the intense feeling inside us both that it was going to work out, no matter what it was that we were doing. An imperturbable faith in our abilities, in the grace of God, in the goodness of people and in the power of positive thinking. It was this faith that allowed us to find fun and humor in any situation. In fact, we soon found out that it was during the most vulnerable, uncompromising and tense times that we generally had the most fun together, when we relied the most heavily on each other. Her smile encouraged and calmed me greatly, made it fun again, but it could not alleviate the lingering fear I had of becoming separated from her.

Finally, the big door swung open. The moment had finally arrived, the crowd of now about 50 squeezed together as we all compressed towards the exit. Karen picked out her two bodyguards and assumed her position between them. I found two more that would work well for me and settled in between them, several feet behind her.

So far so good, I was thinking, when I heard the words that we had been promised wouldn't be said. The guard nearest to me called out, "Have your passes out, please, where we can see them."

Everyone immediately held up their small white I.D. cards as the mass of people began shuffling toward the door. It was too late for us to back out now; the surge of people had caught us and moved us forward whether we wanted to or not. Nothing short of a major effort would have allowed us to go against it in an attempt to escape and certainly not without drawing much attention to ourselves. We had to go.

I looked down at my shuffling feet as my mind raced with wondering what I should do. Should I hold up any piece of white paper and hope he doesn't look too closely at it? Should I just get small and continue on and pray that he doesn't see me at all? I was frantic to decide as I continued looking down to the floor in a desperate attempt to look inconspicuous. Maybe if I shielded my eyes I would become invisible.

I knew it was too late to decide anything though when I heard a voice directly ahead of me ask "Do you have your pass?" I don't know which guard said it or whom he was asking; all I know is that before I could tell myself not to, I instinctively looked up and straight into the face of the security guard that was now only a few feet ahead of me on my left.

To my horrible surprise I found that not only was I already at the doorway but also that the big fellow that was supposed to be covering my left flank had somehow merged into the center when I wasn't looking and had now left me completely unguarded and open to this guard's view. Worse, I was fairly certain that it was this same guard that had just asked the question and that it was indeed me that he was asking it to.

In response to my immediate and total panic, my brain simply ceased any kind of rational thought in that brief moment of eye contact and I didn't know what else to do but to quickly return my gaze to the floor and simply go on as though none of it had happened. I was desperate to believe that if I didn't acknowledge it, it would cease to exist so I just kept on shuffling.

Staring intently now down at my feet, I slowly made my way past the guard and I cringed as I did so for I knew that any moment now I would feel the heavy weight of his hand land on my shoulder and pull me aside. There was no doubt in my mind that this was going to happen and I tried my best to steel myself for it. I was glad that Karen had made it and had all but resigned myself to the brig.

But something very unexpected happened then. More correctly I should say that something didn't happen. For reasons I can't explain, the hand never landed and before I knew it I was walking down the gangway watching Karen's purple shirt bobbing its way down ahead of me. Maybe I had indeed become invisible. I just know that it was the most exhilarating feeling I can ever remember feeling as I made my way down that ramp, almost as much as when we had first gotten on this old girl more than a week ago.

Karen was waiting for me with a big smile when I got to the bottom and landed my first footfall in jolly old England. We'd done it! As truly unbelievable as it was, we actually pulled this thing off and were standing right here in England! We couldn't afford to look too excited just then, though, for fear of blowing our cover, and we still had some big, scary things ahead of us to deal with, like getting through immigration, but that didn't diminish the absolute joy and self-satisfaction that was now swirling through me.

As we filed away with the crowd toward the gate, we heard a holler come from the ship. We looked up to see Kenny there on the Lido deck waving his arms and yelling down to us in congratulations. He was as excited as we were.

We smiled and eagerly waved back. Then, more slowly, he waved us goodbye. So much of the success of this trip was directly because of him, and I was sorry that we hadn't had a chance for a proper goodbye in all the nerves and rush of preparation. Sadness and nostalgia once again intermingled themselves with my excitement as we turned and continued on our way. We never saw him again.

FEETS...Around the World

BRITISH ISLES

We made our way to the gates of the dockyard, the final threshold to our escape. There was a lone sentry guarding our exit but there was no pass checking or searching eyes. Just a perfunctory glance at the crowd in general as we all spilled out into the dark streets of the city.

Passing through the gate, we suddenly found ourselves in a world that we weren't at all prepared for. We had been so preoccupied with the pressing needs of all our shipboard challenges that we'd never given any real thought to what we'd find or what we'd do if we actually made it to this point.

It was now 12:30 in the morning, it was dark and we were in a strange city, a strange country. Much like our arrival in St. Thomas, we stood here at the starting block of a new leg to our trip without a clue as to where we were or where we were to go. At first we just followed the crowd wherever it was headed but when it fanned out too far to follow we broke off and aimed toward the part of town that seemed to be the brightest.

We were both exceedingly exhausted at this point and yet still totally wired as we made our way along the empty streets of Southampton's port district. Karen started to shiver from the cold. Even though it was a summer night here, it felt more like winter to our unacclimated, worn and severely deprived bodies. We had brought hardly any clothes with us, particularly cold weather clothes, so we had little recourse but to put on all that we had and keep moving until we could find a place to hole up in until morning.

We found a cafe in town that was still open and went inside, glad for the shelter and eager to get our bearings in this strange place. We stayed in there as long as we thought we could without appearing too obviously homeless, then headed back outside to wander the streets some more.

We eventually came across a double-sized telephone booth and, after doing a quick time correction in our heads, realized it would be an ideal time to call our homes so we squeezed ourselves in and took turns calling our mothers. Neither of them was at all sure just what to make of our mostly unbelievable story, but we both promised to write them soon and explain it all--once we got our brains back.

After hanging up, we looked back out to the cold, lonely streets and realized that we didn't have anywhere else to go that was any better than where we were, so we just sat down there on the floor of the phone booth and made ourselves comfy for the remainder of the night. We were still too adrenalized, caffeinated and amphetamined to do anything but sit there and talk, though.

Several minutes later an old bum came over and set up his own house in the booth adjoining our own. He was joined soon after by yet another man of the street, and the two of them sat in there all night, yakking and joking. We didn't mind, though. Listening to them carry on provided us with our entertainment for the night and gave us a good distraction until morning light.

It must have worked pretty well, too, for it seemed that daylight came before we knew it, thank God. As soon as it appeared to be at least a little warm outside, we crawled out from the booth and greeted our new world for the first time in the light of day.

There was no reason to hang around Southampton so we decided to just head straight up to London, about 60 miles to the north. That was where the immigration office was that we'd have to go to soon, and it was where Val's brother Mike lived. She had given us his number before leaving the ship, saying that we could stay there if we needed.

We had just sat up through our ninth night in a row without any appreciable sleep and hadn't eaten a real meal since the

Midnight Banquet closed up shop seven days ago. We had quit our chemical stimulant diet the night before and our adrenaline tide was rapidly ebbing as well, revealing the scattered flotsam that was our minds.

We asked around town for directions and were told that the best place to hitchhike from was a particular roundabout way out the north end of town. Forbidden bus fares meant that we were walking so we grabbed up our bags and began the long trek all the way through the fair-sized city and then some ways out the other side before we finally got to the circular intersection where the road to London branched off.

We found ourselves a spot of grass on the side of the road, just past where it split, and promptly stuck our thumbs out. In only minutes someone pulled over for us. Unfortunately, it was a bobby stopping to tell us that we couldn't hitch from here and that we would have to move farther on up the road. Fortunately, he didn't stick around after delivering the message, for we were still just a little jumpy with authority figures right then, and we were wetbacks, after all (in a manner of speaking, anyway). Within minutes of relocating ourselves, another car stopped for us, this one thankfully a regular car, and within the hour we found ourselves in London town.

We made our way to Trafalgar Square and decided to use it as our base of sorts. It was near the city center and full of tourists that we could blend with. We tried to get hold of Mike from a payphone here but there was no answer so we just continued to roam around for a while and then try again later.

We actually tried several times later throughout the rest of the day but we always met with the same results. It became painfully clear to us now that we were going to have to come up with a new plan so we scrounged up a map of the city and began scanning it for any likely-looking spot that we might be able to disappear into for the night. We saw a university listed on there that didn't look too far away and, remembering how good Lewis and Clark had been for us back in Portland, we decided to go check it out.

The British idea of "university," however, turned out to be a much different one than the American idea. There was no campus at all that we could determine; the buildings just scattered around the city streets like any other city buildings. There were no apparent dorms, either, nor student lounges, no libraries for us to melt into. It was obvious that we couldn't hang out anywhere around here so we headed back to the square.

We stopped back into the phone booth there to check the phonebook for any all-night cafes or something but we had no luck. While we were in there, a group of punks came walking down the street toward us and when I first looked up and saw them coming I almost slipped completely from my sanity, as threadbare as it was.

Back in Eureka I had seen a TV special, shortly before we left, on the new punk movement in England, which had forewarned me somewhat of their attitudes and appearance but it couldn't prepare me for seeing them in real life. I had already begun low level hallucinations from the lack of sleep and my chemical imbalances so when I saw these four guys approaching us with their spiked Mohawks and purple Afros on half their heads and safety pins stuck throughout their faces, I was seriously challenged to convince myself that this was real and that I hadn't in fact completely flipped out.

Since we hadn't found anything promising in the phonebook, we took back to roaming the streets again. I was becoming so tired now that I was falling asleep even as we walked, so we stopped to rest for a while.

By 10 p.m. we were no closer to a warm bed than when we'd arrived here 12 hours earlier. We took up a couple of seats on a storefront windowsill together by the side of the street to wait out the night for a while. As we sat there, I looked up to the top of a nearby office building and saw a huge, giant clown up on the roof, peering down at us from about seven stories up. After a quick glance, he'd recoil back out of sight, only to lean over the edge and stare back down at us again a moment later. I sat there for some time watching him, perplexed as to why he was doing that. Glancing over at another building, on the far side of the small plaza that was directly across the street from us, I saw it shooting up out of the ground as though it were an endless ICBM being launched out of a missile silo.

I realized now that I must be hallucinating but just to be sure, I leaned over to Karen and asked her to take a look. She looked over at it and then back at me. "Yeah, so?" "Is it shooting out of the ground?" I asked. She studied it again for a moment before replying dryly, "Yes." "Oh, good," I said to myself half out loud, "I thought I was hallucinating."

I watched it for several more minutes, wondering how it could just keep shooting out like that without ever coming to its end, before my eyes began rolling back up into my head. We picked ourselves up shortly thereafter and continued on until daylight once again illuminated our world.

As soon as it was late enough in the day to not be rude, we resumed our attempts to get hold of Mike but continued to meet with disappointment. We were trapped here now with nowhere to go and nothing to do, all the while our bodies continued to drain themselves of animation. We couldn't leave London until going through immigrations and since we couldn't go through immigrations until they opened again tomorrow morning we had no choice but to keep wandering the streets and hope that one of these times we'd get through to Mike. Of course, we could have spent our money and gotten a hotel or something but our credo was so well ingrained in our psyches by now that the thought never really formed. We spent most of the day loitering around Kew

Gardens and Buckingham Palace. Fortunately, it was a pretty, sunny day, which helped our spirits stay up.

As evening was coming full, we unsuccessfully tried Mike once again and were beginning to fret that it would soon be 11 nights in row with no sleep. We were becoming pretty desperate by now though, so we kept calling every hour. Right around 9 p.m., just as we were thinking that it was useless to keep trying, the bugger finally answered his phone. Our dejection turned to joy when, after a brief explanation of things, he agreed to let us stay the night and gave us directions to his house.

It was way out in the northern suburbs of town, which meant we had to take the tube. Temporarily exempting ourselves from Rule #3, we skipped on down to the nearest underground station and got our tickets. It was our first subway ride ever and it was a little tough trying to figure out the system in our mental condition but we managed and 30 minutes later we were knocking the old boy up.

It was 10 p.m. by now, which didn't leave much time for socializing and considering that our combined I.Q. at the time was somewhere near 15 and dropping, this was fine by us. We couldn't get to bed fast enough. He told us he had to leave for work at seven o'clock in the morning, though, which meant we were only going to get about eight hours of sleep. Eight was a bonanza for us, to be sure, and we were exceedingly grateful for each one of them; still, we were both sorry it couldn't be more like eighteen. In truth though, we were ecstatic to have a bed at all and our bliss grew with each step we took up the stairs to our room until it was with a certain degree of reverence that we climbed into bed for the first time since leaving Sandi's front yard almost a week and half ago.

His guest bed was wonderfully soft and warm and we were both comatose within seconds of hitting its fluffy pillows as we finally allowed ourselves to completely let go for the first time in what seemed like months.

Morning came about forty hours too soon for us that next day. I had sunk into sleep so deeply that I almost needed a couple of electric cardiac paddles to bring me out of it when Mike called upstairs to us that it was time for breakfast (read, time to go). Using all my will, I managed to pry my eyes open and struggle out of it, though it was a monumental effort to leave that bed. Today was Immigration Day, though, a very sensitive and important day for us, and it was imperative that we try and snap some life back into our brains, for we would surely need every neuron we still had that wasn't already past recovery.

This was to be our final and, in many ways, most crucial ordeal of the whole affair. We had to have an entry stamp in our passports if we hoped to get an exit stamp and without an exit stamp we wouldn't be able to leave the country. There was no way that we could avoid having to go down to the immigrations office now, in person, and try to convince them to stamp our passports. Up till now, we'd been pretty much flying by the seat of our pants and relying on our instincts to get us through the obstacles. This was our first encounter where we couldn't just sneak our way through. This time we were going to have to walk into the situation very consciously and deliberately and talk our way through, which is an awful lot harder, and scarier. Not only that but the risks were greater as well. Before we were only violating the policies of a private company but now we were planning on defrauding a first world, sovereign nation. A big difference. We definitely had our work cut out for us today.

After breakfast, Mike showed us on a map how to get to the immigrations office. It was way on the other side of the city, which meant we'd have to take the train there, so we walked on back to the tube station and started our long trek through town. I was glad for the long ride since it gave me just that much more time to come up with a good story and to practice it a few times first. It would be tough, I knew, and I was a bit nervous at the thought of what we were about to do. Not only would I be standing there telling bald-faced lies about something which I knew virtually nothing about but I was going to have to be believable doing it to someone who knew virtually everything about it.

I gave it a lot of thought as we clacked on down the train tracks and, in the end, I felt that I had come up with a somewhat believable story. I wanted to keep it as simple as possible and I figured that the closer it was to the truth the better, for not only would it help lend credibility to our tale but should I have to ad lib at all I would have a lot more material to draw from. The "stupid tourist" ploy had worked so well for us in the past that we decided to stick with it here, too. We figured it was still our best strategy, especially now since, in this case, we really were stupid tourists, albeit lying, cheating, devious ones.

It was late in the morning when we finally arrived at the government building in East Croyden where the main office was and there was already a long line ahead of us waiting to get up to the counter. We fell in at the end and sweated out the long wait. I kept running the story through my head, grateful again for the extra time, so that I'd be as familiar with it as possible when our turn came up. That so much of it was true helped my confidence level tremendously, though not nearly enough to actually make me feel confident.

We were there in line for about a half an hour when our turn came up and the lady at the counter called out, "Next in line." I looked up; the moment of our final ordeal was upon us at last. I swallowed hard as we stepped up to the chest-high counter.

"May I help you?" the lady asked us. Drumming up as much courage, hope and false honesty as I ever had, I made my eyes real big and assumed the stupid look.

With the voice of a perplexed innocent, I replied, "I hope so. I'm afraid we have a problem." I looked over at Karen then back at the lady and continued, "We came in on the QEII last Friday night but we waited until the following afternoon to get off instead of in the morning with the rest of the passengers and when we did the Immigration man had already gone so we couldn't get our passports stamped."

I held my breath. That was it; that was my whole story. I had never dealt with Immigration before and it was entirely possible that in that short little tale I'd already said something that had completely given us away.

The lady eyed us both and chuckled as she said, "Well, I guess you DO have a problem, don't you? Why didn't you get off with everyone else?" I was ready for this one.

"We met a fellow who works on the ship who said he'd give us a ride into London if we waited for him to get off work that afternoon," I replied evenly. It was going well; she seemed to be buying it.

"Well," she came back, "we're going to have to hold your passports here until we get the immigration cards in from the ship."

This one I wasn't ready for and my worst fear now materialized before me. I was going to have to ad lib. I was momentarily stunned but I covered it by making my eyes even bigger yet and looking over at Karen.

"Cards?" I said in mock bewilderment, then, looking back at the lady, "What cards?" "Didn't you fill out the immigration cards on the ship?" she asked. "No," I said slowly, still feigning incredulity. "We didn't see any cards, did we?", I continued as I looked once again over to Karen (who was doing a good job of making big eyes and looking stupid herself).

We, of course, knew exactly what cards she was talking about. We had heard the announcement over the PA system, back aboard the ship, for everyone to be sure and fill out the little, white cards located on our night stands but as we had no night stands we certainly didn't have any little cards either and not having any idea what they were for, we hadn't given them another thought.

"Well," she replied, "now we do have a problem." She paused for a moment as though considering what to do, then excused herself and disappeared into the back of the large office. This was the moment of truth here. The whole of the last 11 days had now come down to this very moment and we were very soon to find out if she was going to bite on our little sack of lies and let us get away with this or not.

A couple of long minutes later, she came back out and asked for our passports. Not sure what this meant or if we'd ever see them again, we promptly handed them over like the obedient supplicants that we hoped she thought we were. She thumbed through each of them and then looked us both over once again, only this time with a more discerning eye. We smiled. So far this could go either way, I was thinking, as she checked the passports again. I was watching her face for any telltale signs of her thoughts but I saw none that would give her away. Then she asked to see our money.

At that moment, I knew in my heart that we had done it. They wouldn't care about our money if they were going to haul us away to the big house, and we eagerly pulled out our huge wad of traveler's checks. We had gotten all of our money converted into 5s, 10s, 20s & 50s back in Charlotte Amalie before we left, which I'm sure made our $1200 look more like $12,000. She riffled through each of our bankrolls then handed them back to us before taking our passports and slipping away to the back office once again. This had to be a good thing. Now our moment was really at hand and the verdict on our fate only a breath away.

She returned a few moments later, still a straight look on her face as she came up to the counter. Then she held out our passports to us, smiled and officially welcomed us into the United Kingdom. Our passports had been stamped and signed, good for six months.

The extreme joy and satisfaction that filled my heart just then fought to emerge but I held them in check as we nonchalantly strolled through the front door of the office and out onto the streets as though this were just another bureaucratic technicality that we'd straightened out. I certainly didn't want to give anything away now.

It was such a tremendous relief, though, to be outside, to be rid of this final burden, to be free and clear. There was no one now to look over our shoulders for, no impending obstacle to plan and prepare for. Suddenly all the anxieties of the past days disappeared into pure joy and glee and a totally exhilarating sense of accomplishment. If my body hadn't been so spent, I would have been jumping up and down and shouting and swinging on lampposts.

But our bodies *were* spent, and our minds numb, so we simply and quietly made our way back to the train station, immersed in the subdued euphoria of knowing that we actually did it. Somehow, beyond all our hopes, we actually pulled this thing off. It was the coup of our lifetimes. I thought of all the naysayers back at Lazio's that had told me I was crazy for thinking I could actually go out into the world with no money and do what I wanted to do. Today, we once again proved them all wrong.

It was with a wonderfully light, if worn, heart that we now clacked back to downtown London on the train. We still had to sign up with the Youth Hostel Association before we could leave town for the rest of the country, and we needed to make some arrangements with the post office so that we could get our things sent up from St. Thomas. It had taken us longer to get through the immigrations, though, than we had planned and by the time we got back to Victoria Station, our stop, it was too late to do either.

It was obvious that we were going to have to spend another night here in London, as much as we hated to admit it. We didn't want to bother Mike again so we resigned ourselves to another night in the cold, deciding this time to just stay there at the train station. We felt perhaps a bit overconfident now that we had a full night's sleep behind us and were legal and we figured we could last one more night on the rough.

And rough it was, too. We had some time to kill so we wandered around in the cold station for a few hours until things finally started to settle down for the night and then found a vacant spot underneath a lamppost to park ourselves until morning. Other young travelers such as us, living on the cheap, had already started to do likewise and find their own spots to unroll their sleeping bags for the night. We were envious of them for their big fluffy bed sacks, for though we too had sleeping bags, ours were still on holiday in the tropics and we had nothing now to shield us from the cold concrete floor of the train station beneath us.

We didn't have a lot of options just now so we simply lay rigid there on the floor like a couple of corpses, with our hands folded over our chests for warmth. After a couple of cold hours of this, Karen got duly inspired and went off to see if she could scavenge us something to lie on. She came back several minutes later with a couple of pieces of cardboard that she'd pulled out of a trash bin somewhere. It wasn't much but it did help soften the cement some and probably even helped insulate too but in both cases, it wasn't really enough to do anything noticeable and the only real benefit, I think, was strictly psychological.

The bobbies that patrolled the station didn't make it any more comfortable there either. Apparently, it was okay to lie about the station but it was illegal to sleep anywhere there so they made it a point as they walked around the place to jostle any sleepers awake, usually by gently kicking them, before walking on. For fear of being hauled away, after all we'd been through so far, we didn't dare let ourselves fall asleep even though, once the bobbies had moved on, most of the other disturbed sleepers simply rolled over and went back to sleep. We did, however, allow ourselves to catch little naps off and on, usually with one of us dozing while the other kept lookout, but somewhere around midnight the bobby patrols all but disappeared so we relaxed some and finally let ourselves attempt some "real" sleep.

I woke up a couple of hours later and realized that our fears had been exaggerated when I saw that virtually the entire floor of this part of the station was lined with brightly colored sleeping bags. They ran along the base of every wall and did wagon wheels around every lamppost. I fell back asleep with the confidence now of knowing that we were at least in good company if not at all in comfort.

It was easy to wake up the next morning as the station came back alive with the jostle and din of people packing up and dashing off to their trains.

We were stiff, tired and cold when we pried our puffy eyes open to the dawn of day but it was with a wonderful sense of peace this morning that we pulled ourselves up from the hard slab that we'd just spent the night on. The peace from knowing that we were free now, that for the first time in what seemed like a long time the day ahead of us was all ours. No longer did we need to bury our already weighted weariness, in that first moment of day, beneath the heavy cloak of wariness before we could allow ourselves to be seen by anyone. No more story rehearsing, no more hiding places, no more scheming and plotting. Our trip belonged to us again and it felt really good, despite the many cricks my body had just discovered.

We packed up our own bags now and left the train station for Trafalgar Square again. There was a post office there that we'd seen earlier, right across the street from the square. Once there, we got ourselves a Poste Restante address (general delivery) and sent off a quick card to Sandi to let her know. After last night, we were pretty eager to get our things back with us.

The postal clerk told us that it would be about a month, though, before anything arrived. This was distressing news but we made the most of it and figured we'd just do a big month-long loop up through England, Scotland, Ireland, Wales and then finally back into London where we'd just grab up our stuff and shoot on over to the continent.

With that settled we set out for our last chore of the day and went off in search of the Youth Hostel office. Luckily, it turned out to be only a few blocks away. Even more luckily, while in there waiting for our turn up at the counter, I spied some odd bits of paper laying on the floor near its base and when I went over and snatched them up I discovered that they were British pound notes, money! About $40 worth, in fact, more than enough to pay for both our membership fees and for a new neck wallet to keep them in. Our first day back in the saddle was getting off to a very good start indeed, I thought.

Now, with our passports and membership cards safely hanging around my neck and under my shirt, we were finally free to leave the big, crowded city of London behind us and go off in search of the bucolic pastures of the rural countryside. Neither of us was much into cities and, after our many months in the tropical sun, the thought of rolling hills of lush, green grass and bleating sheep sounded really good to us right now.

The main artery leading north out of London was the M1 motorway, which was back out near Mike's house so it was a familiar ride for us on the tube. Riding public transportation was now officially back on our taboo list unless, of course, it was free but in this case the only hitching place out of town was at the very edge of town and London was a very BIG town so we made the exception this one last time.

Our good luck was still holding and we got a ride within only a few minutes after getting out there and putting our thumbs up. As we climbed into the guy's car, he asked where we were going and it suddenly occurred to us that we really had no idea where we were going other than "north" so we simply told him that we were going to any town on his way that had a youth hostel in it.

As soon as we were in and moving, Karen and I pulled out our brand-new hostel guidebook to see if we couldn't be a little more specific in our directions and found that virtually every English city had at least one hostel in them, as did most of the towns, it seemed. In fact, there was one coming up in the small village of Copt Oak, we noted, that was conveniently just off the motorway and only a short distance from where our ride was to end.

Our driver knew right where it was and kindly delivered us to its doorstep before wishing us luck and heading off. It was just after 5 p.m. by now, only minutes after the hostel had opened for the evening, and we were the very first ones to register for the night. We signed in, collected our bedsheets and made straight for our respective rooms to pick out our bunks. Since youth hostels keep their dorms segregated, we unfortunately couldn't share a room but under the circumstances that seemed a minor point just now. It was a bed and that was all that mattered.

When I walked into the men's dorm, my pupils dilated at the sight of all those bunk beds scattered around the room. Big, luscious beds. And I could have any one of them that I wanted. [Actually small, saggy beds was more true but at the moment such distinctions did not exist for me]. I chose an upper in the back corner of the room. I wanted to be above and behind any disturbance that the other fellows might inflict to the glorious, unfettered sleep that I was so eagerly anticipating for this night.

In my sleep-lust an element of greed crept into me and I decided to take advantage of the fact that no one else had arrived yet by gathering up several of the extra blankets off the other beds. It was with an ever-growing glee that I spread each

245

one of them over my own until I had a pile of about six heavy, woolen, army-type blankets stacked up on my bed. When I was sufficiently satisfied with the inches-thick stack, I went back out and met up with Karen to fix our dinner. We heated up a can of beans to go on top of our toasted bread and cheese.

It was only about an hour later when we decided to retire for the night. I was so happy at the thought of unlimited, safe sleep and so giddy from the lack of it that, as I crawled under what felt to be about 20 pounds of blanket, the pure joy of the moment caught up to me and I began to giggle uncontrollably. It was a very good thing, I thought, that there was no one else in the room with me (though others by now had checked in), as I surely must have seemed a madman sitting up there in the corner by myself tittering like an excited child. I didn't have long to consider it though for the moment that the last convulsion of giggle quivered from my chest was the very same moment that I fell deeply, divinely asleep.

It wasn't until around nine o'clock the next morning that I finally stirred from my coma. It was so wonderful lounging there in bed afterwards, under all those toasty covers, with no hurries or worries to jab at me and knowing that a hot shower, a real breakfast and my sweetie pie were all waiting for me just on the other side of the wall that I now lay against. The fundaments of reality all boiled down to their very bones for me during those fifteen hours of glorious sleep and I knew now that the simple pleasures in life truly are the ones that make life worth living. Indeed, I believe they just might be the very foundations of happiness itself.

I also learned that absence really does make the heart grow fonder, for I began a love affair that morning with beds and showers that continues with me to this day. So fond was I, in fact, that from that day on I made sure to get anywhere from 12-15 hours of sleep each and every night of the month that we spent here touring through the British Isles and I absolutely adored every single moment of each one.

With our spirits on the mend now and with all the toils and traumas behind us, we hit the road with a renewed, if still bruised, sense of vigor. Life was light again and we were free once more to travel as we felt with unburdened hearts and minds, to explore the new country that was now before us. Other than to the nearby town of Nottingham for the obligatory visit in search of Robin Hood, we didn't know yet where we were going to go but it really didn't matter because for us it was the trip itself that was the adventure, not so much the destinations.

Nottingham proved to be a forgettable place so after an hour or so we took our leave again and continued on our way in the general direction of Scotland, the only real destination we could claim.

When a car stopped for us a few minutes later, and the driver asked us where we were headed we simply shrugged our shoulders and said, "We don't know; where are you headed?" It was a vague answer, to be sure, but it was the only one we could come up with.

As it turned out, though, it was by far the best one we could have hoped to come up with, for it opened up for us such a world of opportunity that would have been otherwise denied us had we given a specific answer. This way we let the people know that we were open to suggestion and allowed them, the ones who knew the area best, to tell us where we should go or where to avoid.

We not only got some great tips and advice this way but, since we likewise didn't have a set time frame to adhere to, it also allowed us the freedom to accept the many kind offers they frequently extended to us along the way.

Sometimes these offers were nothing more than a pint of beer at some roadside pub or an occasional meal. Often we

247

would be treated to our own customized tour of the area. One English fellow told us apologetically that he was on his way home but that if we didn't mind waiting a few minutes while he dropped off his laundry he would take us farther along so that he could show us a few more things he thought we should see. A few times we were even invited along on their own driving holidays, spending the day touring the back roads of remote areas that we'd never have seen otherwise.

It was a wonderful way to travel, for it immersed us into the depths and idiosyncrasies of the people and their country in a way that would have been unavailable to us otherwise. In addition, it gave them the opportunity, and satisfaction, of showing off to a couple of strangers the things that, in their minds, made their country special. Our sincere appreciation of their time and help only seemed to fuel their pride all the more, encouraging them to take us just a little bit farther or to show us just one more thing.

The fellow that picked us up from Nottingham didn't invite us anywhere, nor did he offer anything other than a ride to the town of Matlock Baths, but when he found out how we'd come to England he was so impressed with our story that he slowed down so that he could be sure to hear all of it before dropping us off. We didn't mind though, for we not only enjoyed recounting our exploits but we also much enjoyed the ever-greening countryside that we were passing through on our way to town. We had nothing but time now anyway.

It was early evening by the time we got dropped off in the small, picturesque village of Matlock Baths. A short walk through the quiet town brought us to the hostel where we spent the night.

As nice as the drive into town had been, it was even nicer the next morning when we hiked our way back out along a small winding footpath to the outskirts of town. The intensity that had so recently been such a large part of our daily life was quickly receding now into that of a gentle ramble through the

248

quiet, bucolic pastures that we now found ourselves surrounded by. It was such a delightful relief for us to finally be back in green, rolling countryside again, with trees and rivers and sheep and cows and grass. It had been a year now since we had last seen any of these marvelous things, not since leaving home. In fact, England around here looked quite a lot like Humboldt County. After all that we had been through though, it seemed more like heaven to us right now and our hearts wallowed in all the cool greenness.

We finished up that day in the small town of Castleton, about 40 miles away, and spent another glorious 15-hour night there at its hostel. From there we traveled on through the scenic Peak and Lake Districts as we made our meandering way north, staying at the hostels of Ingleton, Ambleside and Derwent Water before finally reaching the city of Carlisle just across the border of Scotland.

By the end of that first week out of London we were actually approaching normalcy again in the brainwave department. Our rides were easy and good, the hostels numerous and convenient and their beds warm. We were eating cooked food again, too, and regularly. Life slowly returned once again to the carefree nature that was the heart and soul of this trip as we began to settle into the routines of road life.

Even so, it was still a Spartan lifestyle. Living firmly now under the tenets of our Highway Code, we had put ourselves on a five-pound daily budget each (approx. $10) and with the hostels costing around three or four pounds apiece, that only left us another one to two pounds for our food, which ain't much.

In fact, meals were usually little more than bread and cheese. For lunch, we'd normally just eat them straight from the wrapper, often while waiting for rides on the roadside. Originally that's all dinners were as well but that got old pretty fast so we began to make cheese toast instead, just for a little variety. From there we broadened our culinary arts and started putting baked beans on top of that and then finally adding some instant mashed potatoes to crown the whole mess, both of which were available for sale at each hostel. It was actually better than it sounds and after our ocean crossing diet it was grand cuisine for us. Breakfast was usually toast and scavenged jam.

Most of the hostels had a self-serve kitchen, complete with a refrigerator, oven and at least a few banks of hotplates/broilers. One wall of the kitchen was also set up with shelves that were sectioned off into small cubicles. These bins were then used as individual storage cupboards for any of the visitors to use while staying there. Whatever abandoned food that was left over in the kitchen when the hostel closed in the morning was put into a specially marked cupboard and became free to anyone who might want it when the hostel opened up again in the afternoon.

Karen and I made it a point to get to each hostel before it opened for the afternoon so that we could be one of the first ones in. After checking in, while everyone else was running to the bedrooms to grab the good bunks, Karen and I, instead, made straight for the kitchen and scarfed up all the extra tea, sugar, bread, eggs and milk before claiming our beds. It turned out to be a major part of our daily diet and saved us a lot of money.

Indeed, there were many aspects of hostel living that were of great advantage to us. In addition to their abundance, cheap price and free food, they tended to be located in picturesque and often historic buildings and locales. The guide book gave clear directions to all the hostels in the applicable country, making them easy to plan for and to find, and included descriptions of all the local points of interest in the surrounding area, the history, the hiking trails and such. More than all that though, it was a wonderful place to meet other people traveling like ourselves. It was an ever-changing fraternity of kindred souls from all over the world who normally had a wealth of important tips to share about where to go, what to do, who to call or where to look for work. This kind of information was the lifeblood of worldly hobos such as us and there was no single better place to find such quantity and quality of it.

As is usually the case, however, there was a trade-off. Youth hostels, as their name implies, were originally and primarily designed to provide cheap, safe accommodations for young people. In time, though, assumedly in order to fill the surplus beds, they were opened up to all ages, including seniors, but with preference still being given to the young. In truth, however, the great majority of travelers to be found in these hostels were generally in their late teens to late twenties.

Still, in keeping with their original premise they segregated the dorms, lined them with bunk beds and set a curfew of usually around 10 p.m. at which time they locked the doors for the night. Period. If you were unfortunate enough to get locked outside at evening curfew, then you were stuck outside, no exceptions. In the mornings, everyone had to do a "chore" before they could get their membership cards back from the "warden" (manager), normally things like sweeping the floor or wiping down the kitchen appliances, etc. It was hard to feel like an adult under these conditions. We could handle the curfews and chores easily enough but it sure would have been nice to be able to share a room together.

We continued north from Carlisle to Edinburgh and made it there by late afternoon of the same day. There were three regular hostels here in Edinburgh but when we got to the first one we were told that all three were already full for the night. They did have a temporary one set up not far away that they could send us to, however, so off we went.

We found it to be nothing more than an old, rundown boys club in a fairly colorless part of town. The gymnasium had been converted into the boys' dorm with what must have been 50 bunk beds lined up all around the room with two rows running down the middle. It was like camping out in an airplane hangar.

After nabbing what free food was still left and dibbing our beds, we went outside to check out the park next door. It turned out to be a very large lawn-covered lot with a soccer field at one end and a small playground set up in the corner nearest the hostel.

While sitting there in the sunny, late afternoon watching the soccer players, Karen and I digressed into a major wrestle match and thoroughly enjoyed beating each other up. We hadn't wrestled in ages and it instantly took off at least 10 of the 30 years that I had aged since getting on the QEII three weeks earlier. Another ten got knocked off a while later when we went over and put the playground through the hoops.

Karen fell in love with a little girl that was playing there by herself. I think she saw a little bit of herself in this dirty little waif of a girl who was totally lost in her own private garden and just as happy as can be. Karen thought it was her maternal instinct talking. Whatever it was, after watching this smudged little angel in her playful abandon for a few minutes, Karen looked at me and pined, "I waaant onnnnnne."

Back in Florida we had talked about having kids together, after our travels, and had even gone so far as to name them. We'd talked about getting married as well but only if we were to actually have kids. Right now, seeing the longing in Karen's eyes as she watched this little girl, there was nothing more I would have liked to give her than a child of her own. She would be an ideal mother, I thought, and to this day, if I were to ever have kids at all, I would want her to be the one to sprout them.

Our fifteen-hour nights were slowly creeping down to about 12 hours a night now, which allowed us the luxury of staying up that much later before retiring to bed. Being in our first big city hostel we took advantage of our extra time and stayed up in the kitchen that night visiting with our fellow travelers for those few hours before finally heading off to bed.

Sleeping in the gymnasium turned out to be a real treat. Every little noise was annoyingly amplified by the hard, wooden floor, which then echoed throughout the entire room. Snores and grunts rose from every precinct, wafting through the air with nowhere to land, and every time someone rolled over, the squeaking springs of his bed would stir the others who would then roll over themselves creating a self-perpetuating wave of squeaks that would rise into a crescendo before slowly settling back down to give the snores back their turn.

Several months ago, back at the Buccaneer Yacht Club in Florida, I had become casual friends with a couple of construction laborers who were helping with the remodeling of the club's several apartments. They were both aliens working there illegally and when I found out that one of them, Ian, was Scottish, I made it a point to mention that we were hoping to get to Scotland and asked him if he knew of anyplace there where we could likewise find some under the table employment. He couldn't guarantee anything, of course, but he did give me one address and phone number of a friend of his here in Edinburgh (where Ian was from) that might be able to help us out. After taking a day off to explore the wonderful old city, I dug out the crumpled piece of paper with the phone number on it and gave a call to Ian's friend, Douglas. I introduced myself, saying that I too, was a friend of Ian's, and then explained the situation to him.

Douglas listened to my whole spiel and when I was finally done, completely undid my entire prepared delivery when he asked the question that I hadn't planned for. "Ian who?" It wasn't until this moment that I realized I had no idea whatsoever what Ian's last name was and my whole approach here was based on me convincing Douglas that Ian was my good friend.

"You know, Ian," I stumbled as I tried to regain my confidence, "Ian in America."

"Well, I know lots of Ians" he said back to me, flatly, "What does he look like?"

"Uh...," I stammered, "average height, I'd say, um, medium build, you know, pretty regular looking, a real nice guy, you know, Ian."

Actually, I'd all but forgotten Ian in the months since I'd known him and even then it was only very briefly. Fact is, I hadn't a clue what Ian looked like, at least not enough to be able to describe him, but I couldn't let Douglas to know that.

"Well, it might be Ian MacDonald," he suggested after a moment.

"Yes," I jumped in, "that's him. Ian MacDonald, yes!"

Whether it actually was Ian MacDonald or not we never found out but it didn't really matter much because when I called Douglas back a couple of days later, as he'd asked, he offered both of us work anyway. It was for two weeks, packaging bulk foods at his "whole foods" warehouse for resale in his two health food stores, and it was within walking distance from our hostel. It was precisely the kind of job we were hoping for, easy, casual and close. Not only that but there was free food involved, which was always a bonus. I was to start the next day and Karen the day after that.

Karen went roaming around town again by herself that next day while I went off to work. It put her in an off mood for a while but later on she got to play with her little girl in the playground for a few moments which made her happy again.

Work for me that day turned out to be mostly unloading trucks into the warehouse and hauling around big bags and boxes of various foodstuffs. There had just been a big festival of some sort and these were all the leftovers from the booth that Douglas had set up there.

It was a rough start for Karen the next morning. She'd had a very disturbing dream the night before in which her mother died and being as close as she was to her mother, it affected her strongly. She didn't mention it to me though until that evening. Had I known, perhaps I wouldn't have been such a grouch to her that morning as I was. For some reason, things just didn't start out well for either of us that day.

We'd decided to try a shortcut to work that morning that looked good on the map but turned out to be a nightmare in reality. Soon into our trek we came to a disagreement at an intersection in choosing which street we were supposed to take which, in light of our already tenuous dispositions, quickly turned into an argument, a very rare event in our relationship.

Infinitely rarer, however, when she insisted on going her way which I knew to be the wrong way, I lost my temper and yelled at her from across the street, as loud as I've ever yelled at anyone, as she headed away. The only other person to ever see me lose my temper like that was my brother Michael, as he was the only one that could ever provoke me enough to. I suppose it could be argued that feeling comfortable enough in our relationship to scream at her was a sign of closeness but, in my heart, it felt much more ominous than that for some reason and it disturbed me.

Anyway, we continued on, which way I can't now recall, and after picking our way through a hill of thistles we slogged our way through a field of deep mud only to find ourselves stuck on the wrong side of a high fence in a very large train yard. I was wearing my rubber thongs that day and coming up to the yard I stepped on a twig protruding up from the mud, which punctured through my sandal and deep into my foot. We finally got to the warehouse an hour late, muddy, bloody (in my case) and in positively foul moods. Not a very good first day for Karen, I'm afraid.

Later that evening, after returning from work, I went out to the park to lie out in the moonlight and contemplate things. Karen came out a little later and lay down next to me. We both apologized to each other and made up with hugs and kisses. It was all better now as we laid there under our old friend, the moon.

In spite of this reconciliation, however, there seemed now for the first time in our relationship, a slight hint of something amiss on a much deeper level. Though it was unspoken and probably even consciously unrecognized, at least on my part, there seemed to be a vague, impalpable rift developing between us.

We were still having a wonderful, magical time and loved each other more than anything in the world but if there was something missing from our relationship it was here on this day, I think, that the dark seed of disharmony was first cast into our otherwise still bright and shiny relationship. A shine that now glowed, however, with perhaps the faintest hint of tarnish. So faint, in fact, that it only became visible much later when seen through the much clearer eyes of hindsight.

If I had not yet consciously acknowledged something missing in our relationship it was not apparently so for Karen. Her journal entry of the time:

FROM KAREN'S JOURNAL:

[13SEP79] Wanted to talk to Markie the other night, not even real sure what all about but ended up just saying I couldn't talk to him. I just hurt so much sometimes. I'm not sure what I feel and I don't know what he feels and I'm chicken to ask 'cause I won't get an answer of how he really feels or I won't understand it anyway. I don't think that is quite what I want to say so I'll just end that. Goodnight book.

Our jobs turned out to be simple and pleasant enough, if perhaps a bit tedious and boring. We pretty much spent our days there scraping figs out of a big wooden crate and dropping them into individual little bags, or scooping peanut butter out of a five-gallon bucket with an ice cream scooper into glass jars, things like that. There seemed to be a tea break every half hour and there were plenty of free pastries left over from the festival for us to snack on (not to mention all the figs and peanut butter we could handle). The people there were very friendly and accommodating as well. We stayed there at the hostel this first week despite the three-day maximum stay limit imposed by the hostel association. We had become friends with the hostel's two young wardens soon after arriving in town and they knew that we were here to find work so they overlooked the restriction and said we could stay there until the following Sunday when it was to close down for the season.

When closing day arrived, we repaid the favor by volunteering to help break the beds down and clean up the place. We did it to be nice as well as to have something to do that Sunday but we ended up getting our last night's stay for free plus snagging some much needed leftover bits of clothing in the process. We scored a jacket for me, some pants, socks, maps - all kinds of stuff. Since our things from St. Thomas weren't due to arrive for another three weeks, we were grateful for any extra clothing that might help keep us warm in this chilly country.

That Sunday and Monday night we stayed at one of the other youth hostels, one even closer to work, but on Tuesday we moved in with Jackie, a guy we worked with at the warehouse who had offered to rent us a room in his flat. It was cheaper than the hostels and we could share a room together again so we were very happy about it.

He gave us rides to work as well, though it didn't seem to improve our now perpetual tardiness any. As a matter of fact, we had been late to work virtually every single day so far. It went strongly against my own sense of work ethic but it didn't seem to bother anyone else. Indeed, Douglas had even asked us if we could stay on a week or so longer, as he had more work for us if we wanted.

We had already made tentative plans to leave that following Saturday, though, and were looking forward to it, so we politely declined his offer. Two weeks of figs was enough, I thought. We did, however, accept his invitation to come over to his flat for dinner the next evening, with him and his wife, Sandra. We had already agreed to babysit their baby daughter for them that night so that they could go out and enjoy themselves some and they later extended the invitation to include sleeping over afterwards.

Despite staying at the boss's house, we still somehow managed to show up late for work again that next morning. Oh well, we did try. Really.

Things took a very interesting, and rather strange, turn that next night back at Jackie's flat. Not long after the three of us returned home from work, a friend of Jackie's came by unexpectedly. She was a very attractive young German girl and said she needed a place to stay for the night so she asked Jackie if she could crash there. It was fine with him and after introductions went around, the four of us all sat and talked a while.

Suddenly, Jackie got up, saying only that he had to go out for a while, and promptly left us. Not long after that the German girl left the room to go take a shower and was soon followed out by Karen, who went off to our room to write in her journal. I stayed out by myself in the family room by the fireplace.

Several minutes later, the German girl came out from her shower, wearing only a t-shirt and underpants, and lay down on the floor next to me in front of the fire. She lay on her stomach with her feet swaying up in the air above her butt as we talked for a while about ourselves, and it wasn't long before it became obvious what each of us really had on our minds. We retreated a short time later to the living room, closing the door behind us.

Since Karen had told me way back in Florida that she didn't care if I fooled around with other women just as long as it was only recreational and not because I felt that there was something lacking with her. Though I considered this case to be of the former, in retrospect I feel I could have been a little bit more sensitive and discreet. Karen never walked in on us or otherwise interrupted us but she had to know what was going on in there.

This fact became more than obvious to me when we emerged from the living room a while later and went off to our respective rooms. Jackie had since come back home and had quietly gone off to bed already. The German girl went in to join him for the night but immediately came back out, saying that she had to stay in my room because Karen was already in there with him. I hadn't actually made it to my room yet but I knew she couldn't be right. Jackie must have brought someone back with him, I thought, and I didn't believe her but when I went into our room to prove it, it was indeed empty.

Though Karen had the same freedoms as I did in this relationship, I couldn't help but think she was only doing this to get back at me. After her brief fling with the waiter in Portland, I knew that she didn't much care for casual sex and I really didn't think she was at all attracted to Jackie. As nice as he was, I just couldn't see that being the case.

The German girl and I had little choice at this point but to go get into the bed in my room. It was very strange lying in bed with this girl, knowing that Karen was lying in bed with Jackie just on the other side of the wall that I lay there staring at. It was a bad feeling. Something wasn't at all right with this and it held ill portent in my heart. Something felt dirty about all of this and I began to wonder if this was really recreational after all.

The next day was our last at Edinburgh Whole Foods but was otherwise unremarkable. We'd agreed to babysit again that night, this time for Douglas's brother.

It was late when we got back to Jackie's that night so we slept in the following morning to make up for it. We were leaving Edinburgh today and were once again happy to be moving on. As a going away gift, Jackie presented us with some cardboard pieces and a crayon to take with us so to make our hitching signs with. We thanked him for all his help and said our goodbyes before heading off for a "quick" visit downtown to do some last minute shopping before hitting the open road again. I desperately needed to find some new shoes as I had, not too surprisingly, already managed to lose my black cotton Chinese ones from St. Thomas at one of the youth hostels back in England. I had been wearing my old bamboo thongs ever since, but they'd fallen apart so badly by now that it was only a miracle they hadn't crumbled to dust yet. As it was, I could only wear them when I stood still as I dared not walk in them. Karen wanted to get some new shoes, too. She still had her Chinese shoes, as well as some plastic thongs, but now that we were in the real world again she wanted to upgrade to some more normal type shoes.

After checking all the shops on Prince's Street, however, our attempt to re-shoe met with no success and it wasn't until around 4:30 in the afternoon before we finally made it out of Edinburgh.

We got a ride quickly from a young fellow who was very interested in his country's local industries and talked incessantly about them for about a half an hour, pointing out the coal mines, steel factory (largest this side of U.S.), glass works (mostly bottles for Scotch), distillery (Scotch for the bottles), and also the largest chimney in Europe. He did, however, take us to the hostel doorstep in Stirling, which was about 10 miles past his destination so it wasn't so bad. He also threw in a few tads about the local history which we enjoyed.

The hostel was right next to Stirling Castle, one of the main castles in Scotland, and it was quite an old building itself. Many nobles, lords, and princes (later to be kings) had stayed there and is supposedly an architectural showpiece. It was our first stay in a big, stony, medieval place and I found it easy to imagine the lords and ladies of days gone by, walking down the worn steps of the old stone stairway in their big showy costumes as they made their way to some royal party at the castle next door.

The day was cloudy and gray as we left Stirling the next morning for Loch Lomond, our next proposed stop. As was now becoming usual for us, we got rides quickly and found ourselves in the town of Aberfoyle, about 30 miles away, well before lunchtime.

While on a brief break here, we found out that there was a foot trail just outside of town that went straight over the nearby hills and dropped down again right at Loch Lomond and only a mile or so from one of the three hostels that ringed this famous lake of song.

It was still early in the day and we were eager for some exercise so, despite the worsening weather, we opted for a long walk in the country rather than a quick drive and left directly for the trail head, which itself was about a mile away at the relatively small but very pretty Loch Ard.

A light but steady rain had begun to fall by the time we got to the trail head but we'd already come this far so we continued undeterred on our overland trek through the countryside and up the thousand-foot-high shoulder of the mountain known as Ben Lomond that stood between us and the bonny, bonny banks of Loch Lomond. In fact, the rain seemed to fit the countryside very nicely as we ambled through it and, ever since our used clothing bonanza back at the boy's club in Edinburgh, we had plenty of warm clothes now to keep us comfortable if not particularly dry.

For the first several miles the trail was a flat and relatively dry dirt roadway that was easily walked. Occasionally, we had to duck under cover when the rains swelled but never for more than a few minutes. The plastic bags that we were still using for luggage were now much heavier with all our new booty stuffed in them and seemed to grow even more so with each mile we walked. I had to switch my bag from hand to hand as the holes that served as the handles were stretching out thin and began cutting into my fingers if I held it in one place too long. Its weight was also throwing my walking balance off so I ended up carrying Karen's bag for a while, too, just to even me out. Still, dampness and baggage aside, it was a pleasant walk.

After about six miles, however, the trail broke off from the flat roadway and became instead a small, muddy footpath that immediately began a steep four-mile climb up one of the foothills of Ben Lomond. Soon we began to come upon many small to medium creeks running down from the hillsides, severing our path, and at least a couple of places where the trail simply disappeared into a bog, forcing us to pick our way upstream to a point where we could safely wade through it.

It was early evening by the time we finally made it to the top of the ridge and we were relieved now to know that it was all downhill from here. As it turned out, however, this last mile of the mountain trail was by far the most treacherous of all.

It was not only growing dark out now but the wind had whipped up dramatically on this side of the mountain and navigating down the slimy, boulder-strewn trail became a real challenge as the 40 miles an hour gusts slapped us from behind, rudely, and dangerously, testing our balance. I, who sometimes slip but rarely fall, fell twice going down that trail, giving my already soaked clothes a good covering of mud in addition to also wrenching my toe (I was barefoot, of course) and slightly twisting my knee.

Karen, on the other hand, seemed to have no problem at all getting herself down the mountain and was far ahead of me most of the time--in fact, usually out of sight from me. I could always hear her, though. Being playful as ever, she kept taunting me on by singing out "See yoouu laaay-teeeerrrrrr" every few minutes in a sort of Dennis the Menace singsong way as she disappeared farther away into the darkening rain, challenging me to catch up. It worked, too. I became more and more determined to close the distance but, alas, I never did catch her. It also worked once again in keeping our senses of humor about us and making fun out of what would otherwise be a very unpleasant time.

It was about 7 p.m. when we finally got to the roadway at the bottom of the mountain. The hostel was still another mile farther down the road at the north end of the lake, but after what we'd just been through, the flat, paved road we were now on was a breeze.

We were wet, tired, muddy and cold as we walked that twelfth and final mile in the darkness of night, but at the end of it, sitting all alone at the end of the road, the warm lights of the hostel beaconed out through the blackness to welcome us in. I couldn't drop my ten pence pieces into the coin-operated shower fast enough that night and when I crawled into my dry, blanketed bunk, no one could have been more content with the world than I.

The next morning, we gathered our still-wet clothing, put on the only dry spares we had and made our way back down the lonely stretch of road that we had come in on the night before. There were no cars out there and we had to walk a few miles of it before one finally came by. Luckily, the fellow driving it stopped for us and took us down around the bottom of the lake and over to the other side of it where the highway coming north out of Glasgow was.

Though the day had started out sunny, it had quickly turned wet again and by the time we got to the "town" of Tyndrum,

50 miles later, it was raining buckets. We had decided today to head over to the seaside town of Oban, over on the west coast, and this was where we were to change highways for the one going west.

Tyndrum, it turned out, was nothing more than a tourist shop with an adjoining cafeteria, which is where Karen and I immediately set off running for as soon as we got out of the car. We had made some good miles today, so far, and figured we could afford to hang out for a while in there until the rain lessened enough to come back out and continue on our way to the sea.

The place seemed to be designed strictly for casual roadside business and was doing a bang-up business on this gray, rainy day, much of it from the tour bus traffic that stopped here. We managed to find ourselves a table, though, up by the front window where we could sit and watch the rain. Considering all the circumstances we decided that our strict budget could accommodate a couple of teas to enjoy the rain with so we happily went up and ordered ourselves "a cuppa."

Over a half an hour later, with our teas long gone, we found ourselves still waiting for the rain to let up, but with no change in sight. We then got the brilliant idea of hitching from inside the cafeteria rather than out in the cold. There were, after all, many people coming and going from this place and surely at least some of them must be going to Oban. At any rate, we had nothing to lose so we removed ourselves to the small anteroom where the main entrance was, put a cardboard sign on our laps with "Oban" scrawled on it and waited there on a small bench right next to the front door.

Never ones to sit still when we could be playing, we soon lapsed into a sit-down version of rassling right there on the bench, oblivious to those people around us that were busy coming and going, as we poked and tormented each other.

We weren't so lost in our digressions, though, that I didn't notice, briefly, an elderly woman eyeing us from across the room. I figured she was just staring at us in some sort of bewilderment as people, for reasons still unknown to me, were wont to do with us and so relapsed into our frolic. A short while later, a tour group began forming to leave and it became apparent that our "distant admirer" was with this group as they began to file out the door next to us.

We were still sitting there playfully abusing each other as she made her way toward the door. Before exiting, though, she stopped and smiled as she confessed to us that she had indeed been watching us earlier. She told us that we reminded her of her grandchildren. She added that her group was heading for Oban, too, and then flattered us by saying that, if it was up to her, she would let us have the two empty seats on their bus. This was the last thing we expected her to say and we were very surprised and touched by it. She was a sweet woman and we thanked her as best as we could for the thought before she slipped out the door with the rest of her group.

We, of course, immediately resumed our play as soon as she left but were surprised once again, when only a couple of minutes later, the door swung open and our new "grandma" came busting back in.

She hurriedly told us to get our things together, that they were indeed going to give us a ride to Oban and that the bus was waiting for us outside. She explained to us, as we quickly grabbed up our things, that when she'd gotten on board the bus she asked the driver if it wouldn't be okay to take us along. He explained that it wasn't up to him and that she'd have to get permission from all those in the group. So, she then turned and asked this entire busload of people if any of them minded picking up a couple of strays. None of them apparently did so she quickly hopped off the bus and ran in to get us. We were literally dumbstruck as she now ushered us out the door.

As soon as we walked outside, I looked up to see the entire busload of people, sitting there with their faces pressed to the windows, staring at us, undoubtedly trying to figure out just what this lady saw in us.

I'd never before felt so pitiful as I did at that moment, walking up to the door of that bus. We were halfway wet and wearing our old, dirty, torn clothes since our clean ones were still wet from the previous day's washing. I was one week into a new beard and was wearing Karen's two-sizes-too-small, worn pair of red rubber thongs because my bamboo Jap flaps had finally disintegrated. Now here we were, getting onboard a brand new, shiny tour bus with 60 well-dressed old English people out for a week's holiday.

The empty seats were in the very last row of the bus and everyone was still curiously staring at us as we walked down the aisle to take them. They were smiling, though, and greeted us as though we were some kind of celebrities as we went past each row. It was a very strange and awkward moment but we were glad for the ride and the people were all extremely nice to us so we didn't complain at all.

We took our seats in the back, alongside another couple, and we made ourselves comfortable as we prepared to enjoy the ride. Looking up to the front, "grandma" was there smiling and waving at us, obviously very pleased with herself.

Oban was about an hour away so we sat back and enjoyed the rainy day, the comfy bus and all the candy that the couple sitting next to us kept giving us. I think we became everyone's surrogate grandchildren on that ride, as we were immediately accepted as part of the group, although one man did ask us if we were hijackers. He was just joking, though that's certainly what we must have looked like. They asked our names, too, and where we were from. They were all interested to hear that we were from California and the bus driver made some special comments over the loudspeaker about the countryside for the benefit of "the two Californians in the back" as well as a few jokes about sunny California weather (it was still pouring outside).

It was a very interesting ride for me and I found that it gave me a good counterpoint to the trip. As a hitchhiker, you are part of the environment and interactive with it, whereas tourists on a bus generally just sit there staring out the windows with dulled faces as the world shoots past them and never really getting an opportunity to experience any of it. Because of this, I was always a little bit smug about tour busses and never liked them much. Right now, however, as I watched the incessant deluge outside from the comfort of this nice, big, warm and dry shiny bus, I decided that I had participated quite enough with my environment here lately and that, sometimes, being chauffeured through it can indeed be a good thing.

When we got to Oban, the bus driver, while announcing all the pubs and restaurants in town, made it a point let us know where the discos were, too, and was kind enough to let us off on the corner nearest to the youth hostel so that we wouldn't get too wet getting there.

If we had been celebrities when we had gotten on, we were near superstars when we got off. As we walked down the aisle way toward the exit, everyone in turn made it a point to say goodbye and wish us well, a few of them even shaking our hands. We, of course, made sure to stop and thank our new grandma before getting off, who was still very much enjoying her own goodwill.

Once off, they all waved to us again through the windows while we stood waiting for the bus to pull away and even then, as the bus drove away down the street, we saw the old man who we'd sat next to in the back, waving to us backwards, over his shoulder all the way.

It was pretty incredible and I had a hard time, standing there on the rainy sidewalk, accepting how unusually bizarre this day was turning out to be but at the same time was damn glad for it. We walked the two blocks to the hostel, getting totally soaked in the process, of course, and checked ourselves in for the night.

It was a beautiful morning when we woke the next day. The kind of sunny morning that can only come on the heels of a big rainstorm. A fishing village on the Firth of Lorne just before it becomes the Caledonian Canal, Oban proved to be pretty nice on its own accord.

After breakfast, we went and explored the local castle ruin, just down from the hostel, and sat up on its hillside, looking out over the bay and the islands below while catching a much-needed dose of sunshine before resuming the highway. We were heading for the infamous Loch Ness today and ended up hitching from the very same spot where the bus had left us off the day before. We wondered if we would catch it again on its way out. We hoped so.

Though none of them were chauffeured busses, our rides that day were nonetheless easy and we got to the Loch Ness hostel just in time to raid the kitchen cupboards so we had no complaints, excepting maybe the clouds that had moved in. The hostel was quite nice, in a humble sort of way. It was built cabin style to fit the forested, lakeside setting it was in, all paneled in wood and had plenty of windows to sit and monster watch from. Look as we did, though, we never did spot old Nessie.

The sun was ablaze again the next morning and it shone down through the tall evergreen trees around us as we stood there on the highway, right outside the hostel's front door, with our thumbs poised toward Inverness, our next proposed target. We never made it there, though, and ended up, instead, riding off with a couple of Englishmen who were out on a driving holiday of Scotland.

It was a great ride. They took us along with them out through the countryside on a variety of small back roads that we wouldn't have been able to see otherwise. Their plans were indefinite, too, and after stopping at a local pub and treating us each to a beer, they decided on a route that would take us to the small town of Bonar Bridge, whose hostel was located in a castle just outside of town.

Carbisdale Castle has the distinction of being one of the last castles built in Britain, somewhere in the 1800s. Rather than being made of cold, dark blocks of stone like the old castles, this one was painted and full of windows. It was still cold, both in feeling and in appearance but that was mostly because of the desolate and remote part of the country it was in as well as from the many white marble statues that stood so deathlike in the bays of its windows. It would have been more fun, I think, if it had been a dark, old, stony medieval type castle but we enjoyed this one, too, as it was another wet, cold and stormy night.

I couldn't help but think of spooks as the wind howled outside on the lonely, deserted moor, causing the door in my room to rattle and quiver. I really thought of them when my bed made some peculiar noises and movements later, without any help from me.

Leaving Carbisdale Castle that next morning was a virtual repeat of the morning before. It, too, started out sunny and, once again, we got a ride from a couple that were out on a driving holiday. This time, though, it was from a Scotsman who was showing his Israeli woman friend around for the day. They, too, were just cruising around with no place in particular to go and invited us along for the ride. They took us on a wonderful drive up through the rugged and remote northwest corner of Scotland and then partway down the west coast.

Such an intense, yet intriguing sense of desolation hung with me throughout the whole drive as we saw almost no people or civilization during most of it. On top of that, the weather had, as was becoming usual, steadily worsened and by that afternoon it was raining hard with near gale force winds, which only made this whole corner of Scotland seem even more lonely.

We stopped at one place alongside the road to watch a waterfall pouring off a nearby cliff only to have the howling wind catch hold of it and blow it right back up into the sky where it immediately disappeared, scattering into the driving rain.

The rain blasted noisily at our windows as we sat there watching this impressive show and the powerful wind kept batting at the little car, rocking it as though it was trying to knock us out of the way. Watching this swirling tempest outside, I was once again thankful that we were safe from all of it, here inside the warm car. It was definitely not the kind of weather, I thought, that I'd want to be out in.

We continued, winding our way through this remote, barren landscape. We were in Gaelic country here, that part of Scotland so cut off from everyone else that the people who lived here still spoke the old tongue as their primary, and often only, language. Within only a few miles we came up to a marked intersection and, not certain which way to go, our driver pulled over to check his map.

The only sign of human existence here was a single, small house just down the road from us and very oddly, I thought, a bright red London phone booth right next to us on the side of the road. It was very surreal looking, standing out there all by itself, this fire-engine red box glowing against the backdrop of dark, gray sky and wet, brown moor. I tried to imagine what it must be like to live out here in this empty, treeless, storm-tossed land, how terribly lonely it must be.

Suddenly, snapping me out of my musings, our driver looked up from his map and said to us, very matter-of-factly, "This is where you get out."

We were stunned. He'd told us earlier that he was going to take us all the way into Ullapool, a small fishing village on the coast there and the only town anywhere near here that had a hostel. But now, for reasons he didn't share with us, he changed his mind and decided to take his friend the other way instead.

The thought of leaving the safety and warmth of the car, that which only minutes ago I had been so deliciously savoring, and having to stand out in the brutal, intimidating elements that raged around us was not at all a pleasant one. We stalled as much as we could but we had, of course, no say in the matter and so we begrudgingly got our things and climbed out of the car. I had to hold the door tightly with both hands as I got out but I'm not sure now if it was to keep it from blowing off or me from blowing away.

As the car drove away down the road, leaving us feeling very alone and vulnerable, we made a dash toward the phone booth, literally the only shelter that was available to us out here. As bizarre as this contraption seemed, way out here in the middle of nothing, we thanked God for it as we ran up to hop inside. But, alas, we'd said our thanks too early for, to our great dismay, when we anxiously pulled on the door it refused to yield. The blasted thing was locked! We had no choice now but to simply stand behind it instead.

It was fortunate for us now that the wind was blowing so strongly because it was making the rain "fall" straight sideways, allowing us to hide behind the sheltered side. Not so fortunately, however, every time we peeked around the corner of the booth to check for any approaching cars, the rain hit us square in the face, stinging like needles and making it hard to open our eyes enough to see. When we did see a car coming, we'd quickly run out to the roadside and put our thumbs out while bracing ourselves against the wind.

We were definitely a sight to behold out there, two hunched-over Yanks standing in a gale force storm wearing nothing more than jeans, sweaters and our plastic thongs, trying to thumb down a ride in this otherwise deserted no man's land. Needless to say, what few cars did come by only slowed down long enough to gawk at us for a moment before stepping on the gas and speeding away.

Luckily, a lorry (semi-truck) stopped and picked us up before we'd been out there too long and took us all the way on to Ullapool, about 15 miles away. We were so wet and cold by the time we got the ride, though, that when we got in the cab of the truck we completely fogged up the windows, making it nearly impossible to see out of. The driver flipped his defroster on high but our dampness overpowered even this and I was embarrassed every time the poor guy had to lean over the steering wheel to wipe off the windshield enough so he could see the road ahead. I don't think he was too terribly sure of us either. He didn't say very much to us during that half hour ride into Ullapool and would occasionally look over at us with a funny look on his face.

Our next day was a long one and rides were harder to come by as we meandered our way along the still sparsely populated coast. The weather was changing on a regular basis between rain and sun as we hitched and hiked our way toward the village of Torridon, about 75 miles farther down the coast from Ullapool.

On one of our rides, an older fellow who was riding shotgun noticed that I was wearing only my thongs for shoes and asked if I wasn't cold. I told him no but he must not have believed me for a few minutes later he leaned back and gave me a pair of socks to take with me. They were extras, he said, and insisted that I take them, so I did.

Winding down through a long, narrow and very steep valley, we got to the hostel in Torridon late that afternoon, with clouds and rain and mist to greet us. It was a small hostel and looked almost insignificant sitting up all by itself on a barren little hill just before town. It welcomed us in anyway and we were quick to take our showers to warm us up from the dismal weather outside. The whole front of the hostel was done up in big picture windows and we sat there in the main room watching the swirling, gray rain clouds outside as we ate our dinner in comfort before retiring a short while later. It had been a long day.

The morning was awash in brilliant sunshine when I awoke the next day and I was shocked when I saw that those picture windows that had been so gray and drippy the night before now looked directly upon a range of statuesque mountains right square in front of the hostel. In fact, the bright sun made the whole area look like an entirely different place from the night before. The mountains were very steep and devoid of any visible plants or trees. High up on the barren, rocky slopes were caps of gleaming white snow, looking as if someone had just dusted them with a flour sifter. It was all quite beautiful and we very much enjoyed our hike out that morning as we wound our way down through the winding glen at their feet.

Things yet again worsened quickly, though, as the weather turned wet and cold. Rides were even worse today, being short and hard to get and several times we had to hike a few miles in between them.

On one of these hikes a car sped past us and then suddenly stopped. As the car then backed up to us, we could easily see that this little British car was virtually full already and I was surprised to see when it finally reached us that the three people inside looked to be in their fifties and were obviously middle class. Something was peculiar here. They weren't the sort of people that we would normally expect to pick up hitchhikers, especially funny looking ones like us, but a ride is a ride when you're desperate.

After cramming ourselves into the crowded little car, we were even more surprised to find out they were all from New Jersey! This was definitely unlikely and more than just a little bit strange, I thought.

As soon as we started back down the road, though, the driver explained everything to us. They were here, it turned out, on a driving holiday and had passed us on the road earlier that afternoon. He then explained further that he'd long had a personal rule that he would never pass the same person twice on a road without picking him up. It was kind of like an omen or something to him. Whatever it was, we were thankful for it. Particularly later when we stopped at a small seaside town to get out and look around and they treated us to some ice cream and cookies. They ended up taking us all the way into Kyle of Lochalsh, where we spent the night. The hostel there was old and dingy, matching the gray, wet weather very nicely.

After a quick tour the next morning of the landing where the ferryboats to the Isle of Skye dock, we continued on our way south. We were finally back on a main highway again, where rides were once more easy and long. Kyle of Lochalsh was only about 40 miles away from the very same highway that had, four days ago, taken us from Oban to Loch Ness and our first ride of the day brought us to it quickly. When we passed through the small junction town of Invergarry early that day, we completed in that moment our loop around the entire Northwest Highlands and were now back in the mainstream traffic of Scotland.

Our next ride brought us down through Ft. William, the gorgeous area of Glencoe and right through our favorite spot of Tyndrum. Our driver was a fascinating man. He was a Scottish Nationalist and was very proud of his heritage. As we passed through the countryside, he pointed out to us places of historical interest and told us stories of the area. He told anti-English jokes and even played for us a cassette tape he recorded at his family's most recent céilidh (a big, drunken clan party from what we could ascertain). He was a very friendly man and an entertaining and enlightening host. It was a wonderful way to drive through this beautiful countryside.

Ever since arriving in Scotland our rides had consistently warned us to stay out of Glasgow, that it was a dangerous city.

It was now looming ahead of us and as we neared it we became a little worried that we might get stuck in it. Fortunately, we got a ride well north of the big city that took us all the way through it and out the other side, well into the farmlands to the south.

Earlier that day Karen had found a rock on the roadway that for some reason she'd decided she quite liked. She took it up and named it "Jacque, the rock" and it immediately became a special stone for her, though I must confess that it seemed awfully ordinary to me. Standing here now amid the pasturelands, waiting for our next ride, she took it out and started kicking it up and down the highway as if it were a soccer ball while I manned the thumb to the passing cars.

It was only a few minutes later that a car stopped for us and, in the rush to get inside, Karen forgot to collect her rock again and left it behind, sitting all alone in the middle of the road. It wasn't until we stopped for the night in the town of Ayr that she realized that she'd left her treasured stone behind. She felt really bad about it and pined for it all that night.

I didn't realize just how much it meant to her, though, until the next morning when she told me she was going to go back out and get it before we continued on our way south. I thought it was a pretty silly idea; after all it was just a plain stone, but I couldn't very well tell her no and if I said she was crazy it would only make her smile real big. Besides, I was used to her odd bits. In fact, I admired and loved her for them.

She didn't ask me along and it became clear that she intended to go alone so I settled in for the morning with a tea and a book, there in the common room at the hostel, and waited while she hitched the 20 miles or so back to her little rock. I must say that I didn't hold out much hope for her finding it, however.

About an hour later, she came walking back in and answered my unasked but obvious question with a big, self-satisfied smile as she held her precious treasure up for me to see. I looked at it again to see if there was something about this rock that I hadn't noticed before that had made it such a prize to her but, alas, I still thought it looked ordinary.

It was about midday when we arrived in the port town of Stranraer and caught the ferry over to Larne on the east coast of Northern Ireland, arriving there around three o'clock that afternoon. It was windy and rainy when we got there and hitchhiking was very slow. We only made it as far as Ballygally that first night, a mere three miles away, and with the gloom of night already descending.

In the morning, we looked over our map and chose, as our next target, the town of Donegal, about 125 miles away over on the northwestern coast. It was an ambitious goal making up that many miles but we were confident that we could achieve it without much trouble and set out right after breakfast. From there we thought we'd move south through the bottom half of the country to Rosslare and then ferry over from there to Wales, where we'd spend a couple of days touring until it was time to return to London to pick up our things from the post office, which were due to arrive right about that time.

It was a good plan and would've been very enjoyable if it had only worked out that way. As it happened, though, the weather stayed wet and windy and our rides continued to be difficult for some reason. By the end of our first full day here we had made it only to White Park Bay, a whopping 30 miles down the road from where we started that morning.

The hostel was still closed when we arrived there, about a quarter to five, so we just stood out there in the front yard with the other two hostellers that showed up shortly after us, and enjoyed the wonderful view around us.

The hostel here was a small, new one and perched right on the very edge of a steep rock cliff that dropped straight down into the blue bay below. The view from here was absolutely gorgeous, looking up and down the miles of sheer cliffs that are the northern boundaries of this country. Reaching across their tops, and right up to the edges of these cliffs, were the thick green pastures of the local farms. The Autumn sun, which was now trying hard to pry its way from the dark clouds, dropped big columns of sunbeams down here and there to sweep across these fields with the brilliant, yellow light of late day, as if it were scanning the countryside, looking for something lost. A beautiful rainbow appeared over the fields briefly before quickly fading away again. We watched all of this in silence while we waited.

We only made about 20 miles again the next day but mostly, this time, because of a five-mile hike we took along a small foot trail that followed the cliffs along the coast. The hostel we found ourselves at that night was out in the country and had the distinction of being the oldest one in Britain. It was a small, dark, unheated stone house with worn, dirty wooden floors and a thatched roof. It was once a crofter's (shepherd's) house a few hundred years ago and certainly looked the part, I thought.

There was only one guy in there when we arrived, older than most of the people we usually ran into in our limited experience with youth hostels, including ourselves. At first, we thought he was the warden but he told us that no, the warden actually lived farther down the road and that we'd have to go to her house to register for the night. He was just a hostler himself although he was, as it turned out, living there semi-permanently while working at the warden's potato farm. We dropped our things off and then walked on down the quiet, little country road to the warden's farm and up the drive.

As we made our way to the front door, we passed a dilapidated old shed with an ancient-looking tractor parked in its open doorway. Inside, from behind the tractor, a freckly little boy with bushy red hair peeked bashfully out of the shadows and smiled at us as we walked by. The whole scene was straight out of National Geographic magazine, I thought at the time, looking like depression era Appalachia, or at least what I thought it must have looked like. The photographer in me really liked it here.

An old man answered the door and let us in. I was barefooted, as usual, and when he noticed he looked kind of bewildered at my feet and then walked off around the corner to the kitchen, chuckling, leaving Karen and me standing there at the entry way. We heard him talking to someone in there, though we couldn't make out what they were saying. A moment later, as we were standing there waiting, an old woman's head peeked out around the corner at us and then looked down to my feet. It wasn't hard to guess what he'd said.

She then came out from around the corner, chuckling as well, and after a brief discussion about my lack of shoes, said to me in that cheery, Irish lilt, "Well, it'll make ya hardy." She was the only person I'd ever come across in all the years that I'd gone barefooted (which is most of my life) who saw it in the same positive terms that I did, and I much admired her for that.

She turned out to be as cheery as her accent and happily signed us in for the night. We then bade them both goodnight and walked out, past the little boy (who was still peering at us from the shadows), and back up the road for a dark, cold night in our ancient, dirty little cottage. Though it was somewhat squalid, we still did enjoy its otherwise humble charm.

The fellow who was living there told us that we could get work in the potato fields if we wanted and, in truth, the offer was inviting but we were too fresh from work in Edinburgh and didn't want to stop so soon to take another job, so we declined the opportunity. It would've been an interesting stop, though, if cold and muddy, had we chosen to stay and live there in this old house. Maybe next time, I thought.

We finally made it to Donegal that next afternoon, only two days behind schedule. We'd since found out the reason why rides had been so hard for us to get here. Lord Mountbatten, a high-ranking English aristocrat and politician and cousin to the queen, had just been blown up in Northern Ireland by the IRA about a week prior to our arrival, which had raised the tension in the area quite a bit. To make it even worse, the Pope was due to arrive in Ireland in only a week's time hence, which obviously added to the nervousness going around. I guess picking up two young strangers at such a time in their history was not a real safe bet in many people's eyes.

In fact, back in Scotland, we had been worried about how to get ourselves through the dangerous spots of this country and had chosen the ferry to Larne so we could avoid having to take the one that would have landed us in Belfast, a city which we had heard too many bad things about back home. The road from Larne, however, brought us through Londonderry instead, which wasn't exactly unknown to us either, being the proving ground of many mad IRA bombers, and we weren't too sure how we were going to get through it.

We were fortunate though to have gotten a ride from a middle-aged fellow who not only was going all the way through Londonderry but also just happened to be a border guard between the two Irelands. He was stationed at the edge of town and was on his way to work.

He was a friendly guy and we enjoyed chatting with him as we made our way through the city. While driving down one busy street, I was interested to see an English soldier standing on the sidewalk in front of a building holding a machine gun across his chest. I pointed him out to Karen because it was the first time I had seen such a thing in the middle of a big city and we both looked out at him as we drove by. He was obviously guarding the doorway to what must have been an important building but I soon realized that he was doing much more than that for, when he noticed us looking at him as we drove by, he raised his gun and aimed it straight at us. Holding it tightly, he followed us with his gun sight all the way to the end of the street, until we were out of sight.

I knew then that he was really out there guarding his own life, standing there alone on a busy sidewalk, just waiting for someone to drive by and shoot him dead where he stood. In his mind, I'm sure that we, two young people watching him from a passing car and with too much interest, became the ones that just might do it and he wasn't going to take the chance that we weren't.

It was a very sobering realization for me that life in other places, especially modern, civilized cities in modern, civilized countries, could be so tenuous, so threatened, or so violent that it would require machine gunners stationed next to your supermarket to protect it. Americans, I thought right then, were pretty spoiled.

Later that day, while we stood hitching at the roadside on the outskirts of town, a troop truck came past us on its way to somewhere. Looking at the soldiers riding in back as it went by, I was struck by the cold, steely, even frightening, looks on their faces. Looks that I couldn't help but feel were only hiding their fear and resentment, perhaps maybe even hatred.

It was thus easy to see why our rides through this area may not have been so great. In fact, we were so far behind schedule already, and with no change visible in the near future, that we begrudgingly changed our plans that night in Donegal to forego the rest of Ireland and just head back to Scotland via the same route we had just come. It was something we both hated to do, backtracking that is, but there wasn't much alternative for us. Our original plan gave us a week to tour the entire country and now, four days later, we had only barely made it from the northernmost coast.

The sun had come out that next day and we had a real pleasant walk into town after checking out of the hostel that morning. Mostly pleasant, I should say, at least for me, because I was still suffering from the sore foot I'd gotten when I fell on Ben Lomond. It felt as though I had broken a small bone on the little toe side of my foot, which caused me to hobble a little bit on that side of my walk. My other foot had a small puncture on the bottom of it which had collected a small stone in it that I couldn't get out and which made me hobble on the other side as well.

Karen was happy though. She'd found a rainbow colored wool blanket in the hostel the night before that she liked a lot. So much so that she swiped it the next morning and now had it crammed in the little bag that was her suitcase. I'm still not sure how.

We came across a laundromat while walking through the pleasant little town and decided to take advantage of this rare find and do some laundry before heading out early that afternoon. We were aiming for the hostel listed in our book as Learmount Castle. It sounded cool. It wasn't very far, in fact, from the crofter's cottage that we'd stayed in two nights ago.

One of our first rides was from a couple of old men in an old car, and they were a real hoot. They were both in their nineties, bald headed and wearing woolen driving caps. From the back, they looked virtually identical.

They were both quite jolly (in an old, feeblish kind of way) and were laughing and joking the whole time. One of them left his mouth hanging open most of the time. Not in a slobbery, senile way, though. It was more like a long, drawn out laugh, for his eyes never stopped twinkling. I could see in the rearview mirror that the driver, too, had a constant smile on and whenever we said anything about ourselves he would chuckle and say, "Surely to goodness." In fact, he said it so much during the course of our ride that it became our next adopted motto and for months afterwards our standard reply to anyone was "ah, surely to goodness."

A few miles down the road they stopped for a minute at an old farmhouse and honked their horn. We waited there in the car with them wondering what was up when an old, bent woman came out and walked over to us. The two men teased with her a bit before dropping off an empty egg carton and some money while she leered suspiciously at Karen and me in the back seat. Once on the road again they told us she was getting old (80) and had lots of land with no one to follow her. At this remark, the fellow with the hanging mouth started to rub his hands together, in mock greed, and made jokes about getting her to leave it to him, again with a twinkle in his eye. At this, they both started laughing and shaking their heads again. They were something. I just hope I'm that happy when I'm 90. Surely to goodness, I do.

We hitched all afternoon and made it to Learmount Castle just as it was starting to get dark. Once we got inside, we were shocked to find out that a Guru Maharaji meditation group had rented the whole hostel and, although there were several vacant beds, they did not want any outsiders disturbing them and wanted us to leave.

This Rent-A-Hostel scheme was a new idea by the hostel association to bring in some off-season money and the old woman who served as warden here didn't really understand that they had rented the entire hostel and that it was really their choice whether we stayed or not. Not only that, but she thought, somehow, that they were a Christian group and when they said they didn't want anybody else here she really let them have it. She went on for several minutes in a heated monologue, talking of God, brotherhood and the like, and when she was finally done they sheepishly relented and said they would be delighted to have us stay. Not that they were so inspired by this old woman's sense of religious ethics, but I think more just to get some peace and quiet from her.

Actually, had it not been so late and had we not been miles from anywhere else we would have gladly left but as it was, our only other recourse would've been to sleep outside, which we were loath to do. Fortunately, two other hostlers looking for shelter had shown up by this time, so we didn't feel quite so imposing.

After all was settled, Karen and I went for a walk down by the river that ran through the grounds. The sun had just gone down and the gathering gloom of dusk gave a creepy look to the old estate. Adding to the overall effect were hundreds of crows that were for some reason converging on the place and landing in a small clump of nearby trees. Several groups of birds were flying straight in toward us from all directions, silhouetted against the darkening sky, and reminding me, eerily, of the flying monkeys in the Wizard of Oz. Once in the trees, they jumped from limb to limb and tree to tree, several birds at a time. And all the time cawing and squawking. It was bizarre.

We spent a while exploring the mostly forested grounds and then retreated indoors and found that the insides of the hostel did little to dispel the eeriness of the outside. It was a large, old place. Cold and dark and dreary. I went up to my room a short while later and noticed the paint peeling off the walls as I climbed the creaky wooden stairs. The old, faded wallpaper in my room was also peeling off. I climbed into my saggy bunk, with a cacophony of squeaks, to do some reading before turning in for the night but the one gaslight in my room only put out a dim, yellowish light, leaving the corners of the room in shadows, and making it too difficult to read by so I gave up and turned in. I lay there for a while, listening to the creepy sounds of the old manor, thinking again of spooks, before finally falling asleep.

The sun was waiting for us to get up the next morning and after our breakfast we went down to the small river that ran through the grounds and behind the manor to await its rise

283

over the treetops. Across the river was a small meadow surrounded on three sides by the golden-leaved, white-barked trees of the castle's forests. The sun was already shining over there so we tiptoed across the cold, shallow river and laid ourselves out in it. After the coldness of the river (not to mention last night in the castle), it felt wonderful lying there in the warmth of the sun's light, keeping a watchful eye out the whole time for any signs of the wee folk. It was easy for us to see how Ireland could have such stories, for the land actually seemed to be missing something without them.

Off to the right side of the castle building were several acres of planted evergreen forest. It was very dark underneath its closely bound branches but there were spots where the sun managed to find its way through and where it did a small patch of soft, green grass and moss shone brilliantly up from the ground. We went over to investigate one of these sunny islands only to find another one several feet away that drew us away towards it. That one, in turn, led to another and then to another, leading us deeper into the dark woods. It was fun to feel the enchantment and to think it was the leprechauns tricking us. Fortunately for us, the forest wasn't very big.

We stayed that night at the hostel in Cushendall, back on the Northeastern coast. The following day was Sunday, our last in Ireland, and it proved to be just as unpleasant as the first. It was gray, dismal and damp outside and hitchhiking was very slow. We walked about six or seven miles before catching our first ride. It was a long, slow walk on my still sore feet. We got to the ferry dock, though, and just in time to catch the next one heading back to Stranraer.

We were disappointed to be leaving such a beautiful country before having gotten to see much of it but, on the other hand, it was damn good to be on a warm, dry boat heading for a place where we knew the rides were good and fast. Not only that, but we were just that much closer to collecting all of our long-lost belongings from St. Thomas, which were beginning to occupy more and more of our thoughts and conversations.

As the ferry neared the docks of Stranraer, two and a half hours later, we figured it would be wise to be the first ones off the boat so that we could put ourselves and our thumbs in front of all the exiting cars, giving us a better chance to catch a ride. Our strategy worked well, as the very first car that came by stopped for us.

We eagerly climbed inside the big old American car, happy to be back in a land that we knew and where life was easy again. We were even happier when we found out the two guys who were now our hosts of the highway were going all the way to London. This was a great coup for us since London was about 400 miles away and this was going to greatly speed things up, giving us a chance to make up some of the lost miles from Ireland.

The driver of our car was a tall Irishman, about 25-30 years old, who was presently living in London. His name was Sam and he had just bought this car in Ireland and was bringing it over with his friend Arthur, a smallish Pakistani of about the same age. What this old boat of an American car was doing in Northern Ireland we never found out but we nevertheless enjoyed its spacious accommodations and settled into the back seat as we hit the road.

Sam and Arthur were very nice fellows and we enjoyed chatting with them and exchanging stories. Our tale of the Queenie was always a hit with our rides and we earned many a beer from its telling over the past few weeks. We had barely begun to share it, however, when Sam noticed that the car was beginning to overheat. We had gone about 30 miles when Sam, suspecting a stuck thermostat, decided he needed to pull over and inspect it.

We were just coming into a small town as dusk was gathering so Sam turned off into a little parking lot and went out to take a look. There were no tools in the car but he went out anyway to try his luck at taking the thermostat out with his pocketknife. After about a half an hour of futile effort, though, he conceded defeat and got back in the car.

Creetown was a tiny little place, only a few blocks long. Its only pub (that's how small it was) just happened to be right across the road from us. As we sat there thinking of what to do next, Sam looked over and, in true British form, decided that it was time for a quick pint. Afterwards, he announced, we would just limp the car down the motorway as best as we could.

It was dark now as we darted across the roadway to the little pub. We only had time for one beer, Sam told us, because he was due at work in London at seven the next morning, which was still 370 miles away. When we walked in the door, we realized a stranger's worst dream. The room went silent and every one of the half dozen heads in there turned to look at us. Admittedly, we were an odd bunch to see - a tall Irishman, a small, dark-skinned Pakistani, and two Californians all strolling into this remote little pub in the outlands of Scotland, and me still wearing my plastic red thongs.

We picked a table near the front door and very self-consciously ordered our beers. By now the other patrons, all old men, were returning to their conversations, talking in soft tones. I can't imagine what about.

After several minutes of idle conversation amongst ourselves, the old fellow at the table next to us leaned over and said something to us, though neither Karen nor I could understand what. We had to ask Sam to translate for us, for Scottish accents are thick. It was kind of funny to have an Irishman, whom we could barely understand as it was, passing conversations back and forth using his Cockney vernacular for Arthur, his Yankee English for us and his Scottish for our neighbor. There were a few times he even had trouble understanding the Scottie. His efforts weren't for naught, however, for only a short time later we'd become friends with the old guy and soon after that with the rest of the "lads" in the pub.

In fact, just as we were coming up on the bottoms of our beer mugs, engrossed in our new friends, I looked down at the table and was surprised to find a whole new round of beers had been delivered when we weren't paying attention. Seeing the questioning look on our faces, the old guy at the next table lifted his mug with a smile to let us know that he was responsible. We smiled back and thanked him. We really only had time for one beer but since he had been kind enough to treat us strange foreigners we felt obliged to stay and enjoy his hospitality.

As it went, though, just as we were about halfway done with this second round, another full round appeared before us. Over at the bar this time, another old fellow raised his glass to us. Touched at their kindness and generosity, we were nonetheless torn as to what to do about leaving, which we needed to be doing. All to no avail, however, for this kindness was replayed several more times that night and it wasn't until around midnight that we finally managed to crawl out of the place. Even then it was with forced insistence because they were still trying to buy us more as we walked out the door.

By now we were on first-name basis with many of these old lads and it wasn't before saying goodbye, with promises to write to Jock, Curly, Gilly and John, that we made it back to the highway, London-bound once again. Our "quick" beer had lasted only four hours.

In a way, I suppose it was good that, between the four of us, we had put down about three and a half gallons of beer that night, for the car still had a problem of overheating and finding water with which to refill the radiator, in those wee-est hours of the morning, proved to be nearly impossible at times. That Sam and Arthur actually peed into the radiator, however, I have to take on Karen's word since I had long since passed out in the back seat.

I do know, however, that Arthur had very responsibly taken it as his duty as copilot to make sure that Sam stayed awake. Unfortunately for us, the way he chose to do this was by talking incessantly about anything that was dull, mindless and boring and there were several times that we were all ready to strangle him. In fact, it was his droning on and on that helped inspire me to pass out in the first place because I couldn't take it anymore. He did manage to keep Sam's eyes open, however, if not his mind alert.

By 3:30 a.m. everyone was pretty well spent. In spite of all our efforts it was decided that we would pull over some place and get some sleep. We turned off at the first motorway rest stop we came to, bundled up and went to "bed" in our seats, there in the parking lot.

Like our quick beer the night before, our quick nap turned out to be several hours long as well. Upon waking up, we staggered over to the nearby cafe to get some coffee and tea into our heads in an attempt to revitalize ourselves and we met with some success, though not much. Obviously, Sam wasn't going to make his morning roll call at work, since it was now just past 6 a.m., so he called in to let them know he wasn't coming. I don't think he was very high up in the company, though, and I got the feeling that he really couldn't afford this absence from it.

At any rate, we headed out and made it to London at about six that evening. Our eight-hour trip had taken us 24 to achieve. We said our goodbyes to Sam and Arthur and thanked them for the fun ride as we climbed out of the car. From there we went straight to one of the big youth hostels there in town, only blocks far from where we had spent our very first days in this country.

London was much more pleasant, and interesting, this time around, now that we were somewhat normal. It was a very busy and crowded city and with such a diversity of people walking about it. Turbaned Arabs strolled alongside purple-headed punk rockers and nattily dressed businessmen. I found it all fascinating.

Well, our long-awaited visit with the Post Office was tantalizingly close at hand now and we were excited as we made our way to the post office at Trafalgar Square the next day. Our first mail call in a foreign country! We were thrilled when the postman came out with not only a big box, but a telegram and two letters as well. We tore the box open right there only to sadly discover that the box contained only my belongings. There was nothing of Karen's in it at all. She was very disappointed to say the least.

The telegram was from our friend, Sandi, back in St. Thomas, who had sent our things out. In it she explained that she had boxed up and mailed our things separately and that, due to Hurricane David that had come through the island just after we'd left, she wasn't able to get them out till late. The postman there told us now that the hurricane had thrown the trans-Atlantic mail system off and that it would be another four weeks before we could expect Karen's box.

This was bad news for Karen and made it very difficult for her as her only pair of pants had already been mended in about eight places and were still ripping almost daily. We weren't at all sure how we were going to deal with this turn of events. We couldn't very well stay here in England for another month just to pick up her box of clothes and yet, it was all she had and we couldn't very well go off and leave it either.

Back on the plus side, though, one of the letters was from my brother Michael, who was an officer in the U.S. Army and presently stationed in Germany. He'd heard we were over on his side of the ocean and had sent us directions to his quarters in Idar-Oberstein, as well as his door key, with an invitation to come stay with him a while. Having a target and knowing that respite from the road was to be found there made our hearts glad and renewed our spirits. We'd deal with her box later, one way or another.

We had a major disagreement the following morning over something I can't now remember but at the time it briefly threatened to terminate the rest of our trip. We talked it out, however, and came to a resolution just in time to head out for the continent, which was now our destination.

We needed to get ourselves out to one of the ferries on the southern coast. We chose to cross at Ramsgate on the hovercraft that operated there. It was our hope to get a ride from someone going over on the ferry as well so that our fare would be included in the flat rate for cars. That way we wouldn't have to pay the passenger fare ourselves. Our luck didn't hold out, though, and we begrudgingly bought two tickets when we got there for the 40-minute ride across the English Channel to France.

As we passed through Immigration there at Ramsgate, the first time since getting our passports stamped, we noticed the officer checking our entry stamps with unusual interest and occasionally looking at us a little funny. We started to get a a bit nervous right then but a moment later, he apparently satisfied himself with their authenticity and let us through.

We were glad to finally have all that stuff behind us (we thought, anyway) as we boarded the hovercraft and took our seats. It was a fun crossing, skimming over the water like that on the back of this overgrown lawn mower, and we were in France before we knew it.

EUROPE

It was just coming on dusk when we arrived at the ferry docks in Calais, France. The nearest hostel was about 40 miles away to the north, in the city of Dunkerque, so we immediately put our thumbs out so that we might be able to get there before they closed for the night.

France was a little scary for us. We didn't speak the language at all and the country had a completely different feel than Britain had. It wasn't nearly as warm and friendly appearing. In fact, we'd both heard the stories of how arrogant and rude the French people were and this made me feel a little unwelcome here. In spite of all my apprehensions, we actually got a ride fairly quickly and were in Dunkerque in short order.

It was odd, too, and a little uncomfortable, getting into the car and not knowing how to tell the guy where we were going, or being able to chat with him along the way. We'd tried to repay our previous drivers with interesting stories or, at the very least, by showing interest in theirs. We liked to think that we left them at least a little happier for having helped us. Here, though, I felt more like a beggar, just grabbing a free ride and running off afterwards.

We weren't at all sure where this hostel was supposed to be and once we got to town, we had to ask around as best we could for directions. One man we stopped surprised us by not only breaking our prejudged stereotype of French people with his friendliness, but also by the fanciful way he helped us. He spoke no English, as it was, and we, of course, no French so he simply proceeded to act out the directions for us to follow. He played charades with us, indicating the number of traffic signals and road crossings, and at one point even mimicked the pose of a statue that we would need to turn at.

Most of my fears about communicating with foreign speaking people ended right then, when I realized for the first time that there were so many other ways to get one's message across. We found the hostel without a hitch thanks to the kind efforts of this "arrogant and rude" Frenchman. I felt badly when the pen we handed him to draw us a quick map with leaked black ink all over his hands (though it didn't seem to bother him too much).

In keeping with the tone of everything else in this new country, we found the hostel to be a little strange, too. It was much more modern than the ones in Britain and had been, in fact, built expressly to be used as one. It seemed very institutional to us after all the old castles, manors and cottages that we'd become accustomed to.

Making it stranger still was that it was virtually empty when we arrived. This turned out, though, to be to our benefit since the abundance of empty rooms allowed us the rare luxury of actually having our own private room together.

The young man who checked us in at the desk that evening gave me a wry smile when he offered us the option, raising his eyebrow in a way that only a true Frenchman can, and whipered to me that we could be alone to "make....whatever you want." He even asked if we would like a wake-up call in the morning.

We were stunned at such unusual service but happily accepted both offers. He asked what time would be good for us. I told him nine o'clock would be fine and then merci beaucoup'd him as we packed up our things and made for our new honeymoon suite.

After having a good laugh at those strange toilets (laughing, that is, until we had to try and use one), we retired to our "suite" (bunk beds) and took the young man's hint, making...whatever we wanted, that is. It was real nice to be sleeping together again. It had been a while.

Despite the jeune homme's kind offer of a wake-up call, it was 10 a.m. when we finally emerged from our groggy sleep that next morning. Our kind host must have forgotten to wake us, we reasoned, and were wondering at this as we got up and dressed for the day. Our real surprise came a few minutes later, though, when we went out to the kitchen to fix our breakfast and found that not only had the nice fellow not woken us up, but the entire hostel was completely deserted and locked up solid. They had forgotten about us completely!

It was a little unnerving at first, but we got over it quickly and actually had fun cruising around the empty building, checking everything out. That is, until we tried to open the doors and found that they had all been locked from the outside and that there were no latches for them on the inside. We were virtual prisoners of the place. Not only that, but our hostel cards were still locked up in the office and we couldn't leave without them since we couldn't stay in any other hostel without them.

Fortunately, the pane of security glass that dropped down over the front desk, serving as a barrier between the office personnel and the guests, didn't go all the way to the counter top itself, much like in a bank. Karen thought she might be able to fit under it and climbed up on the wooden counter top to give it a try. Her gymnastics classes back at CR came in handy as she twisted and writhed herself under the glass, just barely squeezing through. She made it, though, and grabbed our cards out of the rack before squeezing herself back out through the window. I'm not sure why she didn't just use the door now that she was inside.

With our cards in hand now, all we had left to do was find a way out of the building itself. We walked all around the place trying every door we came to but it was the same everywhere. At length, we found some stairs going down to the basement. Crossing our fingers, we went down, searching for more doors. We wound our way around the various ducts and vents and

293

machinery down there until we came, finally, to a single door, way in the back of the basement, that could be opened from the inside and we made our escape out into the hazy sunshine of the new day.

So far, France was proving itself very interesting. Despite this, however, we had already since decided to head straight for my cousin Don's house just outside of Brussels, Belgium and leave our exploration of France for another day. Brussels wasn't too very far away and we felt it would be an easy day's travel.

Our rides that day were indeed good but our late start caused us to arrive in Brussels at dusk and since our last ride was offering to take us straight to the hostel, we decided to stay there in town that night and try for Don's in the morning. (In fact, our original ride wasn't going into Brussels but he was driving in tandem with another car that was so he pulled up alongside it, flagged his friend down, and then pulled over and did a mid- freeway transfer with us, passing us on to his friend.)

We had a wonderful talk that night in the hostel, mostly about ourselves, and I felt that our relationship was strengthened considerably by it. After the events back in Scotland and our argument that last day in London, it had begun to seem just a little strained and we'd had several moments in the last few weeks that had challenged, even threatened, it. Our talk was a much-needed boost for both us and our trip.

We had an interesting talk, too, the next morning as we sat at the long table in the dining room, eating our breakfast. We had gotten into a conversation with a couple of young English women who were sitting next to us and, in the course of our talk, one of them remarked to us that they couldn't understand the American fascination with old castle ruins.

I explained to her that where we come from, 100 years is about as old as anything gets so seeing these old buildings was a real thrill for us. On hearing this, they both gave a chuckle and replied in a slightly condescending tone that in England they don't consider anything to be "old" until it's been around for at least 400 years.

Sitting directly across the table from the four of us was a young man who had been quietly following our conversation. As soon as the Englishwoman had finished her remark, however, he very politely interrupted and gave her the comeuppance that I couldn't possibly have. He was Egyptian, he told us, and promptly reproved her by saying that in his country 400 years was nothing; that they didn't consider anything old until it was at least 4000 years old! That shut her up quick and I felt totally redeemed as I gave the fellow a slight conspiratorial smile.

After breakfast, and our obligatory household chores around the hostel, we took a quick tour around downtown Brussels before hiking out to the edge of the city and hitching on to Don's house.

Our thought was to wait and give him a call when we had gotten a little closer to his house but our first ride took us almost right to his door before we had a chance to. We didn't want to just barge in unannounced like that so we walked to the nearby town of Waterloo to call from there.

On the way, we spotted some apple trees in a small orchard alongside the road that were full of big yellow apples. Calling forth, once again, the Forage Rule, we changed course and hopped its fence to go for a quick raid.

As we walked up to the trees, we saw that the orchard occupied only a small corner of what turned out to be large farm enclosure and was much more beautiful than it had appeared from the street. In fact, it looked to me just like a jigsaw puzzle picture.

Opposite from us and the orchard, an old, two-story high stone, barn-like building stood right on the edge of a pond that lay in the center of the farmyard. Off to the left of it a little bit, a nearby tree hung out over the water from a small finger of grassy bank that extended out into the pond and where several geese were lounging underneath. The gray, misty daylight that reflected back across the pond's still surface, rather than casting everything in a dismal dress, only added to its old-world look.

There were two horses here as well and they wandered about through the light mist, alternately munching on the fallen apples under the trees and keeping a curious and watchful eye on us as we stood there admiring the scene and picking our own apples.

We found the place so pleasant that, after collecting our booty, we sat down under one of the apple trees a while to enjoy it longer. We had another very nice talk together here before slowly packing up and continuing our way on to Waterloo. Once in town, though, we discovered that we'd brought no money with us at all to call Don with, at least no Belgian money, so we had little choice now but to go against our better nature and just barge in unannounced. Alas, when we got there sometime later, no one was even home and since we had no idea when they might be back we decided to just go back to the hostel in Brussels and try again tomorrow.

By the time tomorrow had come, however, we had changed our whole plan, deciding now to go straight on to Michael's instead. It wasn't that far away and we thought it might be nice to get cleaned up first, especially since I had never met this cousin before and he was some bigwig businessman with ITT who might not appreciate such riffraff invading his home. I could call from Michael's, too, giving me a chance to introduce myself and Karen, and to give them fair warning of our impending visit. We enjoyed our sunny morning hike through the city and out to the hitching grounds at the edge of town, despite the fact that it was several miles away, and our first ride was quickly received once we got there.

Several rides later had brought us into Koblenz, Germany. It was around 9 p.m. now, a lot later than we were used to traveling, and it was odd to be out and homeless in the dark night of a new foreign country. Our last ride dropped us off somewhere in the middle of town, giving us vague directions on how to get back out again and we wasted no time getting started.

His directions, however, turned out to be driving directions, not hiking ones, and after walking through the quiet and mostly deserted streets of the darkened city, we found ourselves hiking along the overpasses and bridges of the autobahn. It was creepy walking through the empty streets at night like that, not to mention dangerous on the autobahn. Before long, though, we were out in the forested countryside, just outside of the city limits.

It's very illegal to walk along the autobahns in Germany and the unlucky person who gets caught doing it is usually issued a hefty, and immediately payable, fine. We learned about this law earlier that very day when we innocently stood on the freeway outside of Aachen, Germany. A few minutes later a car swerved over and the two young men inside hurriedly ushered us into the back seat before speeding away down the freeway. The door hadn't even been closed yet before the driver took off. They then explained to us that, in addition to us being liable for this crime, they could also be heavily fined for even stopping for us which we now appreciated them doing all the more so as bail was definitely not in our budget.

We weren't hitchhiking now, though, and the fear of getting caught as we ambled down the highway added to the mood an air of determined apprehension, if not adventure. Actually, I think it was just me that felt this way, as Karen never seemed to let such things bother her too much. She was the very definition of happy-go-lucky, I think.

Even though the cover of darkness was our only asset out here, we still very much enjoyed watching the full moon rising up in the night sky, silhouetting the steep, forested hilltops, as we walked along the quiet autobahn. Another moon, another month, another world.

It shone bright shafts of silver light into the blackened woods along either side of us, changing their otherwise dark and menacing look instead into a magical and inviting one. We saw one particularly brilliant moonbeam not far inside the forest that pierced down through the thick branches of the evergreen canopy and spot-lit a small clearing there in the trees, beckoning us to come in and explore it. It was just too inviting to resist so we left the roadway behind and let it lure us into the otherwise ebon woods. We reached the clearing and sat ourselves down within its circle of light, letting the moon's luminescence bathe us in its silvery-white shower.

Once again images of little people came into my mind. At the edge of the clearing a narrow dirt road ran off into to the lightless obscurity and alongside it, not far from us, I could see a small pile of newly sawn logs, stacked neatly next to a tree. It, too, was all bathed in moonlight. I don't know if Germany has any legends or stories of Wee Folk but it was very easy for me to imagine a little guy sitting up there on the woodpile, a long pipe smoking from his lips, waiting for the fairy dance to begin in the very moon circle we now occupied. I was certain, as I sat there in my fantasy, that Karen and I had just interrupted the night's events and that he had, in fact, jumped off and run into the woods when he saw us coming.

It was so much fun in here, and so pleasant, that we decided to spend the rest of the night here. It was already chilly out and we only had my one sleeping bag to spread over the both of us but we weren't to be so easily discouraged and we simply resolved to sleep real close together that night and enjoy this wonderful place as best as we could.

298

It was a long, cold and uncomfortable night, to be sure, but, despite the chill and the hard ground we slept on, any discomfort we may have felt was immediately forgotten when we awoke and looked about the beautiful, golden autumn forest that we now found ourselves in. A hazy sun shone through the trees this time but the yellow and brown leaves that thickly carpeted the forest's floor shone back a suggestion of warmth that the morning sun couldn't manage in actuality.

After our breakfast of leftover bread from the day before, we went out exploring more of the woods. When we returned, we were in such good spirits that we spontaneously broke out into another big wrestling match, rolling and tossing in the fallen autumn leaves, before eventually making our way back to the autobahn. Only a little nervously (me again) did we resume our place along the roadside.

Our good luck with rides was still with us, though, and within only a few minutes we were riding down the highway (in a Mercedes Benz, no less) with an off-duty pilot for Lufthansa Airlines. He spoke very good English, of course, and we had a nice time chatting with him as we made our way down the Rhine river towards Mikey's house.

He dropped us off within about 20 miles from the army post in the small town of Idar-Oberstein, where Michael was quartered. One more ride from a young German couple brought us right to the post gate around mid-afternoon.

Michael wasn't home when we got there but his neighbor from across the hall had been forewarned to keep an eye out for us as Michael had since changed apartments and the key he'd sent to us back in London was no good any more. He found us and let us into Michael's new apartment down the hall. We didn't waste any time making ourselves at home by raiding the icebox and flopping ourselves down to watch, for the first time in a very long time, good old American TV.

I hadn't seen my brother in a few years and this was not only my first experience with the army but also my first real day in Germany. Regardless of all this, though, it felt so wonderfully like home to me when we walked into his small apartment that first time. Not that it was so homey, mind you. More that it was a haven to us from the big world outside, a little world that we could hide in for a while, in safety and free from big thoughts and decisions. It was a much-welcomed respite from the road and we grasped it tightly.

Michael wasn't very surprised to see us when he returned home later that evening, even though he really didn't know when we were going to show up (strange how my family is never surprised when I come for a visit). Though I never thought I'd ever say this, it was good to see him again and good to find him the same. I was afraid the army would've changed him, but now I realized just how foolish a notion that was.

Karen and I settled ourselves right in and for those first few days did nothing all day long but eat, sleep, wrestle and watch TV. It was wonderful, in a way, to be back amongst all this Americana, to be surrounded by such familiar little tidbits of the culture that we had grown up in.

On the other hand, this particular slice of Americana was perhaps just a little more suburban than I was used to. Despite the pleasure of being safely holed up here, after these past several weeks of living on various European breads and cheeses, we now found ourselves eating corn flakes, American cheese, and the army's version of Wonder Bread. I don't know, it just seemed to be lacking something now. We weren't complaining though, for it was certainly cheap staying here (free!) and we didn't get thrown out at 10 o'clock every morning like at the hostels. We could cope, I'm sure.

We spent most of Mikey's off hours getting toured through the German countryside with him and his friend Steve. When we'd met Steve earlier in the week, he asked us how we'd come over so we told him, matter-of-factly, that we'd stowed away on the QEII from the Virgin Islands over to England. He just stood there for a moment, looking at us without

300

expression, before turning to Michael and asking, "Are they serious?" Michael, in turn, just shrugged his shoulders and confessed that he didn't really know either. I realized right then that he still wasn't sure himself that we hadn't made up the whole story! Geez, my own brother.

After a weeks' time of lounging around at Club Mikey's, we began preparing ourselves for the northbound leg of our European trip. Our thoughts were to try and outrun the advancing winter and thereby avoid any unnecessary adversity since Karen, of course, still had no provisions for cold weather until her stupid box showed up. We figured a loop trip straight up through Germany to Denmark, then back down through Holland, Belgium again, Luxembourg and back then to Germany would be good and we were soon on our way. Hitchhiking was exceptionally good on our way up, with many nice people.

Our first ride pulled over for us there in Idar-Oberstein before we even had a chance to get our thumbs out. The German couple took us several miles, paying our ferry fare across the Rhine, and then dropped us off just north of Frankfurt, but not before giving us their address and phone number in case we happened back their way and needed a place to stay.

Our next ride came quickly, too, and was from a young German fellow. He was a wine-making student, scion to a long line of family wine-makers but, interestingly, who was soon to be moving to California to study modern wine making. He was excited to have met us. After a few minutes' time, he pulled over and went to the trunk of his car, returning with a bottle of his family's work. He opened it and offered us a toast before passing it around. We had a great time as we made our way north. As soon as we finished a bottle he'd run back and get another, push the cork through (we had no corkscrew), and start a new round. He bought us tea at a roadside cafe that afternoon, too, and then, later, drove us all through the city of Kassel looking for the hostel so that he could drop us off at its door. He even left us with a new bottle to take with us. We snuck it into the hostel with us and enjoyed it later that night. Whoever said that Germans were stern and cold-hearted had obviously never hitchhiked here.

When morning came, we once again got a ride before we could hoist our thumbs out. A succession of rides brought us to within a few miles of the Danish border as late afternoon approached. The place where we were let out didn't look too promising, though.

It was a very sparsely populated piece of countryside here and for the first ten minutes that we stood out there waiting, not a single car came by and I began to think our streak was over. The sky was covered with a thick haze that helped lend a bleak atmosphere to both the environs and our frames of mind, which didn't help any.

Soon, though, a car came around the corner and headed up the autobahn onramp that we were standing on. We quickly assumed the pitiful, desperate look as it accelerated up the ramp toward us. As it got closer, I could see that there were already several people in it so I didn't hold out much hope for it stopping. That is, however, just what it did.

Like Sam's, this one was also a big, old American car and like that previous trip with him and Arthur, it was heading right to our target city, in this case Copenhagen. And like that other trip, too, this one would turn out to be just as memorable.

Since Copenhagen is on an island, Karen and I had already agreed that if we couldn't get a ride all the way there that we'd just have to forego the city altogether since the ferry fare to cross over to it wasn't in our budget. We were therefore very happy to find out, as we climbed into the back seat and took our seats next to a young woman already there, that was exactly where these people were now going.

302

There were three of them in the car. Ulrich (Ulli), the driver, was a German man somewhere in his late twenties or early thirties. Sitting up in the front with him was another young man in about his mid-twenties. This fellow, as it turned out, was from Iceland and the woman in the back with us was his younger sister. They were just finishing up a holiday over here in Germany and were on their way back to Copenhagen for their return flight to Reykjavik.

Ulli had met them in a bar back in Hamburg only the night before and had not only befriended them but also offered to drive them the 300 miles or so up to Denmark to catch their flight home. He was an exceptionally nice fellow, obviously, for doing this but it was, in fact, only a very small sample of his tremendous generosity, as we soon found out.

When we arrived at the ferry dock, the Iceland couple, possibly to repay the charity given them, insisted that they pay our ferry tickets and Ulli, not to be left out, treated everyone to a drink in the snack bar as we made our way across to the island that Copenhagen makes its home on.

It was dark by the time we got to the city and too late to go to a hostel so we had Ulli drop us off at the train station where we figured we'd stay for the remainder of the night. The Icelanders had a friend here in town somewhere that the three of them were going to stay with so we bid them auf Wiedersehen and danke schon and they took their leave of us. Karen and I went inside and set ourselves up for the night on one of the wooden benches there in the middle of the station to await the morning.

At 2 a.m. our long, boring wait was interrupted by an announcement over the intercom that the station was closing now for the night and that everyone here would have to leave. This wasn't good news for us because we really didn't want to spend the night out in the cold (not that the station was all that warm, mind you) and it was very reluctantly that we left to go walk the streets for the few remaining hours until daylight.

While trudging our way out the main entrance to the station, we were startled to see Ulli and the Icelanders trudging their way in. It seems that the Icelanders couldn't remember where their friends lived nor could they call, for some reason, and after driving up and down the streets of Copenhagen for a few hours in a vain attempt to find them, they had finally decided to come join us in the train station.

Now we were all homeless and with only one real alternative. Back to the car we marched, where we spent the rest of the night, all squeezed together, out in the parking lot. We all slept upright with our faces plastered up against the windows except for Karen, who was in the middle of the back seat; she had a slightly softer wall to lean against - me.

Fortunately, dawn was not too far away and with its arrival we once more bade farewell to our friends and parted company. This time, however, we had arranged with Ulli for him to come back and pick us up again after he saw the Icelanders off and take us back down into Germany with him later that day. Copenhagen didn't look all that interesting to us and the thought of a straight ride all the way back to Hamburg was too tempting for us pass up so we just walked around Hans Christian Andersen's town for a couple of uneventful hours and then headed back to the train station to rendezvous with Ulli.

This time, on the way down, he insisted that he now pay for our ferry tickets back across the channel and would not listen to our objections. Just after crossing the border into Germany he treated us to tea at a roadside cafe, as well. While here, he told us that he wanted to stop at his parents' house, just outside of Flensburg, not too much farther, and asked if we didn't mind. It was pretty much on the way and we certainly weren't going to complain, as he had already done so much for us.

It was dark outside by the time we left the cafe with our new destination ahead of us. Despite Ulli's more than generous kindness, in fact, possibly because of it, after about an hour of wending our way down the dark and isolated back-country roads towards his parents' house, my Los Angeles-trained mind began to have suspicions of his motives, particularly when he suddenly pulled off to the side of the road in the middle of nowhere, saying he was out of gas. My suspicions grew to mild apprehension when, as soon as he pulled over, another car immediately pulled over right behind us, its headlights shining through the back window, as Ulli went back to talk to its driver.

After a few moments, though, Ulli came back and told us that the other fellow, a stranger as it turned out, had only pulled over to see if we needed any help and was now going to take Ulli to the nearest station for gas.

While we sat in the car waiting for him to return, I was ashamed of myself for letting my imagination run away like that. He had been nothing but giving to us so far. I guess it was just hard for me to think that people could be as nice to strangers as he was, particularly odd foreign ones like us.

Some while later, Ulli returned with only a few liters of gas (all he had money for, as we learned later) and we were soon back on the road again to Mom and Dad's house. Only about a mile short of their house, though, we ran out of gas again and had no choice now but to leave Ulli's car there on the side of little country lane we were on and walk the rest of the way.

It was very dark outside as we were out in the rural farmlands by now, several miles from town, but as we neared the house I could see that it was a very old and simple one, still with its thatched roof. It looked so perfectly German and was obviously very well tended.

Once inside, Ulli went straight off to talk to his folks, reappearing a few minutes later and surprising us with an invitation for us to stay the night here. This just kept getting better and better. We didn't have to think too long to accept his invitation.

After a nice, hot bath (in a huge tub), an evening cocktail, and an hour or two of playing with Ulli's kitty, we went to bed in the softest, fluffiest, warmest bed I'd ever slept in. After last night in Ulli's car, it was absolutely heavenly and I fell asleep with Karen on my arm and a smile on my face.

We woke from a dead sleep the next morning to a fully spread breakfast laid out for us by Ulli's mother. After introductions had all been made, the three of us took our seats at the table and heartily enjoyed her talents while she sat there with us in the kitchen.

She spoke no English at all so Ulli translated what conversation we could manage between the shovels full of food we were laying into. It was difficult to explain to her why we had to decline the sausages she had prepared. We had noticed that Germans were fond of their meats and I don't think we were entirely successful in explaining to her that we simply chose not to eat animals because we liked them. After that I didn't have the heart to decline her offer of coffee, which I had never learned to drink and didn't like, and tried not to give myself away, smiling as I sipped it down.

We ate until we were stuffed, as only two hobos at a free feast can do, and afterwards retired to the front room to lounge and play with the kitty some more. It seemed only a couple of hours, though, before we were then invited back in the kitchen to find a huge lunch now awaiting us. It must have been that crazed look we had as we devoured breakfast that gave us away. At any rate, yet another stuffing and another reclining before finally heading back out to the autobahn early that afternoon. I felt guilty once again, as we left, for being the recipient of so much attention and hospitality and leaving them with nothing in return but our gratitude.

We arrived in Hamburg in the darkness of late evening and Ulli took us straight to his favorite bar and treated us once again to his generosity by buying us each a couple of beers with the money he had borrowed from his parents. He even put a

306

50pf coin in the jukebox and insisted that I pick out all the songs.

As soon as our beers and songs were all finished, we went on to Ulli's apartment there in town and spent the rest of the night camped out on his living room floor. When morning came and we had packed ourselves up, he then took us out to a small bakery and treated us to a simple breakfast, once again strongly refusing any offer from us to pay for any of it. Afterwards, he drove us out to a rest stop cafe on the autobahn to Holland and insisted on buying us a farewell toast of some unknown German liquor to officially send us on our way.

This man had taken us up and kept us for three days now, seeing to every need or want we came across and never with a single thought for himself, and this in addition to his help for the Icelanders. He was truly a saint, at least when it came to strangers, anyway, and he had a profound effect on not only the way I see the world but in the way I feel about people in general. I came away from all of this more convinced than ever of the inherent goodness of the human heart and that we sometimes need only be given the opportunity to let it show. I know, at least, that I am much kinder now to strangers as I feel that I now have so many kind favors to repay.

It was a very long day hitching once Ulli left us. The truck driver that had given us our last ride dropped us off very late that night right at the border into the Netherlands. We were still several kilometers from Amsterdam by then and there were virtually no other cars on the autobahn so we decided then to just find someplace where we could camp out for the remainder of the night.

There was a patch of bushes right there on the side of the autobahn that looked sufficiently dark enough to hide two bums in until sunrise so we climbed underneath them and scooted the roadside rubbish aside to make a clearing for our bed.

We had to share my sleeping bag between the two of us again that night and the litter-strewn ground around us was cold and hard. This, plus the noise from the morning autobahn traffic only a few feet from where our heads lay, all made for a rough and uncomfortable night but our spirits survived intact and early that next morning we simply shook the dirt off us and crawled back out to the freeway. We walked across the border and promptly caught a ride all the way into Amsterdam.

We tracked down the hostel first thing and checked in for the night before returning to the streets to spend the day exploring the canals of tulip town. It didn't impress us terribly, though, and the aches of last night followed us throughout so we returned early to the hostel, eager to make some horizontal recuperation. We slept a long time that night.

We were off to cousin Don's house again by midmorning. I gave him a call later when we got into Brussels and arranged to meet him at his house the next day. We really enjoyed being back here again. For some reason, every time we came through this city we ended up having a wonderful time together just talking and doing nothing in particular.

Despite never having met Don or his wife Cynthia, we were very warmly welcomed when we arrived later that day. Being from "our world" made it particularly nice. Cynthia showed us to our room, telling us to make ourselves at home and to just help ourselves to anything we wanted.

After all of the polite formalities of our previous guestings, it was so nice to be once again treated "normal." Don't get me wrong, we very much enjoyed all the kindness and hospitality of those we'd met so far, but there is nothing to compare with the easiness of being in the world in which you were raised and familiar with.

Don was, as it turned out, vice president of security for ITT Europe, among other things and their house was very upper class both in its decor and location. He was, on the other hand, born and raised in a small town in Oklahoma and it was this that seemed to set the mood of the place. He was extremely congenial to us. I think we must have reminded him of that part of his life that was simple and fond. After he'd had a couple of drinks, particularly, that faraway glint came to his eyes as he reminisced to us about the good ol' days back in Hess, the tiny town of his youth.

Later, he let us use his "hotline" phone to call our mothers back home. It was his world-wide, toll-free, corporate phone from ITT and was supposedly to be used only on important business. I felt pretty special chatting on it with "me mum". We spent three and a half days here and thoroughly enjoyed them all. Cynthia took us to the nearby Waterloo battlefield and museum the day before we left. I found it all very strange to be standing here at the edge of this beautiful, rolling, green grass field on a quiet, sunny autumn afternoon, trying to imagine the nearly 50,000 bloodied, dead and maimed bodies that covered it those many years ago, the clashing tumult of mortal battle. It was all so serene and calm now, without a single hint as to its brutal and grotesque history.

We also got to go to their son Deke's Homecoming football game at the American high school there and to the big party that followed later that night back at Don and Cynthia's house. The party didn't start until around midnight but we managed somehow to keep ourselves up until it did.

Once word leaked out about Karen's and my adventures, we soon became some kind of celebrities with all of Deke's high school friends and we spent the rest of the night telling and retelling our story for the small groups that kept forming around us until the party finally ended at around 5:30 that morning. I enjoyed my short time as a celebrity.

Our brief sojourn in international, corporate Americana ended with the arrival of Monday morning as Cynthia drove us out to the highway leading back toward Germany.

By that afternoon we had gotten as far as Luxembourg City in Luxembourg. Rides were difficult for us today though, and after an hour or so of freezing our buns off while futilely trying to catch a ride out of town, we changed our minds and decided that staying here at a hostel sounded like a really good idea instead, so we turned around and went back to go track it down.

It was a nice city and we were both glad for the chance to visit it. We got to walk around it some the next morning before making our way back out to the highway for Germany. It was still very cold out and rides were still proving difficult to get.

We had to walk several miles before finally getting one. It was a pretty walk, though, through the colored leaves of autumn and we didn't really mind it much. In fact, Karen made up a song (her "birdie song") on the way and began a helicopter collection (maple tree seeds) to go with her Scotland rock, which was still one of her most prized possessions.

We walked across the border between Luxembourg and Germany, past the guard station which was at the end of a long, high bridge, spanning the Sûre river far below. For some reason seeing that guard station way at the far end evoked again thoughts of those old war movies I watched as a kid. This time I imagined I was part of some cold war prisoner exchange, marching across this highly exposed bridge while some unfortunate prisoner from the other side simultaneously marched the other way, eyeing one another nervously as we passed in the middle. [Indeed, I think I've watched way too many of those old movies. The first time I'd seen a troop of German soldiers walking through the army post, back at Idar-Oberstein, I immediately ducked below the window sill that I was standing at and thought to myself out loud, "Oh no,

310

Krauts!". Michael got a good laugh at this when I told him about it later because not only were we living in what once was a German army facility during World War II, but the Germans were now one of our staunchest allies in the cold war that followed it].

The first real snow of the season had fallen in Idar-Oberstein since our departure a week ago and it greeted us now as we neared the post. It was the first time either one of us had been in snow for quite a long time and after the stifling hot tropics, it was a real pleasure to hear it crunching now under our feet again and to feel the blood collecting in our cheeks. It helped to put our recent coldness into perspective, too, for now it at least looked like it should be cold out.

Michael saw us coming when we returned to the post late that afternoon and welcomed us back as we tromped across the snowy green outside his window by sticking his head out of his second-story window and waving while calling out to us in his best falsetto voice, "Hellllooo therrre." I laughed at the thought of what his troops would think if they could see their fearless and noble lieutenant now.

***

It was good to be back at Michael's again, back in little America. We were going to be staying long enough this time to find ourselves some work. It was time to fatten our coffers before heading for points south and since a recent ruling now made it possible for U.S. citizens to get civilian jobs with the armed forces we decided to take full advantage of the opportunity, especially since we had a free place to stay while here. Strasberg Kasern, the post where Mikey lived, was too small to have any openings so we looked for work several kilometers away at Baumholder, the nearest large Army center.

FROM KAREN'S JOURNAL:

[11Nov79] Two more very lazy yet very fun weeks were spent at Michael's. We did get ourselves up and out each day to look for a job at Baumholder. Not really any chance of that until about the 15th of this month when they hire for Christmas. The days at Michael's are fun, Mark is fun. We rassle each day for our exercise and watch Meter Man and Green Acres on TV. What a life! I feel so close to Mark and so happy! He's such a good person and he's so good for me. He makes me laugh and feel real good inside. To have Mark as my best friend is the bestest thing in the world to me. I love him a lot! Wednesday night, Michael came back from five days in Paris. He came in with little presents for me and Mark. Nice smelly soaps from Paris and a box from my mom! It was like Christmas. I got some beautiful clothes from my mom and another one of these beautiful journal books.

When those first two weeks had passed, we found ourselves faced with a big (and uncomfortable) decision to make. Not only was it time to start working but it was also time to figure out how to get Karen's box back from London. After some serious thinking and discussion, we reluctantly decided that the only solution was for Karen to hitch back to London alone while I started looking for a job. There was a lot more work available for guys and we needed the income badly, plus Karen was very anxious to finally get all of her things again after these past two months of doing without them.

I didn't like the thought of her being out alone like that but, on the other hand, since virtually all of our rides to date had been so extremely nice and so easy to get, I felt confident not only that she would be safe enough but also in her ability to take care of herself. Indeed, it was one of the main reasons I'd wanted to travel with her in the first place and, besides, she wouldn't really be alone anyway. David would be there too. I knew that. Still, it was very hard for me to watch her leave, walking down the road all alone, waving bye to me, as she started her trip of almost 800 miles. Very hard.

FROM KAREN'S JOURNAL:

[08Nov79] Yesterday morning I left Mark for our first separation since we left Eureka. We haven't been apart for more than a few hours at a time since we left! I'd think we'd be sick of each other by now and need a break but boy, do I miss him! I feel very content with Mark, no matter how long we're together. He sure is a very special kind of person and I sure am happy we're friends. Well, I don't really think I needed a break from him, but we got one anyway.

The night before I left, Mark filled me full of warnings and coached me on defense tactics. After a lot of good-byes, I headed off for London and my box. I sat thru the day memorizing my defense tactics as I got rides from very nice people. After 6 rides I was back in dreaded Luxembourg.

After an excruciating long wait of ten minutes, thinking I would never get a ride, I got a ride. The guy was from Luxembourg City and could only take me to the other side of the city. He told me what I already knew, Luxembourg is a bad place to hitchhike. People won't pick you up. He worked at a car rental agency and worried I wouldn't get a ride so he tried to find me a car that had to be taken to Brussels. Unfortunately, there weren't any. Well, he let me off in a good spot and I got a ride pretty fast. And a good ride it was, all the way to Don and Cynthia's front door. I was welcomed with opened arms by the family's m.r. [mental retard] cat. I think he might be Boo Boo's relative [my mother's very eccentric cat - M.B]. *I was welcomed by the rest of the family, too. After a nice chat with Cynthia and good night's sleep, I was up and on my way again. Cynthia, using the excuse she'd rather just drive me to the train station than clear out to the road to Oostende, gave me the money for the train to Oostende. I managed to unknowingly get on the first class section on the train and had to be removed to my proper spot. Oops. How embarrassing.*

Now here I sit waiting for the ferry to Dover, England. I have two hours to wait still and it's not going to much fun without Boogles. [Karen's' nickname for me – MB] *Woe is me, I miss my Boogles.*

[12Nov79] Hi! The ferry finally came. On the ferry I was accompanied by a guy from Washington, D.C. who was living in Antwerp, Belgium, going to school. Nice guy, he was on his way to London, too, and said he would look me up there. Didn't work out that way, my plans changed, in a very good way they did.

I was really hoping the ferry would arrive before it got dark out, but by the time it arrived in Dover it was pitch black out. It's getting dark very early these days! Got to have a baby on the way off the boat, well didn't have one, the baby's mother just borrowed me for a while as a carrier. He was a real cutie, too, was just charming everybody on the boat.

After we were off the boat, I gave the baby back and was moving along through the customs lines, planning to hurry and catch all the lorries and cars and get a ride right up to London. The Immigration man had other plans. He thought I was fishy in some way and questioned me left and right. Counted all my money then questioned me more. He must have liked me a lot cause he personally escorted me to the search table and made sure they checked me out real good. They emptied out my pack and read my address book front to back and read my journal almost word for word. Hee-hee, how embarrassing, he wanted to know who "Boogles" was, hee-hee. He must have figured it was all coded 'cause I'm sure it didn't make much sense to him.

Some of the things I write don't make sense to me. They even smashed on Tattoo! [the small, stuffed animal of un-determined species that she brought with her from home – MB] *To make sure he wasn't loaded, I suppose. Questioned my rock a bit, too, figured he'd crack, I guess, hee-hee. He didn't, though. It all came about, I guess, cause my first stamp into the country isn't quite right. Seems the Immigrations office signed it then the lady stamped it which put his signature in the wrong place. Finally, after one more jab at Tattoo and another little scan at my journal, he let me go and gave me a month in the U.K. Big of him since I still have five months left on my first stamping in.*

I got outside and by then it was 7:30pm and very cold and deserted outside. I went walking along, missing Boogles a lot and thinking I should cry. Everybody from cars and lorries off the boat were long gone. I walked and walked and stood and stood. I tried to screen cars I hitched from, which is a real hard thing to do when the only way to judge their character is by their two headlights. Headlights don't tell a lot about a driver's character.

By 9:00pm I'd gotten about 15 miles down the road. I would have said forget it for the night but the town I was in had no hostel. After a while of standing on a very quiet road a little white mini came along and was going to London. I found out that my biggest problem had been I wasn't on the normal road to London, I was on a small side road. I guess I made a wrong turn somewhere in Dover.

David, the guy who gave me the ride, was going to see a friend in London who was a social worker and had a big house and would gladly put me up for the night, seeing how the hostel would be closed by the time we got there.

We met Bob in a little pub in London, stayed there a while chatting about the QEII, of course.

They both thought it was a very notable thing we did and were quite impressed. Later we went to Bob's house and sat around drinking bottles of wine.

The next morning, Dave took me into London center to the post office. After one step inside the door I thought, Oh God, what if it's sent in Mark's name! There was no need for me to worry about that; it wasn't there at all. Oh woe was me then. I was really wanting to just pick that bugger up and get back to Germany.

[11Nov79] I came out of the post office quite sad to say the least. Dave was outside waiting for me. On the way back to Bob's house we discussed my possibilities. When we got back to Bob's, Bob made a few phone calls and worked everything out for me. I had planned to stay and wait in London if my box hadn't arrived, thinking it would be soon. But now that I was there all I wanted to do was to get back. Bob told me he would pick my box up for me. With many letters now written for Bob and the post office it should work. He is then going to send it to Michael's in Germany. What a guy!

Once we got all that worked out, we started on preparations for the big party. Bob was getting his house ready for a big party that was going to be there that night. He really had nothing to do with the party but somehow got caught up in doing everything with it. After a day of cleaning and shopping Bob's house was ready for a party. As the first guests arrived, Bob, Dave and I left for the nearest pub.

After an evening of a lot of wine and some Chinese food nobody could get me to eat, we went back to Bob's house to find the party still in full swing. As it usually seems to happen in groups, the story of the QEII spread fast and I busied myself telling very short stories about it. At about 4:00 AM the party ended with eight of us crowding into the one warm room of the house to sleep. It was like a slumber party, as soon as the lights *were out the jokes started up and it was another hour till there was silence.*

Next morning, quite late but still way too early for me, Dave and I said our goodbyes to Bob and headed down to Dover. I was tired but boy, did it feel good to be heading back to Mark. A person can really miss a best friend real quick like.

It was cloudy and icy when we got to Dover. Dave went with me to get my ticket and seeing I had a couple of hours till blast off, took me for a tea before I left. Dr. Dave is a real nice guy. I like him. People sure are good and nice, this ole world is a nice place to be.

I managed to get off the ferry quick and got a ride right away all the way to Waterloo and once again to Don and Cynthia's door. Got there about 9:00pm, had a chat with Cynthia, then scooted off to bed.

Cynthia's very nice, they've helped us an awful lot and been really kind to us. Cynthia said when the last of her kids go off to college which is soon, she'd like to help kids that are just traveling like me and Mark. She'd be good at something like that. She's so busy and likes to get involved.

Next morning, I started on my last day of hitching. It was a slow, cold, wet day full of many short and sometimes amusing rides. One Japanese fellow who spoke French thought I would be more than willing to fool around with him because he had heard young Americans wanted to "make love not war." He just couldn't understand it when I said no.

Once past Trier, there was snow on the ground. It was nice to see, haven't seen snow in a long time, it seems longer than it's really been. I got to have a real good look at it 'cause I got left out right into it.

After a brisk stay out in the snow on a very unbusy road as darkness quickly crept up on me, I got a ride by four American army guys. They weren't going very far my way, but somehow in the dark and the fog I managed to mis-steer them right to Strasberg Kasern. It felt so good to go from dark cold night into

Mark's arms. It was so good to see him! It had only been five days, but I sure was missing his smiling face and warm laugh.

While I was gone, Mark got a job at Foodland at Baumholder. Though I would have loved a lazy, warm rasseling day in the apartment with Mark, the next day I gladly went to Baumholder to get myself a job. I was ready to get going.

It was wonderful to have Karen back again and such a relief to have her back safely. After hearing of her adventures, I was warmed to see that David truly had gone with his little sis and had kept such good care of her.

I had since gotten a job at the Army's version of a Seven-Eleven store as a full-time beer stocker, working nights, and Karen soon got herself a job as a part-time I.D. checker at the Post Exchange, working days, so we didn't see much of each other for the two weeks that we worked. At least now I knew where she was, that she was safe and that she'd be there when I got home. That was enough for now.

We both quit our jobs the same day, December 7th, and spent the following three weeks making up for all the time together we'd lost. We had to wait those weeks actually. Wait for our checks to come in from the Army, wait for some money being sent to us from both Karen's mother and my Mamaw and, last but not least, wait for Karen's notorious box to arrive. The next part of our trip was going to be a long, tough one and we would be needing all of these things before we could leave.

By the 14th of December, however, Karen and I were desperate enough that we agreed that if her box wasn't in real soon that we'd just have to leave and forget about it. We certainly didn't want to do this but likewise couldn't afford to waste much more time waiting for what was essentially mostly clothes. It did have her sleeping bag in it as well, though, and it sure would be nice to have it back, especially since it was now well into winter weather outside.

She called Bob to find out what was happening and to her great surprise and relief, he told her that it had just arrived. This was great news! He promised to send it right away. Finally, after all this time and trouble and worry, she was going to get her box.

In the meantime, we continued to wait. One day we went out and had a good time exploring an abandoned old diamond mine not far from the kaserne but the rest of the time we mostly just spent our days, once again, lounging, rassling, and TV watching.

FROM KAREN'S JOURNAL:

[20Dec79] We wake up at 12:00pm, in time for the "Addams Family" and "Green Acres". Music, a few exercises for me, a little studying for Mark til 6pm News, TV and the never ending battle of chess for Mark and Michael til 11:00pm or so. Music and little nothings til 2 or 3 AM and then bedtime. Oh what a life. And of course there's always the Humboldt Times Standard that Michael gets. It's always 2 weeks late, but who cares, it's my hometown newspaper! "Love Boat" is now me and Marks favorite show, oh, the memories.

Though it was an easy and comfortable lifestyle, it was still becoming an awkward situation for everyone. Our original plan of staying only two or three weeks had grown into a month and a half by now (not counting the week we stayed before going up to Denmark) and the strain of our presence was being felt. Michael never complained and as far as I know didn't really mind, but it became heavy on our minds, if not on his, that we were imposing.

On top of that, we were now staying here in Michael's room illegally. He'd had to get clearance for us, at the onset of our arrival, from the guy who supervised the BOQ's (Bachelor

Officers Quarters). We'd only been given permission to stay for two weeks and they, of course, had long since passed so now we had to keep a very low profile during the day, sneaking in and out every time we went somewhere and feeling somewhat like prisoners. At least we were well experienced at it by now. Lurking about, that is.

Christmas was fast approaching now. This would only be Karen's second one away from home now and I'm afraid that one of the presents she got this year was a bad case of homesickness. We waited up until midnight on Christmas Eve to hear the church bells from town ring in Jesus' birthday. Though it had been snowing these past few days and despite the fact that most of our American Christmas traditions come from right here in Germany, it still didn't seem much like the ones she was used to with her family all around.

Michael tried his best, however, to bring in the spirit and at the stroke of midnight that night, he came out from his room in a silly getup that was supposed to resemble Santa Claus, army style. He had cotton balls stuck to his chin and was wearing his army issue, olive drab stocking cap with his army duffel bag tossed over his shoulder. He ho-hoed a couple of times while we all laughed and then he reached in his bag and pulled out presents for all of us there (Karen, me and Steve). He then reached in again, only this time he pulled out three snowballs he'd stashed in there and clobbered each of us. It was fun.

He gave both Karen and me each a Swiss Army knife, which were both greatly appreciated as neither of us had a pocket knife, oddly enough. He also gave me some camera equipment and Karen a very nice knitted cap and scarf. If my brother had ever done anything nice to me in our lives up to this point, this was the moment of it and I was touched at his thoughtfulness (if not the snowballs).

The best Christmas present, however, arrived in the mail two days later. We walked quickly the few kilometers into town where Karen eagerly turned her mail slip in to the Bundes Post and finally got her hands on her long-lost box. We couldn't wait to get it back to the apartment so we opened it right there outside the post office.

One by one Karen pulled all those things out that she hadn't seen since we'd left the islands over four months ago now. It was a tremendous relief to feel intact again. We were free once more and I felt much like I did back in Jensen Beach when I'd finally gotten Otto working again. We excitedly made plans to leave the very next day.

Somewhere around five that next morning, however, while I was fast asleep, one of my wisdom teeth that had been slowly falling apart since the beginning of our trip finally decided to rear its ugly head. The constant droning pain of a severe toothache woke me up several times until I finally got up around 7 a.m. to try and stop it.

I knew I had to have the tooth pulled and that the only place around here to have it done was at the Army's dental office in Baumholder. Michael, however, had to go to work that day and the next bus going from Strasberg Kaserne to Baumholder didn't leave until 10 a.m., another three hours' wait.

I took some aspirin to hold me over until the bus came but it did absolutely no good whatsoever and I found that the only thing that helped alleviate the driving pain was, for some reason, laying on the bed face up while holding my head upside down over the edge. Three hours of that was more than enough for me and I was never happier to see a dentist in my life when I finally got to the dental office to have it pulled.

Actually, I had tried to have it pulled earlier in our visit here but was told that, as a civilian, I was only entitled to emergency dental work and so was denied. It was fortunate for me that it went bad that night and in that way. Any later and I would have been in a part of the world where dental work wasn't easy to get and now that it was an emergency I qualified to have the Army do it for next to nothing.

We postponed our departure until the next day so that I could spend the rest of this one recuperating back at Michael's

It was the first day of a new blizzard when we awoke that next morning but now that Karen was fully equipped we didn't let this deter us from carrying on with our plans. After saying goodbye to Michael and spending the first part of the morning running around Baumholder collecting up our last paychecks, we were blissfully back on the road again.

We left straight from the gates of Baumholder and stood out in the blowing snow on the road heading south, pulling our thumbs out of their warm pockets only in the last possible moments before the cars actually reached us.

The dentist had told me to rinse out my new tooth hole frequently for the next couple days so that morning I had filled my leather boda bag with salt water to bring with me. I knew I wouldn't have much of a chance to rinse and spit once we were in someone's car so I took advantage of the roadside waits between rides to practice my oral hygiene and left behind us a string of small red dots in the snow where I spit my bloody water out. (It was comforting to think, as we stood there in the blinding snow, that if we changed our minds about being out here we could always follow them back to Michael's.)

We had learned well from our travels by now that the more vulnerable a person is (or appears to be) the more likely he is to receive the kindnesses of others. In fact, we were relying on this knowledge today and were only out here because of it. Sure enough, our rides came quick and easy.

Our initial plan was to aim for Munich and then over to Salzburg, Austria to catch a train to Venice, Italy. Because of the snowy, cold conditions in the mountains, and flush now with our new paychecks, we'd decided once again to temporarily overlook our budgetary restraints and actually buy ourselves train tickets to take us through the Alps. Wintertime hitching in the Austrian Alps, we thought, was perhaps just a little too vulnerable at this point in time.

Our last ride, however, was going all the way to Freiburg, right on the German side of the Swiss border, so we changed our plans and decided instead to train from there across the Swiss Alps into Milan, in northern Italy. We had no real itinerary, of course, so it didn't really matter to us either way.

We got to Freiburg just as dusk descended and tramped our way straight to the nearest train station. We found, to our dismay (and after much sign language), that the next train to Milan didn't leave until 10 o'clock the next morning so once again we resigned ourselves to a long, cold night in a train station. And once again, at 10 p.m. this time, the station manager announced that the station was now closing for the remainder of the night and that we'd have to leave. Seeing us sitting there so forlornly on the old wooden bench of the waiting room, though, obviously with no place to go, he let us stay and locked us in for the night.

The station was dark and creepy in its emptiness and the benches weren't at all comfortable but we still had a good time together. The prevailing sense of adventure that had since returned to us allowed us to overlook such insignificant things like beds and baths. Besides, we were pretty well accustomed to doing without these luxuries by now, anyway. In fact, for some reason, the door to the women's toilet was locked that night and when Karen discovered this late that night, for reasons unknown to me, she ended up having to use the urinal in the men's room instead. A complicated feat, I was told, and a first for her.

Switzerland was, of course, absolutely gorgeous as we wound our way through the snowy mountain crags and cozy hamlets. Much like our bus trip back in Scotland, it was easy to appreciate the cold and inclement weather outside as we watched it all pass by from the big windows of the heated train car.

Oddly enough, it was easy for me to tell where the Swiss Alps ended and the Italian Alps began. I didn't know at the time just what it was but, as we rounded a large curve in the tracks, all of a sudden the snow seemed somehow to be tainted now and the buildings went from being nice, neat, alpine-y chalets to being big, dirty-looking villas. Even the quality of the daylight seemed now to be tarnished. It was only when I checked our map, though, that I realized that we had just crossed into Italy and I couldn't help but feel just a little uncomfortable by it for some reason. It was a feeling that, unfortunately, stayed with me throughout the entire week that we were here in Italy.

We arrived in Milano right at nightfall. It was a big train station and very crowded. We made our way out to the street and found it to be just as busy. In front of the station we found a big map of the city and after scanning it carefully, we saw that the youth hostel was clear across town. We set out for it directly and wended our way through the dark city streets. It was very cold outside already and we appreciated the long walk for giving us the opportunity to generate some heat if not for anything else.

We finally arrived at the hostel after about an hour of slowly groping our way through the city but our diligence in finding it went unrewarded when we saw that it was all closed up and dark. A sign on the door sadly informed us that it was closed for the holiday season and would not be open again until after the first of the year.

We were sorely (and coldly) disappointed to learn this. New cities can be intimidating enough as it is but a new city, in a new country, with a new culture and new language, outside on a cold, dark, winter's night with nowhere to go was too much.

Indignant now, I pulled out our hostel directory to check this out and, sure enough, it was indeed listed as being closed. I had no one to blame but myself for not having checked it more closely back at the train station. Worse, though, was that, flipping through the book even further, I discovered that virtually all of the hostels in Italy were closed for the holidays. This wasn't getting better.

Since we didn't want to walk all the way back to the train station for the night and hotels were still off-limits to us, that left us only one real alternative and that was to just keep going.

Karen had wanted particularly to visit Venice while we were here in Italy so she offered the suggestion now that we just head for there tonight. It was getting late but we figured the more miles we made tonight were just that many we wouldn't have to make tomorrow and we set out for the autostrada which was conveniently nearby.

There was a small cafe right next to the on ramp of the autostrada so to help allay our uneasiness at being in this big, cold, strange city, we stopped in and bought ourselves each a cup of "chocolata." It was wonderfully thick and hot, like soup, but sweet and chocolatey. Suddenly everything seemed good again. We began a love affair right then and there for these small cups of Italian manna and never missed an opportunity to engage it.

It was a good thing, too, that we were so energized by our little respite, for as soon as we were back out on the highway, it became clear that, though there was a lot of traffic going by, rides were not going to be easy to get here. It was too dark for us to be seen very well and there was no clear place for a car to pull over and stop. What few cars did pull over for us were all headed somewhere else so we had to let them go.

After an hour or so of fruitless hitching, we decided to quit for the night and find ourselves someplace to camp out until morning. We'd try again then. There was a dark patch of bushes nearby that seemed sufficiently isolated so we went over and rolled out our sleeping bags on the ground behind them.

One of the reasons we had been so eager for Karen's sleeping bag to arrive from St. Thomas was because it was a left-hand zipper designed to match up to my right-hand zipper. This way we could zip them together, essentially making one big sleeping bag and allowing us to sleep together. On this icy night that sounded really good.

Somewhere in the late hours of the night, we were awakened when several cars converged very near us, all with their headlights beaming. Our "isolated" spot turned out instead to be the meeting place for a bunch of teenage partygoers. We lay there in our bags for some time quietly, hoping that they wouldn't discover us, before they finally and noisily left us alone once again to our cold slumber.

Even though we slept virtually on top of each other that night in order to stay warm, we really didn't and when we got up in the morning it was easy to see why. After brushing off the thin layer of ice that had formed on top of us, we walked back up to the autostrada and groggily, shiveringly put our thumbs out.

Our efforts this morning were much better met and we were soon on our way again, rest-stop hopping all the way to Venice. As soon as we were dropped off from a ride, we'd immediately race indoors to the rest stop cafe that was always nearby and order ourselves a couple of chocolatas, savoring every drop of the liquid confection.

One of our rides was from a young student who spoke some English (just about the only Italian we came across that did) and he taught us how to say a few handy Italian words as well as some other helpful hints like how to use our thumb and index finger to specify the number two ("du chocolatas, por favore") and how to insult someone with the way in which you wave to them (palm forward). This last one was a particularly fun one for us and throughout the rest of the trip, whenever either of us wanted to get back at the other, we'd just wave, palm out, and say "oh yeah, well pretend we're in Italy."

We got to Venice early in the afternoon but only had a couple of hours to walk around exploring the city before we had to leave again, this time for Bologne, the nearest city with an open hostel, about 120 miles away.

Our last ride for the day let us out in a foot of snow right on the outskirts of Bologne. It was already nighttime and freezing cold. Karen had gotten well chilled the night before and had never really thawed out since, chocolatas notwithstanding. We walked on into town and meandered our way through the busy city until finally tracking down the train station. We needed to check its big city map to find out where the hostel was.

Again, it turned out to be way out on the opposite side of town. Not wanting to repeat our unfortunate experience in Milan, we agreed that a bus trip was warranted in this case and went out to try and find one that would take us out that way.

We met with little success, however, and what we did get was hard won. We didn't know where to go to catch the bus and no one we approached spoke any English. My newly learned phrase "dove ostello?" (where's the hostel?) only brought us answers that we couldn't understand and we started getting cranky as our stress level slowly rose. Tonight was New Year's Eve, normally a festive and happy time for most people, but this one found us, instead, pissy, lost and much in need of a warm bed.

Finally, after a couple of hours, some bus rides, and a lot of walking around, we made it to the hostel. As we walked up to the door, we noticed that the place seemed unusually dark, even empty. It looked closed. The door was locked when we tried it so we knocked and waited. This wasn't looking very good, I thought. I double-checked my hostel book again and verified that this one was in fact supposed to be open tonight. Dammit, it better be open.

327

We knocked a second time. A moment later we were encouraged to hear footsteps coming up. We were both happy when a woman opened the door for us but our joy was instantly dashed when she then told us quietly that she was sorry but that the hostel was indeed closed, despite what the guidebook said, and that we couldn't stay here tonight.

When she saw the tears that began welling up in Karen's eyes, though, she relented, taking pity on us, and gave us a room anyway. Once inside we gave each other a quick kiss goodnight and then went straight up to our respective showers and beds.

After another roundabout visit through downtown the following morning, as well as another couple of bus rides, we eventually managed to get out and on our way south to Rome. That old saying about all roads leading there is wrong, we found out. On the other hand, though, we also found out that you can ride buses in Italy without having to pay for them, which really made our day (we found out sometime later that the ticket inspectors get on the busses willy-nilly to check for tickets and that we'd only been lucky that they hadn't caught us).

It was another long, freezing day out hitching. We had been real eager, ever since leaving Michael's, to get south into the nicer weather and it was more than frustrating to have the cold, snowy weather follow us almost all the way to Rome, where it then turned into cold, rainy weather. We took full advantage of our new discovery once we got to town and hopped a few more busses (still free!) to get us to the hostel.

We went to tour the city the next day, not really having any idea of where to go. We did think to go visit Vatican City, just because, but we found it to be mostly uninteresting once we got there.

While walking around the grounds there, we noticed a bunch of people making their way through an iron gate with two costumed guards at either side. We didn't know what was in there but figured that if all these people were going in that it must be something more interesting than what we'd seen so far so we decided to go in too. As we got to the gate, however, one of the guards stopped us for some reason and wouldn't let us go through.

Since we had no idea what was in there in the first place, this didn't bother us a bit and we turned to leave. Just as we did, though, an American guy came up behind us and introduced himself as the pastor of a church group that was here from Indiana. Having just seen our rebuff from the guard, he felt obliged to invite us to go in with all of them - to see the pope!

Neither of us being Catholic, nor even religious for that matter, we really wouldn't have been too sorry if we'd missed this treat but it was a kind offer which we in turn felt obliged to accept. We didn't have anything else in particular to do, anyway.

We joined the anxious group of Indianans and filed into the big auditorium where, apparently, the pope shows himself. It was already very crowded inside as the hundreds of people that were there all jammed in.

We were several minutes in there waiting before the shouting of the crowd alerted us to his entrance. It was a good thing they did, too, because we couldn't see the little fellow at all in the midst of all these regular sized people and would never have known otherwise that he'd arrived.

The pontiff eventually made his way through the throng, touching as many of the outstretched hands as he could before finally making it up onto the stage at the end of the room where he took a seat, giving us a better view of this ambassador of God and supreme leader of the Catholic world. Despite all the hoopla and holy ornamentation, I must confess that, even sitting up there before his adoring flock, the little man looked awfully ordinary to me and left me unimpressed.

After a few minutes of politely feigning interest to our hosts, we quietly stole away from the crowd and slipped back outside to a realer world, I thought, eager to continue on our tour of old Rome.

This free bus thing was great and we took them all over town. We went to the Coliseum, St. Peter's Basilica and a few other assorted spots that day before finally heading back to the big, crowded hostel. Karen found a small glass bottle in the Coliseum and carried it with her that day. It wasn't very old but we had fun thinking that it was really an ancient remnant from Caesar's kitchen cupboard. Unfortunately, it broke later that day and she chucked it, so we'll never know.

It was still very cold outside--cold enough to snow, I thought--but the next morning when we made our way to the outskirts of the city, it was an icy rain that we were standing in as we tried to catch a ride down to Naples. Our shoes were soaking wet by the time we got here and, after about an hour or so of luckless hitching (so much for that notion of looking pitiful), I was getting seriously cold and was beginning to shiver. We found an underpass to shelter us while we hitched but it did nothing to alleviate our distress since we were already soaked. Only seconds before giving up and going back, though, a fellow finally stopped for us and we made it all the way to Naples by that afternoon.

Rome was pretty much the midpoint of our Italian "vacation" and I was real glad that we were now on our way out of the country. My initial feelings of discomfort about Italy had followed us throughout and getting out of this country increasingly became my prime concern. I'm not really sure why I felt this way. The weather, of course, didn't help any, nor did our difficulty with the language and with getting rides but I felt as though these were only adding to the feeling, not creating it. Indeed, my illness of ease and apprehension while here seemed to be pre-existing. It seemed to be the place itself.

Our homesickness during this time was growing stronger, too, making it all the harder to appreciate being away in the first place. In fact, this first morning here in Naples I awoke with yet another sore tooth and I began feeling anxious about it. The thought of getting dental work done down here wasn't a fun one for me and I found myself actually thinking seriously about how nice it would be to go home. This was the first time I actually admitted these feelings to myself and once I did it seemed to take the gut out of my ability to enjoy being here. Once I was up and around, my toothache subsided and never returned but the effect it had on me never left.

Our plans today were to head for the town of Brindisi, over on the east coast, and from there to catch a ferry across the Adriatic to Greece. We got our first view of the Mediterranean that morning on our way out of town when we stopped for a while on the shore of the Bay of Naples. We sat and watched the ships coming in to port with the snowy Mt. Vesuvius as their backdrop. Thankfully, we had finally made it far enough south to be out of the rain although it was still overcast out and the day colorless.

A few short rides had brought us, by mid-afternoon, to a rest stop in the snow-covered foothills of the mountains that ran down the middle of the country here. We employed our Oban tactic again here and hitched from the warm entryway of the cafe.

Before long, we had managed to get a ride from a little, crusty looking truck driver. He spoke no English at all so we had to rely on pointing to the map to tell him where we were going and his ambiguous response made us unsure if that was anywhere near where he was going or whether he even understood us at all, for that matter. He didn't say no, though, and we didn't want to get stuck in this rest stop so we climbed in the cab of his truck and spent the rest of the afternoon quietly watching the trees go by in the lightly falling snow as we continued up the mountain.

By dusk, the snowfall had become more of a blizzard and the long line of cars and trucks on the autostrada was going ever more slowly now. Soon after, the eastbound side of the roadway came to a complete standstill. We ended up turning around to head back down the way we had just come.

Within only a few minutes, however, we started to slip on the ice as we were climbing one of the hills so the old man pulled the truck over to the side of the road and hopped out to put his chains on. After several minutes of trying to fit them on, Karen suggested to me that I go out and offer to help. I didn't really want to, it was cold out there and he didn't seem very nice, but I went out anyway. After all, he was doing us a favor. As it was, though, there was nothing I could really do for him and the only thing I managed to accomplish out there was to lower my body temperature by 30 or 40 degrees.

Alas, our efforts were all too late anyhow and, despite the one set of chains that we (he) managed to finally get on, it was clear that the storm was going to win this contest after all and we all backed up into a long, stalled line of traffic. We had no choice now but to just sit and wait. For what I wasn't sure, I just knew that it was all we could do.

At about 11 o'clock that night, the plows and policemen finally came through in an attempt to clear the road but they were in too much of a hurry, I suppose, because they got so far ahead of the truck pack that we now belonged to that the road iced right back up again before we could drive over it and on the very next hill we all came to yet another stall. Apparently for good this time, too, since our driver promptly hopped into the bed that was back in the sleeper booth of his cab and went to sleep.

Taking our cue from him, we then tried to make ourselves comfortable for the night by wrapping up in our sleeping bags and leaning against the door of his 18-wheeler, a position that was becoming very familiar to us on this trip. It turned out to be yet another memorable night for us but I'll let Karen tell about this one:

FROM KAREN'S JOURNAL:

[06Jan80] What a mess it was! And it was looking like a blizzard outside now. The little man got into his bed and me and Mark got into our bags to sleep the night away. I was laying there thinking about home and heading to dreamland when I felt a hand touch my leg. Then he started pinching and rubbing his hands all over and trying to get into my sleeping bag. I just didn't know what to do. I was real upset and more so mad. I laid there squished against Mark trying to ignore him. I didn't want to upset him and be thrown out but I was mad. Finally, I pulled my bag way over my head and pulled farther away from him and he left me alone. I know Italians are aggressive but come on. I was so upset I couldn't go to sleep.

A few hours later when it got light out the plows came again and I changed places with Mark so I was by the door. By then I figured it was over and done and that's just the way Italians were so I just ignored the guy and pretended like nothing happened.

Pretty soon we were on our way; they even managed to be smart enough and keep the snow plows and salters right in front of the trucks as they went down the road. We got turned around and heading the right way and had ourselves a convoy slowly going towards Bari.

The time went by and the roads cleared up and the snow started disappearing as we got close the east coast. Then about 40 kilometers from Bari the little twerp pulled into a deserted

333

parking area, fooled around with his truck a while, then promptly got [in] on my side of the truck and tried to grab me again. I was sitting right next to Mark and he wanted me to sit on his lap and fool around while Mark just ignored him.

Well, me and Mark had very different ideas about that! I slapped his hand away, he jumped out of the truck and ordered us out and he was very upset. I gladly jumped out of the truck and as Mark was getting the stuff, he grabbed me again! This time I punched him in the chest and Mark yelled at him so he left us alone. Dang little, nervy twerp! We left the truck while he screamed at us till he drove away. And I'd thought he was a nice little man.

Well, somehow a car picked us up right off the motorway in record time. It was good to be out of his truck! Not only to be away from him but we'd been in it for almost 24 hours.

That day while me and Mark were in twerpo's truck, we decided something: we'd been away from home for too long. Traveling was good and neither of us really wanted to stop, but home was calling us to come now. We decided we were going to head home right away. It made me feel good thinking about being home right soon and I'm real happy about our decision. We decided to still go to Greece and Kenya real fast but then home.

As if to make up for its recent past failings, our trip seemed to pick up momentum from the very moment we jumped out of "twerpo's" truck. Still, I came away from the whole incident with my ill feelings about this place fully charged. Even though we got picked up almost immediately after he dropped us off, a feeling of drear (or was it dread) followed me all the way to Brindisi and I wanted nothing more than to just leave this country as soon as possible. It was an irrational anxiety. I couldn't explain why I felt it, only that I did. It felt like a holdover from some past life trauma suffered here.

Perhaps it was just David again, helping as he could, but things seemed to be lining up all of a sudden to ensure that I got my wish of hasty exit. We easily got to Brindisi by early that evening. Though our ride into town didn't speak any English and couldn't have understood our questions about the location of the hostel, he just happened to let us out directly across the street from it. We went in and registered for the night, thankful that we didn't have to trudge around town looking for this place, and then went off to claim our beds and relax in our rooms for a while.

The fellow that checked us in was a slightly odd Englishman named George. Though this job was normally one for the warden to do, I got the impression that he was more of a semi-permanent resident than anything else. Either way, as soon as we mentioned to him that we were looking for a cheap way to Greece he immediately went into action. He told us that the ferry leaving tonight at 10 p.m. was the last one for the next three days and said that we'd have to move fast.

George checked us back out of the hostel while we packed ourselves up again and when we returned to the desk he then gave us not only a price list for the ferry but also a map of the city. On it he had circled the docks (so we could find our way there), the police station (so we could get their official okay for us to leave) and a grocery store (so that we could provision up for the 20-hour ride). He also told us what bus to take to get us to all these places and warned us to hurry because all this took time and we had to check in with the ferry company early if we wanted to get on.

With great (and many) thanks to odd George, by 10 o'clock that night we were happily on our way to Greece.

FROM KAREN'S JOURNAL:

[06Jan80]   Before boarding the ferry, people that had just come across filled us with warnings that the ride was terrible. It took 20 hours and the seas were really rough and everyone got sick. Our trip over was quite smooth and easy though.

The ride was quite unexciting but I got in my sleeping bag all dressed and slept not only warmly but I was even hot. Oh what joy!

It was good to see Italy go, things just never seemed to go right there. Most of the people were nice enough and Rome and Venice were real nice to see but things worked out wrong there for some reason. We were always very cold and wet and hitching was hard and slow, and the hostels were always a fight to get to. It was just nice to say good-by.

We slept outside on the deck that night in our sleeping bags with the several dozen other budget travelers that were also making the crossing with us. We awoke in the morning to the first bright, warm day we'd seen in a very long time.

The fog in my head, I soon realized, had finally lifted too. I wasn't at all surprised when I checked my map a while later and found that we had just crossed the mid-sea border out of Italy and into Grecian waters. Strange.

The morning sun was rising up from the sea through the pinkened horizon, chasing away the still bright moon, as we made our way past the small island of Kerkirya (Corfu). It all seemed to me as though a final affirmation that this dreary Italian leg of our trip was indeed finally over.

The ferry landed us in the port city of Patras, Greece, down on the Peloponnese, at about six that evening. It was still cold outside but not nearly as bad as Italy had been and certainly much drier. Darkness was descending as we walked through town and then out to the far edge to find ourselves a place to sleep. We came by a small vacant lot that would do and unrolled our sleeping bags.

I lay there for some time, in my sleeping bag, watching all the stars as they slowly introduced themselves to the nighttime sky. It was just like I had done a million times before and it gave me solace to recognize them as the same ones I knew back home, so many miles away. It surprised me though, this time, when I started to call off their names to myself and realized that this was their home. I was lying here in the very land, this dirt, where their names and myths had been created so many centuries ago, where their adventurous exploits and heroic deeds had taken place.

It was so much more fun now to look up upon them and to know that I was seeing them in much the same way as those original mythmakers had. It somehow made them all seem more real to me. I liked feeling this way and I went to sleep for the first time in a long time with a contented heart and a sense of peace. But then, maybe that was just because I wasn't in Italy anymore; I don't know.

When we left Patras that following morning to thumb our way up to Athens, it was with the thought of taking our time and meandering our way there. The big rush to get out of the cold weather was no longer necessary here in this very Mediterranean climate we were now enjoying. Our rides, however, had other ideas and we got to Athens by two o'clock that same afternoon, record time. It seemed that the surge in momentum our trip had taken recently was still with us.

What with last nights newly realized astral connections, I now enjoyed the notion that perhaps Hermes himself, the Greek god of travel and a traveler in his own right, had taken up company with us back at that roadside pullout in Italy and that it was really he, not David this time, that was now moving things so quickly for us. Maybe he was late for reunion with his big sis, Athena, and was eager to get there, bringing us along for the ride.

We went straight to the hostel and dropped our things off there, checked the city map and headed back out to explore

337

the old city. We spent the whole of the afternoon lounging around the Acropolis and touring through the ruins of the ancient marketplace below it.

It was a sunny, warm day, a very lazy day for us. We spent a good part of it just sitting up on the wall by the Parthenon, looking out at the city, with our backs to the old temple, while discussing all the fun stuff we wanted to do once we got back home.

In fact, we sat now and talked as excitedly about home as we'd once sat back on the hillside overlooking the college, talking about the rest of the world. This observation wasn't lost on me and only confirmed in my own mind that it was indeed time for us to go home.

Visiting Kenya, however, was a lifelong dream of Karen's and certainly one of this trip's main attractions for her, and we didn't want to end it before she'd had a chance to go there. Especially being so close now, relatively speaking anyway.

With this in mind, it was with only half a heart the next day that we put ourselves to the task of devising a plan that would satisfy our seemingly contradicting feelings. We looked at maps, read books, counted our money and checked at all the cheap travel offices in town for fares. We then looked at more maps, made lists, formulated possible routes and counted our money again. Finally, we came up with what we thought was a workable plan, if only barely.

We had tried to figure a way to get us back home without having to backtrack. We still wanted to arrive in California from across the Pacific, in the west, so that we could join that elite club of world circumnavigators but, under the circumstances, this would mean flying most of the way back and that was just too expensive for us. In the end, we reluctantly accepted that it was far cheaper and easier to just go back the way we came.

The overall plan now called for us to fly to Egypt, train down through the Sudan and into Kenya, visit the wildlife parks and then turn around and head back to Athens in reverse order. From here we would simply fly back to the U.S., collect Otto (who was still unsold and waiting for us back in Florida) and drive back home. It would still be expensive this way, we knew, and we'd be arriving back to the States with virtually no money but we could do it and that was all we really needed to know.

Now that this had all been worked out we immediately set about the next morning getting everything in order. Our first task was to get our appropriate visa applications submitted since they would take anywhere from a few to several days to get processed and returned.

With the help of the youth hostel's big city map, we easily tracked down both the Egyptian and the Sudanese embassies. We dropped off our paperwork at the Egyptian embassy but when we got to the small suite that served as the Sudanese consulate we found them closed so we spent the rest of the day, instead, exploring the city again and supremely enjoying the warm, sunny day we again had. This definitely wasn't Italy anymore.

As things went, by the following afternoon our plans had changed once again. Since visiting the game parks in Kenya was so important to Karen, we now thought that it would be far better to come back and visit them when we had more time to fully experience and enjoy them. With that thought in mind we decided now to forego the Kenya leg and to just fly on down to Egypt and spend some time traveling around there for a while. We immediately went into town and picked up a couple of round-trip tickets to Cairo.

It was probably just the mounting excitement of getting so close to coming home, but by nightfall everything had changed yet again. Our feeling now was that spending all that money to fly across the Mediterranean just to spend a few days in Egypt was really kind of foolish. After all, since we were going to be coming all the way back here in only a few months to visit

Kenya, we could easily throw in a trip to Egypt as well. In fact, we might even have to go through Egypt to get there in the first place. With this thought now expressed, we decided that very same moment to simply suspend the rest of our trip altogether, right here and now, and to just go straight home. Tomorrow would be good.

In order to allay any feelings of remorse for not having made it all the way around the world, we sat down and worked out the plans for two more trips that would ultimately get us to all the places we'd always been wanting to go to but were now foregoing. We weren't tired of traveling, you see, just homesick, and there were still many, many places left for us to explore and conquer. We went down and exchanged our Cairo tickets for two one-ways to New York. Unfortunately, we couldn't get on the flight leaving the next day, Thursday, and had to book ourselves on the flight that left on Saturday, instead. It was disappointing for more reasons that just the extra wait, though.

The airline we were flying on was Royal Air Maroc, the nationally owned and operated airline of Morocco. In order to promote tourism in their country, they offered really cheap flights to various places but only on the condition that you spend some time in Morocco on the way.

To make it even easier, they supplied free room and board in Casablanca to boot. The Thursday flight was the better one since it included lodging for that first night, all day Friday and then Friday night before leaving again on Saturday morning. All extras included in the price. Saturday's flight out of Athens, however, only provided lodging for that one night and then breakfast the next morning before flying out Sunday morning. In our flush of excitement at the thought of going home, we weren't about to wait around another week just for one extra day in Casablanca. Saturday would just have to do, I guessed.

It felt so good to hold those two pieces of paper in my hands when they handed over our new tickets, to know that we were actually going to be on our way home in only three more days. We left the travel agency on wings (the last unintended pun) and headed straight into the heart of the tourist part of town.

Since our trip was more or less over now, we reasoned, we no longer had any need to watch our money as closely as we had been. Finally allowing ourselves to discard our trusty "rules of the road," they that had served us so well, we went merrily off to go spend it without a care on souvenirs for all our family and friends back home. We shopped all the rest of the day and most of the following one. It was great fun.

GOING HOME

Saturday finally arrived and we excitedly packed up, checked out and made our way through town to the airport. We were going home. That's all I could think of as the jet raced its way down the runway and into the sky. We were on our way home.

We landed at the airport in Casablanca just before dusk. I looked around for Humphrey Bogart as we got out but all I could see was a hill of beans. We were about a half an hour's drive from town so the airline provided us with a bus to take us in to the hotel they were putting us up in.

We had both been real disappointed that we weren't able to take the Thursday flight here because we thought it would've been the perfect way to end this first trip together, spending the day cruising around a romantically foreign place like Morocco but, as we drove through it and I saw how truly fascinating this country was, I was painfully sorry. It was even more exotic than I'd imagined and it was only the thought that I would catch it on the next trip that kept me from changing our plans again and staying on here for a while. As it turned out, we almost got a chance to anyway though it wasn't really by our choice.

The very nice hotel they provided for us collected up everyone's passport when we checked in that evening, assumedly as a security measure. They would return them, we were told, when we checked back out the following morning. It wasn't until we were standing in line at the airport that next morning, however, waiting to check in for our flight home, when I suddenly realized to my horror that I had forgotten to re-collect mine before we'd left to come here. Our plane was due to leave in within the hour and I knew that it would be at least an hour round-trip to go back and get it. I didn't know at all what to do now but the thought of panicking immediately came to mind.

I obviously had to tell somebody and it was with much nervous anxiety that I approached the airline guy that was shepherding us through the procedures to inform him of what had happened. As far as I knew, this was the only flight out of here for New York until next Saturday, six days hence.

By now, we only had about 50 dollars left between us and the thought of us getting stranded here in this strange country without any money wasn't at all a pleasant one. The image of the swarthy looking customs man who'd just checked my bags was still with me as I considered our unfortunate situation. He had leered at me very sinisterly, I thought, and chuckled as he poked and fondled my bags. As he did so, he said slowly to me in his heavily Moroccan accented English, "What you got in here...druuuugs?"

It was an unsettling feeling I'd gotten when he said that and my mind flashed back to a scene in the movie "Midnight Express" that I'd seen back in Florida. A true story where a young American man, not unlike myself, had had a similar experience trying to get out of Turkey. In it he had been arrested for smuggling drugs and sent to a medieval Turkish prison where he suffered horrible conditions for several years before finally escaping.

No, this wasn't at all where I wanted to get stranded, I thought, as I recalled all this.

As soon as I'd explained my problem to him, the airline agent told me that the only thing I could do was to call a taxi back in Casablanca and have the driver pick up my passport and deliver it here to the airport. To my relief he then told me that another man in our group had also forgotten his passport. At least I wasn't the only fool. The only thing was, he continued, was that this other guy had called and made his arrangements some time ago and that it might be too late for this to be of any help. If I was lucky, though, I might be able to still catch the cabbie before he left the hotel and have him bring mine out as well.

I knew from plenty of recently past experiences that the odds of me being lucky were pretty good but even so, our plane was due to leave in only minutes, long before the taxi could get here, assuming I could even catch it in time. I found a phone and hurriedly called the hotel. Yes! My luck was indeed holding; the taxi driver hadn't left yet and the clerk said he would make sure my passport would be included. All I could do now was to wait and hope.

We waited ever more anxiously as the departure time for the plane crept up and then passed. We were given a temporary reprieve when an announcement went out that the plane was going to be delayed for a few minutes for unspecified reasons. We waited. Those few minutes had now come and gone, too. We waited some more. This was getting way too close for me.

Just when I thought the plane would surely leave without us, that we would be stranded here and thrown into prison for being penniless vagrants if not drug-smuggling, imperialist, American spies, a taxi driver finally walked into the airport lobby and in his hands, he carried our two long-lost passports. The other fellow and I split both the fare and the generous tip to the driver before grabbing them up and quickly getting stamped out of the country.

He, Karen and I finally boarded the still delayed plane and gratefully took our seats. We weren't on board two minutes, however, before the pilot announced that the delay was now over, coincidentally enough, and that we were cleared for takeoff, buckle up. Whew, that was a close one.

As we taxied down the runway and lifted off the tarmac, I felt certain that they had actually held the plane over for us that extra half an hour, though nobody had said so. We were thankful, though, either way and very glad to be on our way again.

The flight back to New York was a very happy, yet sad one for us. Much like our flight out of Norman's Cay back in the Bahamas, we quietly watched out the window of the plane as our whole trip was replayed back to us in the merest fraction of the time it took to live it. Only this time there was so much more of it to rewind. All the thousands of miles and so many months, zipping past us now faster than we could remember them all. It was all undone in eight short hours.

We were back in New York City in time for a late lunch, as odd as that sounds, but we went straight to the Greyhound bus terminal. By six that evening we were on a bus headed for Florida. It was such a strange feeling for me to be thinking about all of this now, Morocco in the morning and Maryland by nightfall, the cultural clash. It all happened so fast. I almost felt that all the planning, preparing and dreaming that we'd done, the time and effort and even the reward itself had somehow been stolen from me by the simple act of turning around and flying back. I felt cheated.

It was strange, too, once I realized that we were traveling down the very same highway that Karen and I had driven Otto down, way back at the beginning of our adventure, nearly 16 months ago. Our trip was just gearing up then. We were so innocent on that drive, it seemed to me now, and infused with such a wonderful sense of adventure and freedom, of expectant excitement. The world was in front of us.

This time, however, it was all winding down, the world behind us. I felt so much wiser now, so much more aware of life. So very contented and satisfied. For we had done it, Karen and me. Maybe not around the world, not this time, but at least we knew now that we could've done it, that we still could do it, and whenever we wanted to. The world was free to us now. Those words I had spoken to my mother's coworkers, so innocuously all those months ago, had proven truer than I could ever have hoped or dreamt. The world truly had been ours for the taking. We had but to go and get it and now, returning, I was bringing it all back with me. It was all in my heart now.

Despite this odd confliction of feelings, it was also a little fun driving back down I-95 again, passing by all of our old breakdown spots and reflecting on them; the rest stop in Laurel, the motel in Fayetteville. And adding even more to this quiet gyre of emotions, was a bit of sadness too, the kind of sadness that comes with the awareness that your once bright-eyed innocence was now spent, that life would never again appear the same.

Thirty-five hours of bittersweet reflection later, we finally arrived in Stuart, Florida by 11:30 the next night. It was too late for us to go over to my grandmother's, especially since we hadn't even told her we were coming, so we went over to Sambo's and hung out there all night, eating pancakes just like in the old days, and waited out the morning. The culture clash hit me pretty hard here. Only two nights ago we were in Casablanca, Morocco, Africa for heaven's sake, and now here we were loitering in Sambo's in Stuart, Florida. It was really, really strange.

When the light of morning finally showed several hours later, we slowly trudged our tired way along the few remaining miles to Mamaw's house, letting the pretty dawn take our minds off the heavy and overly stuffed packs we now had to carry for this, our very last march.

Since we had wanted to surprise everyone with our return, we hadn't bothered to warn anybody of it and Mamaw was, indeed, surprised to see us so early that morning. I think Irving must have realized now that we weren't the innocent kids we'd been before because he was unusually civil and deferent to us this time.

We stayed here for a couple of days to catch up on our sleep and get good ol' Otto checked out for the drive home. It was wonderful to plant my butt once again on those seats, feeling for the first time since returning, that I truly was back home again.

We decided to take the southern route this time, and our drive through the Gulf states and across the deserts was much more relaxed and reflective than our first crossing. It was mostly uneventful, too, although Otto did break down again, right in the middle of Texas. It was only temporary, though, and didn't stop us for long.

After all those months of being carless, it felt great being behind the wheel again, out on the highway, and once again in control of where we went and when. Freedom of mobility is a great thing.

In only a matter of days, we had managed to unwind a year and a half of the most incredible living I could have wished upon myself and we were back in Eureka before the week was out. Curiously, virtually no one was surprised to see us when we returned. They were all extremely happy to see us both come home after all this time, of course, and in good health and spirits, just not very surprised, for some reason.

No one, though, was happier than Karen. She was finally home again. Home to her family, her friends and her animals.

A home that she has never left since.

EPILOGUE

It was 10 years from the trip's dramatic beginning, almost to the day, that I started this writing this and I am surprised to notice that it's been 15 years, almost to the day, since its quiet end that I now finish it. Karen and I split up long ago, shortly after returning home, for reasons that I am still unsure of, and though she lives only about 20 miles away I seldom see her and only hear from her maybe once or twice a year. It seems strange for me to be saying this in light of what is contained in this story and perhaps someday I'll understand how it came to be.

I do know that once Karen set foot again on her old home ground she was so happy to be back that she knew in that moment that she could never leave it again. There would be no more world trips for the two of us, no Kenya, no Himalayas; she did offer that much to me.

I know, too, that I wasn't as prepared as she to spend the rest of my life here in Eureka. I had seen too much of the world now to be able to sit so still and there was still so much more of it left to be explored, so much more life to be experienced. Six months later, Karen drove me back down to Los Angeles, on what would be our very last trip together, to send me off on the start of another adventure. I was flying back to England to share my newfound world with my old friend Doug (from Portland) before continuing on, solo.

I cried, deeply at times, as we drove past some of the places that we'd shared together on this, our very first, and now last, highway. Though we'd not formally split up, I guess I knew in my heart that it was all over now, somehow, and it saddened me like nothing ever had before, or has since. Indeed, my eyes are misting even as I write this now.

I guess my mother put it best when she said that we simply had a difference of priorities, which was certainly true all of a sudden, but rationales could never alleviate the horrendous pain I felt in my soul whenever I thought that we might not be together for the rest of our lives. All I really know is that, as I stood there by the side of the road watching her and Otto make their way up the onramp to go back home, my heart was driving away with her. In all these years since that day, never has it fully returned.